D1234795

HARVARD HISTORICAL STUDIES

PUBLISHED UNDER THE DIRECTION OF
THE DEPARTMENT OF HISTORY

FROM THE INCOME OF
THE HENRY WARREN TORREY FUND

VOLUME XLVIII

HARVARD HISTORICAL STUDIES

HARVARD UNIVERSITY PRESS
CAMBRIDGE, MASS., U. S. A.

The Reign of King Pym

BY

J. H. HEXTER

Queens College of the College of the City of New York

CAMBRIDGE

HARVARD UNIVERSITY PRESS

LONDON : HUMPHREY MILFORD

OXFORD UNIVERSITY PRESS

1941

COPYRIGHT, 1941
BY THE PRESIDENT AND FELLOWS OF HARVARD COLLEGE

PRINTED AT THE HARVARD UNIVERSITY PRESS
CAMBRIDGE, MASSACHUSETTS, U.S.A.

To

W. C. ABBOTT

MY TEACHER AND MY FRIEND

ACKNOWLEDGMENTS

In writing any book, but especially in writing one's first book, one incurs a great number of obligations to a great number of kind people. Any list of one's creditors must seem incomplete and perfunctory. Nevertheless, I wish to thank, for aid rendered me in various ways on various occasions, Professor C. H. Mc-Ilwain, Professor W. K. Jordan, Professor Crane Brinton, Sir Harry Verney, Miss Veronica Wedgewood, Miss Marion Daughaday, Mr. Irving Wechsler, and the staffs of the libraries of the British Museum and Harvard University. Some special gratitude I owe to Professor David Owen and Dr. Elliott Perkins, who read the manuscript of this book in longhand. To my grandmother, whose own imperturbability gave me courage in very dark days, I owe a debt I can never adequately pay. This is equally true of my debt to the teacher and friend to whom I gratefully dedicate this book.

J. H. H.

NEW YORK
MAY, 1940

CONTENTS

THE REIGN OF KING PYM

PROLOGUE: THE DEATH OF A LEADER

On December 15, 1643, ten men carried John Pym to his grave in Westminster Abbey. Royalists at Oxford celebrated with festivities and a bonfire. London mourned and feared. Stephen Marshall, preaching Pym's funeral sermon, tried to hearten men downcast and perplexed by the loss of their leader. "The enemy," he said, "rejoices, as if our cause were not good, or as if we should lose it for want of hands and heads to carry it on. No, no, beloved! this cause must prosper, . . . this cause must prevail." [1] To Royalists, Pym was "the promoter of the present rebellion and director of the whole machine." [2] To Marshall and to many who heard his sermon, Pym was the symbol of "the Cause," the dynamic embodiment of the opposition to Charles I.

Other men had been symbols of the Cause of Parliament before Pym. Edward Coke, who came to the House of Commons in 1621, took the leadership of the Commons by a sort of natural right. He had fought the prerogative, the arbitrary power of the King, from his stronghold in the Court of Commons Pleas, and when routed from there resumed the struggle as Chief Justice of the King's Bench. Since James had taken from him his judicial office, in 1621 he resumed the duel as champion of the Common Law against the prerogative in the only arena left open to him — Parliament. Sir John Eliot won his place as leader almost as soon as he won his seat in the House. In 1624 the concentrated zeal that drove him found an outlet in words in the lower house, words so compelling that, although he knew little of the ways of the Commons, he soon became spokesman for his fellow members. Coke and Eliot took the Commons by storm, Pym attained the pinnacle he stood on at his death by a long slow climb in the House

[1] Stephen Marshall, *Threnodia* (1644), p. 39.
[2] *C. S. P. Venetian*, XXVII, 53.

itself. He was nearly forty years old when he first came to
Parliament. He was almost sixty, with only three years of
life ahead of him, before he became the recognized leader of
the Commons.

In all the Parliaments that Coke pontificated to and Eliot
electrified, Pym sat. He sat, and he worked with a capacity for
work given to few men. He acted on committees and conferred
with members of the House of Lords and prepared reports
and spoke when he thought speaking might help to get what
he wanted. He saw the auspicious opening of the Parliament
of 1621 and assisted in the prosecution of one of the hated
monopolists. He saw a cloud of doubt, no bigger than a man's
hand, about the King's foreign policy grow to blot out all
the hopes men had cherished of the new Parliament. He appeared prominently in the proceedings that led up to the
Protestation of the Commons, asserting more definitely than
it had ever been asserted before the right of the Commons to
debate whatever matters they deemed important to the Commonwealth. He sat in the confused last Parliament of James
and in the equally confused first Parliament of Charles. In
Charles's second Parliament he watched the smoldering shame
of the gentry at the role of England in the German war spring
to flame when Eliot turned their anger on Buckingham, the
King's favorite. Pym aided Eliot in this work that forever
alienated Charles from his Parliaments. In 1628 Pym took
his place alongside the other great leaders of the quest for an
affirmance of the subjects' liberties against arbitrary royal
seizure of their persons and property. In the struggle for the
Petition of Right Pym played no less a role than Coke and
Eliot. When Charles I dissolved Parliament in 1629, eleven
years of prerogative rule began, and Pym's political apprentice-
ship ended. He had learned his trade as no man of his generation learned it, and his trade was the management of the
House of Commons. For a decade it seemed that all his lore
might be dead antiquarianism. While Pym busied himself with
the management of an unsatisfactory colonial enterprise,

Charles ruled England without Parliament, collected ship-money without Parliamentary grant to finance the state, and won approval for his levy in court in the case against Pym's friend John Hampden.

While Pym and his friends in England dreamed of a haven from Laudianism in the New World, Archbishop Laud unwittingly prepared a dark doom for his beloved King in Scotland. The Scots rose against the defilement of their Kirk by Popish ceremonial as they would never rise against abuses in the state, and the troubles in Scotland had to be paid for out of the pockets of Englishmen. To open those pockets Charles I called a Parliament in 1640. From the first day of the Short Parliament Pym came into his own and found the reward of long years of experience in an almost unbearable burden of thankless toil. Yet day by day as the House of Commons exercised that initiative which it had developed and learned to use in the twenties, the man who could lead the House displaced the King as the active center of the state. King Pym displaced King Charles. Ship-money was condemned; the prerogative courts fell; the Earl of Strafford, Charles's faithful servant, went to the scaffold; regular Parliaments were made certain, tunnage and poundage became Parliamentary grants, all under Pym's guidance. Then Parliament split asunder. Some men followed the King; the rest stayed at Westminster. Over those who stayed King Pym still reigned, the symbol of the Cause of Parliament.

When Pym died in December 1643, the Cause of Parliament, at least for a time, died with him. In place of one cause came deep confusion, painful cross purposes, many causes. The divisions imminent in the Civil War Parliament were fittingly presaged among the pallbearers of Pym. Among them were two of those eleven commoners that the army forced out of the House in 1647,[3] and three who a little later signed an engagement to live and die with that same army.[4] When in 1648

---

[3] Holles, Clotworthy.
[4] St. John, Vane, Haselrig.

Colonel Pride purged the House of Commons of members favorable to a peace with the King, four of Pym's pallbearers were among the forty he arrested,[5] and he barred another from entering the House.[6] Within a month two of the other pall-bearers had engaged their faith to a kingless Commonwealth of England,[7] and yet another was Lord Chief Justice of that Commonwealth.[8] Of the four of Pym's pallbearers arrested in Pride's Purge one sat in Cromwell's House of Commons and became a Knight of the Bath at the Restoration,[9] a second sat in Cromwell's House of Lords and became a baronet at the Restoration,[10] and a third fattened off the confiscated estates of the Irish Royalists after the Cromwellian conquest, and be-came a viscount at the Restoration.[11] For two of Pym's pall-bearers the return of the Stuarts brought elevation to the peerage; [12] for another it meant flight from England and life-long exile.[13] And for two of the pallbearers the triumph of Charles II spelled a traitor's death on the block.[14] Unwittingly Parliament chose these men of divers destinies, these leaders of many causes, to do last honors to the leader of a single cause which, though the mourners did not know it, he carried with him to the grave.

We do not know and cannot guess whether Pym himself could have reconciled the factions, diverging in ideal and pur-pose, that emerged in Parliament after his death; we only know that after his death the factions quickly became and remained irreconcilably hostile to one another. To understand how Pym postponed the perhaps inevitable schism, we must try to learn how he, "the director of the whole machine," controlled Par-liament.

[5] Clotworthy, Gerard, Holles, Knightly.
[6] Sir Neville Poole.
[7] Haselrig, Vane.
[8] St. John.
[9] Knightly.
[10] Gerard.
[11] Clotworthy. For his connection with Irish land see *C. S. P. Ireland, Charles I and the Commonwealth,* III, 522, 546, 645, IV, 141, 218.
[12] Clotworthy, Holles.
[13] St. John.   [14] Haselrig, Vane.

The two-hundred-odd men that Pym had to work through were pitifully inadequate material for the task he had at hand. Many of them did not want to fight; most had not the vaguest notion how to organize the unwieldy club of landlords called Parliament into an effective bureau for war administration; and some who understood what must be done did not have the heart and stomach to do it. Since June men all over England had been taking up arms for the King or for Parliament. Late in October the King's army met the Parliamentary forces in an indecisive battle at Edgehill. All hopes of an early peace were blown away with the haze of that battle. Some of the hitherto feckless optimists in Parliament suffered a rude shock, especially those who maintained "at the beginning of our warfare that it would be only to show ourselves in the field with a few forces, and then all would be presently ended." [15] Parliament's feeble moves toward preparedness had been made with the persistent faith that the war would be short, or under the pathetic illusion that there would not really be a war at all.[16] After Edgehill hope, faith, and illusion had to make way for the reality of a king in arms and undefeated, who considered the members of Parliament at Westminster enemies, rebels, perhaps traitors. Those members must now either negotiate with Charles for peace, or make ready for a serious war of uncertain duration, or both.

Partisans on both sides had failed to see in the events of 1642 the signs of an inevitable trend toward cataclysm. On the contrary, many of them found in the course of events a dim, improbable, almost nightmarish quality that left them frightened, surprised, and confused. Bulstrode Whitelock, who was stodgy and pompous, but surely no fool, reflected a prevalent

[15] *Rushworth*, v, 386.
[16] This delusion appears in a dozen contemporary letters. For example, Cowper MSS ii, *H. M. C. Report XII*, app. ii, *passim*; Verney MSS, *H. M. C. Report VII*, app. i, pp. 431–508; *C. S. P. Domestic*, Charles I, XVII *passim*. As late as June 22, 1642, Henry Manners wrote Lord Montague from London: "I trust we shall have no blood. Undoubtedly it will not begin from hence, and of the King's disposition . . . I cannot expect anything but good." (Beaulieu MSS, *H. M. C. Report*, p. 154.)

feeling when a few weeks after the outbreak of hostilities he
spoke with perplexity of how Parliament had

insensibly slipped into this beginning of a civil war by one unexpected
accident after another, as waves of the sea which have brought us
thus far, and we scarce know how; but from paper combats by
declarations, notes, messages, and replies we are now come to the
question of raising forces. . . .[17]

Against the drift of circumstances leading them into open
combat with their rightful king the more conservative members
of Parliament reacted sharply. Men still sitting in the House
of Commons, who later went over to the Royalists,[18] would
have accepted peace at almost any price. Others shared their
yearning for peace, though not their willingness to forsake
or betray Parliament to attain it. Sir Benjamin Rudyerd, an
ex-courtier and latterly a Puritan commercial entrepreneur,[19]
cried out in the House for an end to fratricidal bloodshed.[20]
Bulstrode Whitelock solemnly warned his fellow members of
the inevitable evils of civil war, of dark days impending when
reason, honor, and justice would leave the land, when laws and
liberties must be surrendered into the hands of insolent mer-
cenaries, and "the ignoble will rule the noble." [21] The queru-
lous antiquarian, Sir Simond Dewes, his understanding of
present realities dimmed by a too-long adoring contemplation
of the common law, actually voted against fortifying a town
menaced by a Royalist attack, because, he said, to fortify it
would be illegal.[22]

The faction that wanted a quick peace — almost any peace

[17] *Whitelock*, p. 58.
[18] Among the future renegades still members in good standing in November
1642 were Sir Guy Palmes (*C. J.*, III, 34), Sir Hugh Cholmeley (*W.*, fol. 29),
Sir Robert Crane (*D.*, 164, fol. 274), Edmund Waller (*D.*, 164, fol. 352),
William Constantine (*D.*, 164, fol. 243), and the Hothams (*D.*, 164, fol. 354).
[19] Samuel Rawson Gardiner, *History of England, 1603–1642*, 10 vols.
(1883–84), IV, 235, 342; A. P. Newton, *Colonizing Activity of the English
Puritans* (1914), pp. 41, 67–68.
[20] *Sir Benjamin Rudyerd His Speech for Propositions of Peace* (1642), pp.
1–6.
[21] *Rushworth*, v, 160–161.
[22] *D.*, 164, fol. 303.

would do if it were quick enough — found a leader in one of
the five members whose impeachment the King had sought
when he broke in on the House of Commons in January 1642.
In the first year of the Long Parliament, Denzil Holles had
been fiery enough to stand out in the King's mind as a leader
of the radicals; but early in the war Holles had got stuck in
the mud in a futile siege of Sherborne Castle. At the sound
of a bullet the raw levies he led "fell flat on their bellies" in
fright or simply ran away, and the man whom Charles II was
to make Baron Holles of Ifield discovered in himself a reluctance to die for any cause "like a fool in the company of
heartless beasts, with whom we had no more wit than to engage
our honors and lives." [23] Contempt for his own soldiers and
painful forebodings of the ultimate fate of an army composed
of such men brought Holles by the way of disgust and despair
to thoughts of accommodation with the King. Such at least is
the most charitable explanation of the change in Denzil Holles,
although earlier in 1642 a letter-writer, observing a slackening
in Holles's ardor, attributed it to his marriage to "a bitch
wife." [24] Whether the causes for his transmutation were martial
or marital, Holles on the morrow of Edgehill was at the head
of a faction in Parliament anxiously seeking conciliation with
Charles I.

At the other extreme were men who would have peace only
on terms that the King could not possibly grant, and men who
in their hearts did not want peace with the King at all. Alexander Rigby proclaimed the right of the Houses to levy what
taxes they pleased for whatever purposes they pleased,[25] and
Sir Henry Ludlow maintained that the two Houses were above
the King.[26] Henry Martin looked forward to an English republic or at least a change of dynasty.[27] Between the extremes
represented by Martin's treason to the royal house and Edmund

[23] Braye MSS, *H. M. C. Report X*, app. vi, pp. 147–148.
[24] Cowper MSS ii, *H. M. C. Report XII*, app. ii, p. 314.
[25] *D.*, 164, fol. 113.
[26] *Y.*, 18777, fol. 54.
[27] *Clar. H. R.*, bk. v, par. 280 and n. 1.

Waller's treachery to Parliament were ranged the rest of the members. How they were grouped remains to be seen.

During the early months of the Civil War no one seriously challenged John Pym's leadership of Parliament. In the confusion of fear, hope, and rancor that seized the members of both Houses after Edgehill, the influence of a great and effective leader might determine the course Parliament should take. Pym could employ his influence to press Parliament along one of three possible lines of action. He could use all his prestige in favor of a quick peace. Or he could trust the boldness of the more fiery spirit to leaven the more lumpish mass of members and force a vigorous war policy. Or he might try to balance the extreme parties with a middle group. The last alternative demanded great patience, great effort, and great finesse since it involved controlling the centrifugal forces that manifest themselves when the bounds and bands of political society are broken.

PART ONE

PYM AND THE MIDDLE GROUP

CHAPTER I

PYM AS POLITICAL ARTIST

FROM Clarendon [1] to the latest potboiling biographer of the leader of the Civil War Parliament,[2] authority stands behind the thesis that John Pym led the "war party"; or, by implication, that at the head of the most violent and militant members of the House of Commons, he cut ruthlessly through to his goal of an effective Parliament-in-arms. Before we can verify or modify this hypothesis we must examine Pym's policy as it developed after the Civil War broke out. Ideal for the purpose of such an examination are the dreary months of bickering and haggling over peace terms and peace negotiations that followed the indecisive battle of Edgehill. Pym was at the height of his power, and he faced a prolonged crisis fit to test that power and perhaps to destroy it.

Ordinary run-of-the-mine citizens can rarely contemplate with equanimity the prospect of cutting one another's throats, and few men in England relished the thought of plunging deeper into the chaos of civil war. They wanted first to test the possibilities of arriving at a peaceful settlement.[3] The issue before the House in the autumn of 1642 was really not whether Parliament should treat with the King, but on what terms it should treat, and what it should do during the preparation and progress of the treaty. On both these questions there existed a vague sort of unanimity. The Earl of Essex, the Lord General of the parliamentary forces, favored only a treaty in which Parliament should accept no unreasonable terms, and the City of London would have only such a peace as was consistent with the security of religion, the reformation of Church and

[1] *Clar. H. R.*, bk. VII, par. 413.
[2] C. E. Wade, *John Pym* (1912), pp. 286–308.
[3] *C. S. P. Venetian*, XXVI, 159–175.

State, and the privileges of Parliament.[4] But in the actual formulation of the peace proposals it was not Essex nor the city fathers, nor any warlike group in the Houses, that gave content to those shadowy phantasms, "privileges of Parliament, reformation of Church and State, security of religion." The pacific Holles and his allies worked out most of the propositions ultimately presented to the King at Oxford.[5] Before even discussing the terms of the treaty the House of Commons decided its own course during the period of negotiation. It resolved not to permit the treaty to interfere with the necessary military preparations.[6] This resolution put Pym in a sound strategic position. With one hand he could make peaceful gestures to the Royalists, and with the other industriously mold the administrative weapons that Parliament, if the treaty came to nothing, might turn against the King.

Skillful politicians rarely receive their just due from the historians. Frequently they are not inspiring, eye-catching, heart-moving figures. They do not, they cannot afford to, indulge in splendid gestures or bold deeds. Chatham making fine speeches, daring greatly, and going mad at intervals, is more exciting than his laborious, cautious, competent son. Sir John Eliot, uttering noble sentiments and dying in prison a conspicuous martyr, is more entertaining and also less effective than the black-letter lawyers of the early Stuart Parliaments, who said little and showed no yearning for the martyr's crown. Unfortunately for the great politician, the nature of his work forbids him to indulge in imperial gestures. He is merely the manipulator, the economizer of whatever material the uncontrolled drift of affairs brings within his reach. Such a one was John Pym. He had the dull but useful knack of squeezing the maximum political energy out of the most unpromising raw materials and of applying that energy at the time and in the

[4] C. W., I, 54; C. S. P. Venetian, XXVI, 222; House of Lords MSS, H. M. C. Report V, app. i, p. 62.
[5] Holles's speeches, Y., 18777, fols. 64–64v, 65, 66; Glynn's speeches, ibid., fols. 66, 66v, 67; Whitelock's speech, ibid., fol. 66.
[6] L. J., V, 431.

place where it would be most effective; somehow or other he kept things going. His performance was often awkward and sometimes downright crude; but, then, few men succeed in running an obstacle race gracefully, and those who do are rarely winners.

The obstacles confronting Pym would have given pause to a less stubborn man. The fraction of Parliament left at Westminster was engaged in an unpromising conflict with its anointed lord and king. By November 1642 this segment at Westminster had gone so far in preparing for a serious war as to appoint a commander-in-chief for what it optimistically called its forces. Beyond that it had yet to pass even the most necessary and obvious measures for the successful prosecution of a war. It had seized on the customs of the Port of London, but the civil turmoil had reduced the income from those customs to a trickle.[7] Besides this thin trickle Parliament had no source of regular revenue, nor did it have any administrative machinery for the collection of taxes. It had little administrative machinery for any purpose whatsoever. It had no ally ready to come to its aid, should the King press too hard. It did not have even the skeleton of a permanent military organization; it had merely a volunteer army paid — or more often not paid — by voluntary contributions. Nothing was done; all was to do. Each step in the doing was rankly illegal; yet each had to be passed on by lawyers and country gentlemen whose hardest complaint against the King had been that his government was arbitrary and against the law.[8] To succeed in these precarious circumstances a leader in Parliament needed a minute knowledge of the balance of forces in both Houses, tact in the handling of perplexed men, and mastery of the craft of political timing. Working with material as recalcitrant as the members at Westminster against time and a determined enemy, a competent leader might fail and be

---

[7] *C. S. P. Venetian*, XXVI, 7.

[8] Samuel Rawson Gardiner, *Constitutional Documents of the Puritan Revolution, 1628–1660* (1888), pp. 202–232, the Grand Remonstrance.

pardoned his failure. Pym did not fail. Between November 6, 1642, when the King on a flimsy pretext slighted the first overtures of Parliament after Edgehill,[9] and the middle of the following April, when the treaty between Charles and Parliament at Oxford was broken off, Pym had either pushed through or thrown open to discussion almost every important administrative, fiscal, and military ordinance enacted by Parliament during the Civil War.[10] During the few months of life remaining to him after the treaty collapsed all his proposed measures were adopted.[11] He left Parliament with an administrative organization in the counties, with an ally ready to march in arms to its assistance, and with three armies of its own to take the field against the King.

Parliament needed allies, armies, and an administration, but first and foremost it needed money. Its most serious ailment, at once chronic and acute, was insufficient funds. To this deficiency Pym gave his special attention in the waning months of 1642. He was fortunate to find someone to lend him powerful assistance in his work, assistance both unsolicited and involuntary. He had as an auxiliary Charles I, King of England. Pym utilized the momentary indignation of otherwise cautious members at some fresh evidences of the King's bad faith or bad opinions to persuade Parliament to add one story after another to its crazy, ramshackle, yet somehow usable financial structure. The first money bill was the hardest. The scruples of the Houses might have indefinitely postponed its passage, had His Majesty spent less energy after Edgehill convincing the members at Westminster that the only

---

[9] Y., 18777, fols. 51–52.

[10] Measures enacted to April 30, 1643: martial law, 9 November 1642 (A. O. I., 1, 37); assessment of London, 26 November 1642 (A. O. I., 1, 38–40); association of counties, 31 December 1642 (A. O. I., 1, 49–55); weekly assessment, 24 February 1643 (A. O. I., 1, 85–100); sequestration of delinquents' estates, 27 March 1643 (A. O. I., 1, 106–117).

[11] Assessment of the fifth and twentieth, 7 May 1643 (A. O. I., 1, 145); Vow and Covenant, 9 June 1643 (A. O. I., 1, 175–176); Assembly of Divines, 12 June 1643 (A. O. I., 1, 180–187); alliance with Scotland, 19 July 1643 (A. O. I., 1, 202–215; excise, 22 July 1643 (A. O. I., 1, 202–214); Solemn League and Covenant (Rushworth, v, 478).

way he could be made to see a point was at the end of a pike, and that if they wanted a settlement at terms better than surrender they would have to fight for it.

On November 6 Charles refused to receive a peace delegation from Parliament because he had previously proclaimed one of the delegates a traitor.[12] Having provoked them by his refusal to receive their emissaries of peace, Charles a few days later threw the members into a rage by attacking Brentford, just west of London, while plans for a treaty were in progress.[13] The House of Commons was not quite angry enough to discard the idea of conciliation; when Charles offered a lame explanation of the Brentford affair, it voted to continue negotiations with him.[14] But at least the majority was shocked into listening to the pessimists who had suggested all along that it was unwise to rely solely on the King's sweet reasonableness. On the same day that the resumption of the treaty was voted, the *soi-disant* "most active and religious part of the city" providentially brought in a petition. The active and religious gentlemen begged that some way to raise money be found that would not put all the expense of the war on the "good and godly party," that is, on those good enough and godly enough to contribute voluntarily to the cause.[15] This request harmonized so well with Pym's known wishes that an unfriendly witness might have suspected the assiduous John of lending Providence a helping hand in the production of the petition.[16]

Thus Pym, with the aid of Charles I and the citizens of London, prepared the minds of the members of Parliament for a money-making scheme. He needed only a little more help from the King to make them accept it. Charles did not fail him; on November 24 he rejected the four proposals on which Parliament wished to treat. Whatever opposition there

[12] *L. J.*, v, 435–436.

[13] *C. S. P. Venetian*, XXVI, 201–202.

[14] *C. S. P. Domestic*, Charles I, XVII, 406; *C. J.*, II, 858–861.

[15] *C. J.*, II, 857.

[16] Dewes on a later occasion accused Pym of using his City friends to petition for the things he wanted (*D.*, 164, fol. 303*v*).

may have been to the plans of Pym and his good and godly friends vanished. On November 25 the Commons read, passed, and sent up to the Lords an ordinance for an assessment to be levied on London. On the following day the Lords passed it with the same startling dispatch. The measure was a revolution in its own rights. The Houses had taken it upon themselves to raise money without the consent of the King and to coerce those who refused to contribute.[17] Pym had coaxed Parliament into its first step toward an adequate system of war finance. The first step was the hardest.

The first step was the hardest, but the next few steps were not easy. The Houses were still shaky and hesitant. Pym and his friends did not give the rest of the members too much time to measure the gravity of their actions. For the next few months they crammed the agenda of the House with proposals for raising money — confiscations, land taxes, personal property taxes, general assessments, excises. Projects for financing the war came so thick and fast that they seemed to perplex even the clerk of the House. A bill for a weekly assessment, a bill for a monthly assessment, a bill for assessing non-contributors, a bill sequestering the estates of Royalists, followed by a confused barrage of directive resolutions, pop into and out of committee almost daily, so that it is well-nigh impossible to follow in detail their legislative history.[18]

To tide the armies over during the critical weeks while the committees shaped the great money ordinances Pym got Parliament to approve temporary financial expedients. The House extended the application of the London assessment piecemeal to other sections of parliamentary England.[19] They passed a permissive ordinance to allow the deputy lieutenants to raise

[17] Gardiner calls the measure of November 26 a tax (*C. W.*, 1, 65). The ordinance was badly drafted (*C. J.*, II, 858, 863; *L. J.*, v, 460, 462–463), and it was necessary for the Houses to pass an explanatory ordinance three days later (*C. J.*, II, 867; *L. J.*, v, 467), and another two weeks after (*L. J.*, v, 471). The implication of these measures seems to be that the original law was intended to be not strictly a tax, but a forced loan with promise of repayment.

[18] *C. J.*, II, 875–993.

[19] *C. J.*, II, 893, 932.

money in their own counties.[20] They tried to squeeze a little more money out of the customs.[21] Such measures were palliatives. They did not commit Parliament to a permanent scheme of illegal taxation. They might bring in a little cash for a little while. Half-hearted measures suited the half-hearted men in the House, men who hoped they would not have to go further and believed they would not, because the King must surely accept the peace proposals they were getting ready to offer him.

Pym had little faith in the likelihood that Charles would accept the proposals of the House and no faith whatever in the utility of palliatives. Armies demand permanent revenue, not half measures. It seemed to Pym only too likely that, when the time came, Parliament would find itself without peace and without the wherewithal to wage war. Parliament must have a regular supply of money, or the cause of Parliament must perish. Viewing the situation from Oxford, Charles I came to the same conclusion. He tried to work on the timidity and hesitance he detected among his enemies. He declared illegal the levy of customs in London and the raising of taxes by the Houses without royal consent.[22] Pym answered the King's declaration by brazenly begging the question. He said that the Houses raised taxes by the same right that they raised an army.[23] To a Royalist this was no answer to the King's accusation, but merely another way of phrasing it. But Pym had to fight back and take his arguments where he found them. He had to fight back because the King's attempt to scare the House away from the money bills threatened to succeed. Time after time the Commons recommitted the weekly assessment, the assessment of those not contributing to Parliament, the sequestration ordinance.[24] On February 1 not

---

[20] *L. J.*, v, 482.

[21] *C. J.*, II, 901–927. The custom receipts, however, were assigned to the navy (II, 928).

[22] *C. J.*, II, 903; *Rushworth*, v, 114–116.

[23] *Rushworth*, v, 115.

[24] *C. J.*, II, 875, 878, 886, 899, 900.

one of the three ordinances had got the approval of the House, although all three had been under consideration for more than a month.[25]

Pym and his friends did what they could to shake the House from its torpor. They pointed out that the King was levying taxes in the counties under his control. When His Majesty rejected the overtures of the City requesting him to come to London and settle peace, Pym used the refusal to press the need for a more vigorous prosecution of the war.[26] The City helped him. A Common Hall — the assembly of all the livery-men of all the Companies of London — put itself on record in favor of an assessment.[27] At last the legislative jam showed signs of breaking. A little more pressure might thrust several of the money bills through the House. That little more was supplied, as usual, by the King. Slowly and patiently during December and January Parliament had worked out its peace terms.[28] By the beginning of February it had them ready. Just a little before the committee of the Houses left for Oxford with the propositions, Lord Fairfax, Parliament's commander in the north, intercepted some letters from the King. On January 30 they were read in both Houses. They proved the prevalence of Popery in the Duke of Newcastle's Royalist army and indicated that Charles wanted nothing done to discourage the enlistment of Papists under the Duke's standard.[29] The men at Westminster agreed unanimously on almost nothing; but in their hatred of Roman Catholicism the most moderate members did not yield to the most violent. There they stood on common ground.[30] All believed they saw in

[25] The House of Commons started to work on the general problem of supply early in December (*C. J.*, II, 870).
[26] *C. S. P. Venetian*, XXVI, 234.
[27] *Perfect Diurnall*, January 9–16.
[28] *D.*, 164, fols. 243–287; *Y.*, 18777, fols. 70v–139.
[29] *L. J.*, v, 580; *Rushworth*, v, 125–126.
[30] *Y.*, 18777, fols. 112–114v. If in this debate on the menace of Popery Yonge had not indicated the names of the speakers, nothing in the speeches would enable us to distinguish the words of the peaceful Holles and Rudyerd from those of the bellicose Rigby and Blakistone.

His Majesty's letters evidence of what they must expect and fear if the peace proposals failed and the King triumphed in the war [31] — the toleration, perhaps the triumph of Popery. So February began with the majority in Parliament hoping for a successful treaty, but suspicious of the King's good faith, and aware of the danger to the Cause, should peace not ensue.

Pym and his aides now had their chance to press the House of Commons into action on its own declared policy: treat for peace and prepare for war.[32] On the day that Parliament's commissioners at Oxford presented their proposals to the King,[33] Sir Gilbert Gerard was telling the members the sad tale of misery and want in their army and exhaustion and emptiness in their war chest. He also pointed the moral of the tale. It was no longer possible to fill the chest or supply the army out of voluntary contributions. They must find some regular general source of revenue to take the place of free-will offerings.[34] Gerard made his appeal on the first day of February. The House of Commons did not even wait for their commissioners to return from Oxford. The members released the ordinance for an assessment of non-contributors and passed it.[35] Then they stayed for Charles's answer to their peace proposals. It arrived on the sixth of February. Pym could have hoped for nothing better. The King declared that whoever was responsible for the propositions only desired "to make things worse and worse." To the proposals of Parliament which he would not accept he answered with counter proposals of his own that Parliament could not accept.[36] In effect he asked the Houses to withdraw all their demands and trust in God and their King.[37] He thus ensured the passage of the new money measures through the House of Commons. He had taught the members to have more faith in God and dry powder than in the King's word. At Westminster men might still debate the expediency of resuming the treaty. In

[31] *D.*, 164, fol. 286.
[32] See, above, pp. 13–14.
[33] *Whitelock*, p. 67.
[34] *D.*, 164, fol. 287.

[35] *C. J.*, II, 955.
[36] *Whitelock*, p. 67.
[37] *Rushworth*, v, 169.

view of His Majesty's reply to their propositions they could no longer doubt that they must prepare for the worst — war *à l'outrance*. They passed the bill for a weekly assessment.[38] In seven days Pym had seen the Commons approve two great general tax ordinances and send them to the Lords.[39] The "promoter of the rebellion" could congratulate himself on a good week's work.

Still the job was something less than half done. The ordinance for sequestering the estates of Royalists was still in committee in the House of Commons, and the Lords had not yet consented to either the weekly assessment or the assessment on non-contributors. The sequestration ordinance had about it an aroma of confiscation which might make it unpopular in an assembly of landlords. Pym let it rest in committee a while and concentrated on winning the assent of the Lords to the assessment bills. A steady procession of messengers from the lower house begged the peers to act quickly on the measures.[40] They pointed out that a loan for war expenses had to be raised in the City, and that the City financiers would expect a security more tangible than the good faith of Parliament. They reasoned and cajoled in vain. The Commons had on February 11 turned down the Lords' suggestion to resume negotiations before disbanding the armies.[41] Now in reprisal the Lords held up all the money ordinances.[42] The younger Vane and his friends wanted to make the recalcitrance of the peers a pretext for an open breach with them.[43] Pym counseled moderation.[44] His friend and collaborator, Sir Philip Stapleton, proposed a compromise.[45] It conceded much to the Lords and would bring about a resumption of negotiations with the King. The Commons accepted Stapleton's proposal; the Lords next day passed the weekly assessment ordinance.[46]

[38] *C. J.*, II, 958.
[39] *L. J.*, V, 597.
[40] *C. J.*, II, 963, 967, 968.
[41] *C. J.*, II, 961, 962.
[42] *L. J.*, V, 608–610.
[43] *Y.*, 18777, fols. 157–157v.
[44] *Y.*, 18777, fol. 157.
[45] *Y.*, 18777, fol. 158.
[46] *L. J.*, V, 610.

Having finally seen one of the general tax bills through both Houses, Pym let up on the Lords and set about bringing the sequestration ordinance before the Commons. He had hardly got the measure out of committee when Charles, ever obliging, incensed the Commons by proclaiming their county associations traitorous,[47] and even aroused the Lords by returning to their proposals for a cessation of armed hostilities an answer as uncompromising as the one he had formerly given to their peace propositions.[48] The peers thereupon notified the Commons that they were resolved "if a just peace with the security of religion and liberty cannot by fair means be obtained, to go on in such a way as may evidence to the world their constancy to the cause." [49] The day after they received this resolution the Commons passed the new sequestration bill.[50] The peers, at last awake to the difficulty of making terms with Charles I, were further enlightened by two intercepted letters. In one the King revealed that he regarded the Oxford treaty less as a means to peace than as a vehicle to show forth his own magnanimity and the stubbornness of the rebel Parliament, and that he had many "fine designs" for taking advantage of "the distraction of the rebels." [51] The second royal letter proved to Parliament's satisfaction that in Ireland the King had identified his interests with the triumph of the Papists over the Protestants.[52] The letters had a profound effect. When the King showed signs of consuming yet more time over new proposals which even the exacting Dewes regarded as models of "justice and equalibrancy," [53] and when some moderate members of the Commons had pointed out to the peers that their scruples about confiscating the revenues of the Royalists were not shared by the King in his dealings with

[47] *Y.,* 18777, fol. 169.
[48] *L. J.,* v, 638–639, 641.
[49] *C. J.,* II, 991.
[50] *C. J.,* II, 993.
[51] *Letters of Queen Henrietta Maria* . . . , ed. M. A. E. Green (1857), pp. 174–175.
[52] *D.,* 164, fols. 329–329v.
[53] *D.,* 164, fol. 334.

the estates of the Parliamentarians,[54] the upper house followed the lower in consenting to the ordinance for sequestering the estates of delinquents.[55] Two weeks after Pym with the inadvertent assistance of the King had slipped the sequestration ordinance through Parliament, the Oxford treaty collapsed.[56]

The months of weary negotiation had thus seen the passage of three money bills of the utmost importance, one establishing the precedent for forced levies by ordinance of the Houses, the other two opening up sources of revenue that Parliament would continue to tap for many years. The weekly assessment and sequestration ordinances did more than that. They set up the system of county committees, which was the standard and universal organ of central control over local administration until the Restoration.

When Parliament's effort to bring peace by treaty failed, there was still an item of unfinished business on Pym's agenda — the ordinance assessing one-fifth of the income from land and one-twentieth of the personal property of all who had not voluntarily contributed to Parliament. When the bill was first introduced in the House of Commons it had given Sir Simond Dewes "heartburnings" and other symptoms of a slightly dyspeptic conservatism.[57] It limped and tottered through the Houses, pushed aside now for the debate on the peace proposals, now for more promising revenue bills. For months after the Commons passed it in the burst of energy that came after the opening of negotiations at Oxford, it lay neglected and apparently quite dead in the House of Lords. When the Oxford treaty was no longer more than an irritating memory, the lower house, at the instigation of some of Pym's friends,[58] reminded the Lords of the ordinance for assessing non-contributors; and almost half a year after the Commons had first taken up the measure, the peers made it law for the counties held by Parliament.[59]

[54] D., 164, fols. 344v–345.
[55] A. O. I., I, 106–117.
[58] Gerard (D., 164, fol. 380v); Mildmay (D., 164, fol. 381).
[59] A. O. I., I, 145–155; L. J., VI, 33.

[56] C. W., I, 108.
[57] D., 164, fol. 243.

Like an industrious hen, Pym, when he was not busy hatching one batch of schemes, set about laying another. So during the winter negotiations he did not limit his attention to maneuvering the money bills introduced in February along their devious course. Even those bills did not supply Parliament with funds adequate to maintain its armies, nor did they exhaust Pym's expedients for raising money. No sooner had the House of Lords assented to the sequestration ordinance than Pym sprung an excise scheme in the House of Commons. On a smaller scale it raised in the House just such an uproar as the excise scheme of another great commoner, Robert Walpole, was to raise throughout the country a hundred years later. Members rose to condemn Pym's proposal as "an unjust, scandalous, and destructive project," [60] and with his wonted patience Pym did not press his point.[61] Pym's excise plan, however, did not ultimately share the ignominious fate which overtook Walpole's. When the Oxford treaty had run its futile course, the same House that had so roundly condemned the excise revived it; [62] and ere many months passed, it had become, with the assessment, the land tax, and the delinquents' sequestrations, one of the main financial props of the Parliamentary cause.[63]

The four great money bills along with the customs and an occasional special assessment levied on a county [64] or on London [65] completed Pym's plan for supplying Parliament with

[60] *D.*, 164, fol. 346.

[61] Dewes has it that the scheme was rejected (*D.*, 164, fol. 346*v*). Whitaker's version that discussion of it was postponed seems more probable in the light of subsequent developments (*W.*, fol. 38).

[62] A committee to consider an excise was appointed on April 12 (*W.*, fol. 42*v*). Pym was not a member of it (*C. J.*, III, 41). It is worthy of note that Strode had already suggested an excise on luxuries in January. There is no evidence in the surviving accounts of the Commons' debates that the slightest attention was given to his proposal at the time (*Y.*, 18777, fol. 133*v*).

[63] *A. O. I.*, I, 202–214.

[64] E.g., assessment of Warwickshire (*A. O. I.*, I, 56); Northamptonshire, Huntingdonshire, Rutlandshire, Leicestershire, Nottinghamshire, Bedfordshire, Derbyshire, Buckinghamshire (*ibid.*, I, 61–62); Devonshire (*ibid.*, 164); Somerset (*ibid.*, I, 69); Gloucestershire (*ibid.*, I, 79). Most of the county assessments were modeled on the first London assessment (*ibid.*, I, 38–41).

[65] Assessments on London (*A. O. I.*, I, 38–41, 77–79, 267–271, 321–322).

the sinews of war. The program was hasty, slapdash, tentative. The excise was a source of chronic irritation to the Londoners, irritation that occasionally expressed itself in riot.[66] The ordinance for the fifth and twentieth part was even worse. The assessment of a fifth of the rent of non-contributors required elaborate machinery to identify the non-contributors and to determine the assessment. It opened the way to all manner of chicanery, tyranny, petty vengeance, and favoritism on the part of assessors and collectors. And for all the trouble it gave, the yield was pitifully low.[67] Administrative difficulties, similar to those that made the assessment of non-contributors Pym's least successful fiscal experiment, forced a modification in the management of estates seized under the sequestration ordinance. The encumbrance of debts and claims against some Royalist estates, the difficulty of inducing tenants to pay their rents to Parliament, the danger of a land-glutted market if confiscation went too far, the splendid opportunities open to sequestrators for corruption and connivance, convinced Parliament that a less drastic scheme might be more effective. Sequestration continued under the ordinance, but Royalists were allowed to redeem their estates after taking an oath never to bear arms against Parliament and paying a large fine in composition for their so-called delinquency.[68] Even the weekly assessment had a defect. For the county committees the collection of trifling sums every week was simply a nuisance. In 1645 Parliament changed the assessment from a weekly to a monthly basis.

Yet a part of Pym's seemingly jerry-built structure survived all the shocks of civil war. The excise produced a flexible

---

[66] C. W., III, 216.

[67] C. S. P. Committee for the Advance of Money, I–III, is a calendar of the proceedings of the central committee charged with administration of the ordinance of the fifth and twentieth part. The measure in a year brought in about £260,000, less than one-fifth of what had been demanded (loc. cit., I, vii).

[68] The proceedings of the committee for compounding fill five volumes of the Calendar of State Papers (C. S. P. Committee for Compounding, I–v). The development of the procedure is related in the introduction to the first volume.

revenue that could be regulated according to need by expanding or contracting the list of excisable commodities. The Committee for the Advance of Monies for years squeezed small driblets of cash out of the assessment of non-contributors. The sequestration ordinance continued to function as the necessary preliminary to the imposition of redemption fines on the Royalists. Cromwell's great New Model Army lived on a monthly assessment levied in lump on each county and apportioned to individual property owners by the local authorities, a measure differing from the old weekly assessment only in its greater efficiency. Finally the county committees of local magnates, employed by Parliament for both assessment and sequestration, remained until the Restoration the principal link between Parliament and the country, charged with heavy responsibilities in their own neighborhoods for the success of the Parliamentary cause. We need hardly be surprised that experience suggested alterations in the superstructure of Pym's financial system. The history of the past hundred years has taught us that laws seldom spring all perfect from the mind that conceives them. What is really surprising is the durability of the foundations of the system Pym laid out so hastily.

So Pym ministered to the fiscal needs of the Cause; but he realized that wars are not won with money alone. Pounds sterling buy ammunition, but they do not shoot guns. For some of the measures he deemed essential to the success of the Cause, Pym had to wait on the course of events; Parliament was not ready for them. It was only after a full year of war that the specter of defeat, with all defeat means to men whom their enemies regard as traitors, confronted the members of Parliament. Until fear had done its work on his colleagues, Pym could only point to the course he knew they eventually must take. This he did assiduously. Save impressment, every important project for defense that Parliament adopted until the time of his death Pym broached once or several times between the opening of negotiations with Charles and the collapse of the Oxford treaty in April.

Such a project was the excise of which we have already written. Such also were the alliance with Scotland and the oath of association. Of all the schemes Pym's fertile brain brought forth, these two were most dear to his heart. He had taken the lead in putting through the Protestation of Parliament of 1641 — the Tennis Court Oath of the Puritan Revolution.[69] Pym believed that the principle of association should be extended beyond the Houses. The outbreak of hostilities enhanced the importance of a covenant among men of good will to maintain their religion and liberties against all odds and any force whatever. Pym proposed an oath of association to the House a few days before Edgehill,[70] but he got no hearing. The clamor of that battle had scarce died away, and the clamor of the opposing sides claiming victory had not yet risen, when Pym again submitted the form of an oath to the Commons.[71] Although some members found the form of the association too moderate,[72] the proposal was quickly heard; the Houses quickly decided to publish their resolve to "unite with all the well-affected . . . of His Majesty's dominion" at hazard of their lives to defend the cause; [73] and quickly they forget about their resolution, and nothing came of it. Pym did not therefore quit plugging. A few weeks later he returned to the charge. He tried to commit the House in advance to an association should the peace treaty with Charles come to nothing.[74] Again the House was ostensibly receptive, and resolved that "in case the King shall not accept of our petition we shall enter into an association to defend our religion, laws, and liberties." It took many months of weary haggling barren of consequence to convince the majority in Commons against its will that Charles would not accede to its

[69] Gardiner, *History of England*, IX, 353.

[70] *D.*, 164, fol. 324v.

[71] *Y.*, 18777, fol. 41; *L. J.*, v, 412.

[72] Martin objected to the inclusion of the protection of the King's person among the objects of the association (*Y.*, 18777, fol. 40v).

[73] *L. J.*, v, 418–419.

[74] Pym made his proposal on November 10 between the King's rejection of Evelyn as commissioner and the attack on Brentford (*Y.*, 18777, fol. 53v).

demands, and in the meantime Pym had again put forward a plan of association. He gave the scheme a new twist. Seeking to capitalize on the indignation of the members at Charles's refusal to discourage Popery in Newcastle's army, Pym threw out the suggestion that now was the appropriate time for a covenant among the pure in spirit against the Catholic menace. By way of good measure he proposed that Scotland be brought into the anti-Catholic association.[75] At the same time he was using the King's correspondence with Newcastle as an argument for his tax measures; [76] it was a characteristic attempt to squeeze the very last drop of advantage out of a situation; but Pym overestimated the political potential of the anti-Catholic hysteria in the House. Popery was good for a lush forensic outburst against the Painted Woman and a batch of antiquated expedients directed against recusancy; [77] but that was all. Pym's little scheme was drowned in a flood of oratory in which the more voluble members of the House indicated their unqualified disapprobation of the Antichrist.[78]

Though Parliament was as yet stony ground for Pym's favorite project, in the City it took root and flourished exceedingly. Ministers in London wrote pamphlets in favor of an association.[79] The City fathers petitioned for "a religious covenant to be entered into," and reminded the House of its former resolution to bind the godly together.[80] They even tried a sort of political blackmail, covertly threatening to withhold necessary loans until the House acceded to their request.[81] Pym acted as the City's spokesman in the House of Commons.[82] Still Parliament remained cold and indifferent to the oath of association.

It showed a similar lack of interest in an alliance with the Scots, a measure which Pym insisted on with his wonted per-

[75] *Y.*, 18777, fol. 112.

[76] See, above, pp. 20–21.

[77] *C. J.*, II, 913.

[78] *Y.*, 18777, fols. 112–114*v*. Only Rigby and Whitelock are recorded as rallying to Pym's scheme.

[79] Edward Bowles, *Plaine Englishe* (1643).   [81] *D.*, 164, fol. 381.

[80] *C. J.*, II, 976; *Y.*, 18777, fol. 162.   [82] *D.*, 164, fol. 324.

sistence and vigor. Onto the abortive resolution for a covenant
that he slipped through Parliament in October, he tacked a
clause expressing the expectation that "our brethren of Scotland . . . will help and assist us in defence of this cause."[83]
A few days later the Houses resolved to call for Scottish aid.[84]
Pym even got John Pickering sent to Scotland with Parliament's resolution and a rather vague commission "to solicit
the affecting of it."[85] The fear he expressed at that time that
Parliament might fail to pursue its course with regard to the
Scottish alliance was justified. We have seen how little interest the proposed alliance evoked in February when Pym
presented it to the members along with a plan for a covenant.
When the negotiation with the King ended in the spring of
1643, Pym, gauging accurately the sentiment of the House
on both issues, adopted a policy of quiet waiting.[86] The projects were not dead but sleeping. The golden chance for resusci-
tating the scheme of association came in June. Pym and his
friends exposed the plot of Edmund Waller, John Hampden's
cousin, still sitting in Parliament, to betray London to the King.
Prominent citizens were implicated in the conspiracy, and
men suspected that Waller was not the only member of Parliament acting the role of enemy within the gates. Pym took
advantage of the momentary panic that the exposure of Waller
evoked in the House to bring the association into being under
the form of a vow and covenant;[87] but only its imminent defeat
and destruction, foreshadowed by the catastrophic overthrows
of its northern and western armies at Adwalton Moor and
Roundway Down, set Parliament on the road that led to the
amalgamation of the league with Scotland and the covenant
among the well-affected into one great Solemn League and
Covenant — Pym's last legislative masterpiece — which saved
the parliamentary cause for a time and ultimately destroyed it.

[83] *L. J.*, v, 419; *C. J.*, II, 832.
[84] *L. J.*, v, 430–431, 437.
[85] *C. J.*, II, 854; *Y.*, 18777, fol. 55.
[86] *D.*, 164, fol. 324.
[87] *D.*, 164, fols. 210–210*v*; *D.*, 165, fols. 93–97*v*; *D.*, 164, fols. 396–399.

CHAPTER II

THE MIDDLE GROUP

JOHN PYM'S most conspicuous talent was his skill in getting the approval of a parliamentary majority for his elaborate and novel program of defense. Less conspicuous, but perhaps more important for an understanding of the man, was his ability to get what he wanted without doing irreparable hurt to the *esprit de corps* of Parliament as a whole, without completely disrupting its morale. Sir Simond Dewes, who opposed him at every turn, quite unintentionally testifies to the deftness with which Pym used this second talent. Dewes derives a sort of morbid pleasure from recording in his diary the successive outrages perpetrated in the Civil War Parliament on the body of his beloved mistress, the common law. Naturally he said hard things about Pym's money bills when they were first proposed.[1] One might reasonably expect yet harsher things when the bills passed. In the early days of February 1643 we listen attentively for a lament from the diarist, for then in one week the House of Commons passed the bill for a weekly assessment and the bill for the assessment of the fifth and twentieth part, both measures outrageous from Dewes's point of view. We listen in vain; Dewes says nothing about the gross illegality of the bills; indeed he does not even take note of their passage.[2] Either he himself no longer objected to the bills or else the general opposition to them had so dwindled as not to warrant mention of it by a diarist who delighted in the trivial. Dewes thought an oath of association wicked, too, and in May characterized a project for such an oath as "a dangerous and ungodly snare."[3] In June Pym exposed the inept plot of Edmund Waller — member of Parliament, cousin of John

[1] *D.*, 164, fol. 113; *D.*, 164, fol. 243.
[2] *D.*, 164, fols. 287–293*v*.
[3] *D.*, 164, fol. 381.

Hampden, and poet of a sort — to raise a faction in the City against the Houses and open London to the Royalists. Pym took advantage of the fervent pro-Parliament spirit that the revelation of the City conspiracy evoked to induce the Houses to impose a vow and covenant along the lines of the oath of association which he had long advocated. That ardent opponent of oaths of association, Sir Simond Dewes, remarked that the Vow and Covenant was both "modest and sober," [4] and took it without a qualm.

The failure of the opponents of Pym's general defense program to rise in their wrath at the crucial moment when the House voted was a constant feature of the entire legislative history of that program. Although at one time or another there was indifference or positive hostility in the House to every measure Pym proposed, although every measure was of a controversial nature, in the end they all went through the House with surprising ease. To the sequestration ordinance alone was the last ditch opposition strenuous enough to warrant a division in the Commons; and there is reason to believe that Pym's more impetuous lieutenants took the management of that bill out of his hands, and jammed it through, when Pym, given a little time, would have eased it by without friction or division.[5] The rest of Pym's projects — assessment, excise, land tax, association, and Scottish alliance — slid gently through the House of Commons without so much as provoking a poll of the members.

[4] *D.*, 164, fol. 399.

[5] It is conjecture, of course, to say that Pym had nothing to do with the forcing through of the sequestration ordinance; but in favor of the conjecture there is the following evidence:

1. The moderate Lewis was a teller in favor of the ordinance, a fact which indicates that it was in no real danger of defeat (*C. J.*, II, 993).

2. Pym's handling of every other important ordinance shows that it was not his policy hastily to force through measures whose ultimate success was in any case certain.

3. Pym is not mentioned as a participant in the crucial debate by Yonge (*V.*, 18777, fols. 175–176v) or Dewes (*D.*, 164, fols. 315–316v). This is particularly significant in the case of Dewes, who rarely failed to see Pym's machinations in anything that he disliked as much as he disliked the tactics used to pass the sequestration ordinance.

The smoothness, regularity, and facility with which Pym slipped ordinance after ordinance through the House contrast with the unruly catch-as-catch-can business that the legislative process degenerated into after he died. In the eighteen months between his death and the battle of Naseby, Parliament considered only two really important projects involving changes in general policy — in 1644 the ordinances establishing and settling the powers of the Committee of Both Kingdoms and in 1645 the army reforms. There were four divisions — actual counts of the House — on the committee ordinances,[6] and at least four more on the army reforms.[7] In less than half eighteen months Pym had steered through the House of Commons six measures no less radical than those passed after he died, and on only one of the six was it necessary to poll the House. This is all the more remarkable because the factors which minimize the number of formal divisions in modern representative legislatures did not operate effectively in any English Parliament during the seventeenth century and did not operate at all in the Civil War Parliament. Today bills often pass without a division because legislators are chary of alienating one or another interest group in their constituency by appearing on either side of a division list. In the seventeenth century no record was kept, official or otherwise, of the individual votes in a division; but in the early Parliaments of Charles I the members occasionally exhibited a wholesome fear of the questions their constituents might ask them when they went home.[8] The members of the Civil War Parliament faced no such ordeal. According to a clause in the Act of 1641 Parliament could only be dissolved with the consent of both Houses. Only

---

[6] Divisions on the Committee of Both Kingdoms, *C. J.*, III, 391, 443, 483, 503.

[7] Divisions on the army reforms, *C. J.*, III, 726; IV, 26, 43, 48.

[8] For example, in the debates on the Petition of Right in 1628 Roger North, opposing the Court's proposal of a bill confirming earlier acts of Parliament on taxation and imprisonment, remarked, "They ask us, when we come home, what relief we have brought them. We tell them that we have confirmed the old statutes; they ask us when they were repealed" (Frances H. Relf, "The Petition of Right," *University of Minnesota Studies in the Social Sciences*, VIII, 34).

defeat in the Civil War could pry the members out of Westminster against their will; and if the King won, those members would have more important matters to worry about than
the temper of their constituencies. Since the Civil War House
of Commons was under no external pressure to avoid a division,
a dearth of divisions on major issues can result only from
conditions within the House. Positive certainty that one will
suffer defeat is the sole plausible reason for not demanding a
poll of the members. Apparently the opposition to most of
Pym's program was too small to be worth numbering. By the
time his projects came to a vote he had the vast bulk of the
House behind him.

Pym made a remarkable success of getting the support of
most of the House of Commons for the measures that he deemed
necessary. An explanation of this success, an explanation of
his ability to make an essentially cranky parliamentary machine
run with very little friction, would greatly aid our understanding of Pym's policy and his methods. Part of his achievement
was the result of political agility and sense of timing, of that
sixth sense which tells a skillful politician just when to jump
and just where. But finesse will account for only a portion of
the solid backing which Pym won for his program. Two other
members of the House, Oliver St. John and young Sir Henry
Vane, had political dexterity comparable to John Pym's. But
it was Vane and St. John, capturing control after Pym's death,
who had to shove and haul the ordinances for a Committee
of Both Kingdoms and the ordinances for new-modeling the
army through the House of Commons under a barrage of close
divisions. ·

According to Gardiner, whose thesis in the matter has never
been challenged, a month after Edgehill "there were once
more two parties in the House," a peace party led by Holles
and a war party led by Pym.[9] If we accept this separation of
Parliament into war party and peace party during Pym's
ascendancy, his legislative facility as contrasted with the legis-

[9] *C. W.*, I, 61.

lative difficulties of Vane and St. John becomes entirely incomprehensible. Had the cleavage between the extremes been sharp and unbridged, Pym's legislative program could not possibly have rolled through the House as easily as it did. It is certain that all his projects aimed at a more effective prosecution of the war. It is equally certain that in February 1643 more than a hundred men voted to continue a peace treaty with the King despite his unfavorable answer to Parliament's proposal.[10] It is difficult to believe that a really cohesive peace group, which in a crucial poll of the House could muster over a hundred votes, let a war party, which in the same poll could count less than eighty-five votes, drive war legislation through the Commons without even bothering to ask for a division. The two-party analysis, at this point at any rate, seems incongruous with the facts. An investigation of the political actions of some of the members during the period of Pym's ascendancy in the House of Commons may enable us to test the validity of the two-party analysis which we have just seen cause to suspect.

Concerning the attitude of individual members on particular issues we have two major sources of information: 1. There are no true division lists for the Long Parliament; but, when the House divided, two members from each side counted the votes. The names of these members — the tellers — and the side they took are indicated in the official *Journal of the House of Commons*. 2. Through the first year of the Civil War three members kept diaries of proceedings in the House that have survived. Laurence Whitaker rarely set down more than the general sense of the House, and so gives little information beyond what is in the official *Journal*; but Walter Yonge and Sir Simond Dewes frequently noted the names and actions and sometimes the opinions and arguments of individual members.[11] From the *Journal* and the diaries together we can get

[10] *C. J.*, II, 960.
[11] Between the battle of Edgehill and the death of Pym there are occasional gaps in the diaries of both Yonge and Dewes. The worst are the two

an idea of the position of some of the members on many
issues.

A member might reveal his judgment about war and peace
in three ways: by his attitude on negotiations and treaties,
by his attitude toward the King and toward groups aiming at
pacification, and by his stand on measures of war administration. Thus a "war-party" man would oppose the initiation,
continuation, or resumption of peace treaties; he would favor
resolutions that might annoy the King or harass and embarrass
the peace party; and he would support, regardless of their
legality, ordinances to increase Parliament's military effectiveness. A "peace-party" man would favor treaties, defend pacific
groups, seek to placate the King, and oppose illegal war
measures.

Now if a distinct cleavage separated war party from peace
party, given the side a member took on one question involving
war or peace, we should be able to predict his position in regard to any other question involving the same issue. For
example, if a member voted against a treaty of peace in February, that would identify him as one of the war party. We
should then expect that in July as well as in February he
would oppose a treaty, that he would support the weekly assessment ordinance, that he would attempt to brand all petitioners
for peace as potential traitors, and that he would refuse Charles's
servant a pass to go from London to Oxford with fresh bed
linen and nightshirts for the King.[12] Let us try the powers of
prediction with which this hypothesis endows us on the stubborn facts that we find in the *Journals* and in the diaries of the
Civil War Parliament.

On February 17, 1643, the House of Commons was rounding
out its first week of intramural wrangling as to the advisability

in Dewes from October 23 to November 21, 1642, and from September 21 to
October 28, 1643; and the one in Yonge from March 4 to July 20, 1643. It is on
Yonge that we must rely for the arguments of the Commoners; Dewes showed
interest in the details of the speeches of only one member — Sir Simond Dewes.

[12] There was actually a division on this momentous question in November
1642 (*C. J.*, II, 862).

of treating with the King before disbanding the armies. Someone proposed a compromise to make possible the resumption
of the treaty.[13] On a division of the House Sir John Clotworthy
was a teller in favor of accepting the compromise proposal and
renewing the negotiations.[14] Sir John, then, appears to be one
of the peace party; and we shall expect him hereafter to use
all his ability to guide Parliament along the path of appeasement. In May the House debated a bill for making a new
Great Seal to replace the one Lord Keeper Lyttleton had carried off with him to Oxford. The Venetian secretary in London thought the measure radical,[15] and Royalists found in it
evidences of the determination of the House to fight to the
finish against their King.[16] Maynard, a consistent peace-party
man, said in debate that the Seal was "an inseparable flower
of the Crown, and there was no end in making a new Great
Seal unless they intended to make a new King." [17] Here was
a chance for Sir John Clotworthy to show his firmness in the
cause of peace by opposing a violent measure that would
diminish the likelihood of an early settlement. He chose instead to take a flower from the Crown. He voted in favor of
making a new Great Seal.[18] This is perhaps confusing, but
not nearly so confusing as Sir John could be when he set his
hand to it. One morning while the fiery spirits in the House
inveighed against a letter from Charles I asking an extension
of time for the Oxford treaty, Clotworthy in the face of their
invective moved to grant the royal request.[19] The same after-
noon certain Commoners broke into Somerset House, invaded
the chapel of the Queen's Capuchins, "burned altar cloths,
defaced pictures, and broke statues and superstitious relics."
The perpetrators of this act, says Dewes, were "some of our

[13] *D.*, 164, fol. 301*v*.
[14] *C. J.*, II, 969.
[15] *C. S. P. Venetian*, XXVI, 277.
[16] *Mercurius Aulicus*, May 14–20. For a critical evaluation of *Mercurius Aulicus*, see Appendix A.
[17] *D.*, 164, fol. 389.
[18] *C. J.*, III, 86.
[19] *D.*, 164, fols. 347*v*–348.

fiery spirits . . . Mr. Bond, formerly a tradesman . . . John
Gurdon, a man of mean parts, . . . and Sir John Clotworthy,
an Irishman." [20] Sir John thus enjoys the rare distinction of
being a peace-party man and a fiery spirit, all within the com-
pass of a single day. With the Irish knight our powers of
divination seemed to have failed us. We will leave him in his
distinguished and anomalous position and turn to Mr. Recorder
Glynn.

There is not much doubt where John Glynn stood on measures for ensuring effective military action. He was for them.
All the violent projects that at one time or another seared
Dewes's law-abiding soul had Glynn's backing. He favored a
general assessment on land [21] and the sequestering of the estates
of delinquents.[22] He was for making a new Great Seal, [23] and
he was a co-author of the Vow and Covenant.[24] In odd moments
he framed, proposed, or supported minor measures calculated
to set the teeth of the peaceful on edge.[25] So John Glynn was
patently a war-party man. And that makes it seem odd that
he should be — as he was — the ablest proponent of the Oxford treaty. He waxed eloquent in his advocacy of settlement
by negotiation as against settlement by arms.[26] He persuaded
the radical Commons to tone down the proposition of the
pacific Lords on the disposal of the militia, so as to make it
more acceptable to the King; [27] and he was mainly responsible
for the moderate tone of Parliament's proposals.[28] He even ran
directly counter to Pym in speaking for a treaty without disbanding the armies.[29] So Glynn was for a militant policy;
and he was also for peace — in February. In August he was
for war. At that time he delivered a very effective and logical
onslaught on some proposals for a treaty that the peers had

---

[20] D., 164, fol. 348v.
[21] Y., 18777, fols. 101v–102.
[22] D., 164, fol. 344v.
[23] D., 164, fol. 389.
[24] D., 164, fol. 399.
[25] D., 165, fol. 103v, 169.   [27] Y., 18777, fols. 126–126v.
[26] Y., 18777, fol. 53v.   [28] Y., 18777, fols. 66, 66v, 67–67v.
[29] Pym's view, Y., 18777, fol. 153; Glynn's view, D., 164, fol. 245v.

sent down; [30] and a few hours later the Commons by a narrow margin refused to consider those proposals.[31] Glynn's speech may have turned the scale against negotiation.[32] Thus John Glynn, the supporter of all Pym's war measures, was the zealous advocate of peace — in February; and Glynn, the zealous advocate of peace in February, was the ardent opponent of a treaty — in August. So he joins that pacific fiery spirit, Sir John Clotworthy, both of them defying neat classification in a two-party scheme.

In this they are not alone. There is Sir William Lewis, whom the violent party in the City once planned to kidnap because of his annoying partiality for treaties of peace.[33] Yet Sir William was a teller in favor of the sequestration ordinance against the peace party leaders, Holles and Maynard.[34] There is Bulstrode Whitelock, outspoken in his opposition to the sequestration ordinance that Lewis approved,[35] and suspected by the fiery spirits of complicity in Edmund Waller's plot against Parliament,[36] who nevertheless supported Pym's proposal for a covenant with the Scots when the bulk of Parliament was altogether apathetic to it.[37] There is Sir Christopher Yelverton, who at one time tried in vain to induce the House to start on a new treaty with the King,[38] and at another tried more suc-

[30] *Y.*, 18778, fols. 9v–10. He argued (1) that the propositions of the peers made no provision for any of the objectives that Parliament claimed to be fighting for, (2) that a treaty would betray Parliament's new allies, the Scots.
[31] Seven votes in a House of 169 (*C. J.*, III, 197).
[32] This suggestion may seem to indicate a greater faith than I actually have in the efficiency of merely logical onslaughts on the average legislative skull. The Civil War House was unique, however, in that it could not be dissolved without its own consent, so the members had to fear no accounting with constituency or patron. This put the members in a good position to hearken to the voice of corruption, but also to the voice of reason. And in this particular instance four votes told the tale.
[33] *D.*, 164, fol. 307v.
[34] *C. J.*, II, 993.
[35] *D.*, 165, fol. 145v.
[36] *Whitelock*, p. 66.
[37] Among the twelve speakers between Pym's motion for the covenant (*Y.*, 18777, fol. 112) and Whitelock's support of it (*Y.*, 18777, fol. 114), only one spoke to the motion.
[38] *C. J.*, III, 97.

cessfully to prevent the House from starting on a new treaty
with the King.[39] Finally there is Sir Philip Stapleton, one of
the Lord General's intimate advisers,[40] in February the most
intransigent enemy of a treaty in the House of Commons,[41] in
May himself involved in a surreptitious negotiation with the
Queen,[42] and in July vehement "for the furthering of a treaty
of peace." [43]

That six solid and substantial members of the House should
shift from war party to peace party and back in such a fluid
and insubstantial way is awkward and disconcerting. It becomes more disconcerting when we realize that the six are in
all probability merely obvious examples of a more general
phenomenon. After all, our information on the doings of individual members of the Civil War Parliament is scanty. Behind
many cold entries of orders and resolutions in the *Journal* were
heated debates and vehement outbursts of which in the diaries
we do not even hear an echo. If our information on the proceedings of Parliament in 1643 were as complete as it is, say,
for 1843, if we had a full record of the debates and real division lists, might we not then find as many members between
the stools of war party and peace party as there were members
clearly on one side or the other?

The metaphor involves a difficulty; it prejudges the case.
Falling between the stools is the sort of gaucherie we usually
associate with the socially and politically awkward. Perhaps
the inconsistent course that Glynn and Whitelock and Clotworthy and Yelverton pursued had no method in it; perhaps
it was merely erratic, the outward and visible sign of sheer
political ineptitude and denseness. If these men got stuck
between the parties of 1643 because they knew no better, we
can justly expect their later activities to exhibit the same sort

[39] *D.*, 165, fol. 148v.

[40] Bulstrode Whitelock, "Memorials," British Museum, Additional MSS,
37343, fols. 298.

[41] He spoke thrice (*Y.*, 18777, fols. 146v, 148, 152v), and acted six times
as teller (*C. J.*, ii, 959, 960, 961, 962, 969) against continuing the Oxford treaty.

[42] M. A. E. Green, *Letters of Queen Henrietta Maria*, pp. 193–194.

[43] *D.*, 165, fol. 123v.

of inconsequential fecklessness. But if on an examination of their careers they turn out to be hard-bitten, hard-headed politicians who in the long run do reasonably well for themselves, we shall have to seek further for an explanation of their curious behavior in the first year of the Civil War. Among the errant members of the House of Commons (from a two-party point of view) John Glynn and Sir John Clotworthy fell between the stools with the greatest frequency and verve. If we follow their later vagaries, we may discover whether we can attribute their singular conduct in 1643 to anything but stupidity.

Glynn's career was fantastic. Recorder for the City of London, member of the Committee of Safety with Pym and of the Committee of Both Kingdoms after Pym's death, he was one of the eleven members the army impeached in 1647. Instead of running away with most of the others, he faced out the impeachment. Imprisoned before a trial which never took place, he resumed his seat in the House in time to be made a commissioner in the last desperate treaty with Charles I at Newport; and his efforts there to bring about an agreement between the King and Parliament [44] might have led to his arrest in London during Pride's Purge, had he not managed to be conveniently and comfortably elsewhere at the appropriate moment. The execution of the King and the founding of the Commonwealth abruptly halted his public career; [45] but under the Protectorate he burgeoned wondrously. Starting from scratch as a lawyer whose political principles, if any, were suspect, he became in three quick jumps serjeant-at-law, Protector's serjeant, and justice-in-eyre. On circuit he took over the job of trying Penruddock, leader of a futile Royalist rising in the west. He condemned Penruddock to death. It looked just a little bit like hangman's pay when Glynn received from Cromwell the post lately resigned by Judge Rolle — the

---

[44] *C. S. P. Domestic*, Charles I, xx, 297.

[45] In this period with John Maynard he undertook the thankless job of defending the Royalist Lord Chandos before the High Court of Justice (*C. S. P. Domestic*, Interregnum, iii, 150).

chief justiceship of the Upper Bench. He had made the climb
from ordinary barrister to the highest judicial rank in the land
in a little more than a year, a competent performance for a
middle-aged man starting his public life anew. Now a trusted
councillor of the Lord Protector, he played a leading role in
the attempt to make Cromwell king; yet he did not bother to
conceal from that all-powerful military man his civilian contempt for military rule.[46] With many another opponent of the
dominance of the army he served the Protectorate in Cromwell's House of Lords. When the Restoration came, the old
Royalists waited with bitter joy for the chastisement of this
man who served too many causes.[47] They waited in vain; they
overestimated the vindictiveness of Charles II and under-
estimated John Glynn's happy knack of landing on his feet.
When Charles II made his triumphal entry into London,
Glynn rode in the royal retinue. In 1661 the lawyer who
under Cromwell tried the Royalist Penruddock for his rising
in favor of the Stuarts became one of the King's counsel
learned in the law; late Protector's serjeant Glynn became
King's serjeant Glynn and a knight to boot.[48]

The most significant fact for our present purpose about this
man of law, who never allowed his long robe to interfere with
his political agility, is his election to the recordership of London. The position was one of great importance, the recorder
acting as a sort of liaison officer between Parliament and its
most fervent and affluent supporter, the City of London. The
Commons recommended Glynn to the City for the post.[49]
We may surmise that Pym had some influence in this choice.
Yet twice on major issues Glynn took sides against Pym,[50]
and he could not have been *persona grata* to the more belli-

[46] Sutherland MSS, *H. M. C. Report V*, app. i, pp. 163, 181.

[47] Sutherland MSS, *H. M. C. Report V*, app. i, p. 153.

[48] The salient events of Glynn's career can be found in the *D. N. B.*, article
Glynne, John (1603–1666), and in Edward Foss, *The Judges of England* (1848–
64), VI, 434–440.

[49] *C. J.*, II, 889. Glynn is first referred to as Mr. Recorder on June 6, 1643
(*C. J.*, III, 117). His election to the office is dated at May 1643 in the *D. N. B.*,
but no citation of authority is there given.

[50] Pym opposed a treaty before disbanding in February; Glynn favored it

cose members of the House. Indeed at the very time that the House recommended him for the recordership he was earning the dislike of the party of force by his active efforts for a treaty of peace.[51] Of course, running with the hare and hunting with the hounds was a pastime not unknown even in the seventeenth century. Judging Glynn by his later record we might well suspect him of indulging in such sport. He was a master of the fine art of changing sides at the moment best calculated to forward the personal interests of John Glynn. But why in the conspicuous arena of open debate in the House of Commons did he weave so aimlessly from peace party to war party and back again, and why in the name of political sense did either party let him get away with it? Discreet fellows with their own interests to push do not ordinarily make a show of their political inconstancy, nor are political groups wont to reward such inconstancy with the juicy plums of patronage. Yet John Glynn was a very discreet fellow, and the recordership of London was a very juicy plum. We are reduced to the conclusion that our analogy of the hare and the hounds does not hold, that in 1643 it is foolish to talk of running with the hare and hunting with the hounds, since at that stage in the political evolution of the Civil War Parliament hare and hound were not completely differentiated species.

We must now turn to that other political anomaly, Sir John Clotworthy. He was one of Pym's pallbearers. He was also one of the eleven members impeached by the army in 1647, and one of the forty arrested by Pride in 1648. He spent most of the Commonwealth era in prison, bluntly refusing to recognize the legality of the Rump Parliament.[52] He nevertheless made a good thing out of the Cromwellian settlement of Ireland [53] by purchasing confiscated land, and a better thing still out of the Restoration by becoming a privy councillor and

---

(Y., 18777, fol. 153; D., 165, fol. 142v). In September Pym wished to include the provision for extirpating episcopacy in the body of the Covenant; Glynn thought a note in the margin sufficient (Y., 18778, fols. 29v–30).

[51] Y., 18777, fol. 53v.

[52] Portland MSS, III, H. M. C. Report XIV, app. ii, p. 195.

[53] See, above, p. 6.

Viscount Massereene in the Irish peerage. He seems to have
been a man with an eye to the main chance; but in 1643 he
twice gave open support to a policy of conciliation with the
King at junctures when the more belligerent members wanted
to make an end to treaties and negotiations.[54] Only a little
less surprising than Clotworthy's conduct in the House is his
presence there, for he was an Irishman sitting in the English
Parliament a century and a half before the Act of Union.
Clarendon hints darkly that Clotworthy owed his seat to "the
contrivance and recommendation of some powerful persons," [55]
who used him against the Earl of Strafford. Clarendon does
not name the powerful contrivers; but on the basis of a few
scraps of evidence we can, perhaps, guess their identity. Whatever Clotworthy's political vagaries, he was a consistent Puritan. He remained a Puritan even at the Restoration, when nice
religious scruples went out of fashion.[56] He was on friendly
terms with prominent Puritans in the eastern counties, a cor-
respondent of John Winthrop, the governor of the Bay Colony,[57] and of Sir Thomas Barrington.[58] In the godly county
of Essex there was only one Puritan more influential than Sir
Thomas Barrington, and that was Barrington's old friend,
business associate, and political ally, the Earl of Warwick.[59]
The Earl treated Essex as his private political preserve and,
being Lord Lieutenant of the county, employed the captains
of the train bands under his command to make the voters
see things his way in the Essex elections of 1640.[60] In 1640
Irish Sir John Clotworthy was returned to Parliament for the

[54] C. J., II, 969; D., 164, fols. 347v–348.
[55] Clar. H. R., bk. III, par. 5. There are brief biographies of Clotworthy in
D. N. B. (under Clotworthy, Sir John, Viscount Massareene) and in G. E.
C(okayne), Complete Peerage, 8 vols. (1887–98), under Massareene, Sir John
Clotworthy, 1st Viscount.
[56] C. S. P. Domestic, Charles II, II, 71.
[57] M. H. S. Collections, 4th ser., VII, 203; 5th ser., I, 208.
[58] B., 2647, fol. 43.
[59] For the business connection of Barrington and Warwick, see C. S. P.
Colonial, America and West Indies, 1574–1711, I, 123, 125; for their political
coöperation, see Victoria History of the County of Essex (1903–), II, 229.
[60] Victoria History of . . . Essex, II, 229.

borough of Maldon in Essex by "the contrivance . . . of . . . powerful persons."

The linking of Sir John to Sir Thomas and the Earl almost irresistibly suggests a tie with another intimate friend, business associate, and political ally of the Essex Puritan grandees — John Pym. Barrington, Warwick, and Pym had long been joined together in an expensive colonial venture; [61] in 1640 Pym helped frame the petition of the twelve peers for a Parliament, a petition Warwick signed; [62] Pym's long friendship with Sir Thomas was soon to be sealed by the marriage of his nephew into the Barrington family,[63] and Pym helped manage the Strafford trial in which Clotworthy took an important part. A correspondence, recently published, furnishes direct proof of the connection between Pym and Clotworthy. The letters are from John Pickering in Edinburgh, where Parliament had sent him. Officially he was the agent of the two Houses in the Scottish capital "to negotiate various businesses of importance concerning the good of this Kingdom." [64] His letters indicate that his sojourn in the northern kingdom had a second purpose, unofficial but more significant than his official duties. On January 9, 1643, he wrote at length to John Pym. To one unfamiliar with the misty chaos of Scottish politics in the days of the Covenanters the letter is partly gibberish. These are dark words of Nidry making peace with Clermont and putting off his mask, of Forester's being led by the nose, of Cockburne's valor, and of the momentous truth that "Quinsey and Gibbey if Godfrey give them notice will see that he pass not Mantua." A few of these names we can identify.[65] The rest are doubtless cipher designations for some of the more prominent noble ruffians involved in the plots and

[61] *C. S. P. Colonial*, America and West Indies, 1574–1711, vol. 1, *passim*.
[62] Gardiner, *History of England*, IX, 199.
[63] B., 2646, fols. 279–279v; B., 2647, fol. 97.
[64] *L. J.*, v, 469.
[65] Cockburne is Adam Cockburne, Forrester Lord Forrester, and Nidry Sir John Wauchope of Niddrie (Duke of Hamilton MSS, supplementary report, *H. M. C. Report*, pp. 209, 217, 237).

counterplots of Scottish politics at that time. To attach particular names to particular ruffians is beyond our ability; nor does it matter much, since the essential purpose of the letter is not hard to fathom.

The pivot on which Scottish politics turned in 1643 was the problem of Scottish relations with England. More specifically, the crucial questions were whether, when, and on what conditions the Scots should come to the aid of the English Parliament. To John Pym, who had made an alliance with the Scottish Covenanters an integral part of his program, Pickering was writing from the political center of Scotland detailed accounts of the political situation north of the Tweed. The unofficial aspect of Pickering's mission is therein clearly revealed. With information garnered from Pickering's reports Pym at the proper time would know just what wires to pull to bring Scotland into the war on the side of Parliament. Pickering's letter to Pym ends with an exhortation. "The coals now want only blowing from England and this Kingdom will soon be on fire. . . . I solemnly protest to you in the presence of God that you are guilty of . . . the ruin of religion . . . in that you have not used all . . . means for drawing this Kingdom to your assistance." [66] On the same day he posted his message to Pym, Pickering wrote another letter in the same tone. "A little quickening from London would set us agog. I hope you will not be unmindful. Delays are now most dangerous. It will be too late to strike if the iron grow cold again." This letter begins with an apology for its brevity, "I have writ largely to Mr. Pym, which will cut your letter short." [67] The letter is addressed to Sir John Clotworthy.

The Pickering correspondence patently has a bearing on our problem of the relationship of Clotworthy to Pym. Twice in the face of opposition from the more bellicose members Clotworthy openly espoused a policy of conciliation with the King. Yet his pacific leanings did not alienate Pym from him.

[66] Hamilton MSS, supplementary, *H. M. C. Report*, pp. 65–67.
[67] Hamilton MSS, supplementary, *H. M. C. Report*, p. 67.

Nor is Sir John a mere casual supporter of Pym's Scottish policy. On the contrary, he is obviously an insider. He knows the real purpose of Pickering's mission to Scotland; it is expected that he can and will actively help Pym coax Parliament into a league with Scotland. Clotworthy was an ally of John Pym familiar with the secret details of his cherished projects.

At last, perhaps, we are in a position to clarify our ideas about the arrangements of political groups in the Long Parliament during the Civil War. There was nothing fundamentally unsound about the analogy of the two stools. Only our hypothesis defined war party and peace party so as to allow no crossing over. But men actually did cross over, and to that fact we must adapt our conception of parties in Parliament. We have assumed an abyss between war party and peace party; but in Pym's day no such abyss existed. A member might cross from one side to the other, incurring no odium whatever and encountering as little trouble in transit as he would in crossing the Thames from London to Southwark. Commoners like Glynn and Clotworthy could and did shift whenever they chose, as interest or reason or conscience dictated, without doing any discernible damage to their political careers. Some members, of course, never did change stools; there were immutable war-party men and immutable peace-party men. But there were also members, considerable in number and importance, who moved freely from one side to the other. These mobile Commoners, these trimmers, I have called with sufficient vagueness the "middle group."

CHAPTER III

PYM AND THE PARTIES

THE discovery of the "middle group" with Glynn and Clotworthy as typical members solves one set of problems about the structure of parties in the Long Parliament; but it poses another set of problems. Pym allows an honorable and politically important office to be presented to John Glynn, and he concerts measures with Sir John Clotworthy. Yet neither Glynn nor Clotworthy shows that enthusiasm for war which we expect to find among the friends and allies of "the promoter of the present rebellion and the director of the whole machine." If we accept Gardiner's conclusion [1] that Pym led the war party, his association with two "middle group" men is hard to explain. If his association with the middle group was permanent and regular, then it makes no sense to set him down as the head of the war party. The question of Pym's relation to the various groups in the House of Commons constitutes an intricate problem, and we must set ourselves to unraveling it, starting with the preparations for the Oxford negotiation.

The first serious peace parley between Parliament and the King had trouble getting under way. In the House of Commons in the three months before the treaty at Oxford there was a great deal of vigorous activity with little to show for it. In the midst of all the furious starting and stalling Pym was curiously passive. Once he had induced both Houses to lay an assessment on London he became almost completely quiescent. Of course there were always routine matters for him to tend to — easing minor tensions within Parliament,[2] soothing the irritable Lord General Essex,[3] judiciously flattering present

[1] C. W., I, 61–62.
[2] D., 164, fol. 276v.   [3] Y., 18777, fol. 85.

allies,[4] preserving amicable relations with potential allies of
Parliament,[5] making the regular monthly motion for an oath
of association,[6] and devising schemes for raising money. But,
after all, the main issue before the House was not whether the
furniture taken from Essex's sister's house by overzealous
Roundheads should be returned to her. Nor was it whether
someone should tell the City fathers that Parliament still had
their best interests at heart. The main issue was war and
peace; and a casual student of the record for December 1642
and January 1643 would not hesitate to select Martin, Rigby,
and Vane as leaders of the war party,[7] and Maynard as leader
of the peace party.[8] The same casual student would also pick
out Pym as a conscientious busybody with a finger not very
deep in a number of not very important pies. Yet Pym was
beyond doubt the one real leader in the House of Commons,
and when in February he actively reasserted his leadership
there was none to say him nay. It can be maintained that
Pym was inactive in December and January; it cannot be said
that he was strictly neutral. When one stands by while a
strong man thrashes his weak neighbor, that is not strict neutrality. Inactivity in such circumstances implies approval of
the aims of the stronger party or at least indifference to the
fate of the weaker. In the House of Commons in December
and January the members favoring negotiation with Charles I
were the stronger party, and they promptly and firmly squelched
several attempts of the opponents of a speedy peace to block
a treaty with the King.[9] From November to January a majority of the members of the House of Commons supported the
policy of treating with the King; but the events of February
showed up the essential instability of that majority.[10] Had

---

[4] *Y.*, 18777, fol. 57.
[5] *D.*, 164, fol. 270*v*.
[6] *Y.*, 18777, fol. 112.
[7] *D.*, 164, fols. 245*v*, 248, 273*v*, 290*v*; *Y.*, 18777, fol. 101, 103, 103*v*.
[8] *D.*, 164, fol. 279; *Y.*, 18777, fol. 77*v*, 115.
[9] *D.*, 164, fol. 270*v*; *Y*, 18777, fol. 101.
[10] See, below, pp. 67–70.

Pym chosen to throw the full weight of his influence against a treaty, he might have carried enough votes with him to break the preponderance of the peace group, but he did not choose to do so. By his hands-off policy, which must be described as benevolent rather than impartial neutrality, Pym gave the members anxious for a treaty their chance, a chance they used to frame the most moderate proposals presented to the King during the whole course of the war — milder than the Propositions of Uxbridge and Newcastle and Newport, milder than the Heads of the Proposals of the New Model Army, milder even than the Nineteen Propositions of June 1642, drawn up before the fighting started.[11]

Only once in three months did Pym do anything that might be construed into direct opposition to a treaty of peace. Early in November Parliament asked the King for a safe conduct for their commissioners to come to him and discuss a negotiation. Charles refused the safe conduct on the grounds that he had already proclaimed one of the commissioners a traitor.[12] Whereupon Pym moved that the King's answer was unsatisfactory.[13] Other members were aroused to greater asperity by Charles's want of tact. One moved that the King's answer about the treaty "is intended for a denial"; another that the House "should send presently into the City and show them that it appears by this answer that the King's ears are shut up against all access for us."[14] For the first motion Henry Martin was responsible; for the second, Denzil Holles. When the most violent member of the House joins with a leader of the peace party to condemn a royal act, the condemnation is not a party measure. On the basis of his role in this episode we cannot say that Pym led the war party or even that he generally opposed a treaty. On the other hand, Pym had two

----

[11] All these plans for peace save the one presented at Newport are in Gardiner, *Constitutional Documents*, pp. 249–254, 262–267, 275–286, 291–306, 316–326. The Newport proposals are very like those of Newcastle.

[12] *C. W.*, I, 54.

[13] *Y.*, 18777, fol. 51. Motion carried without a division.

[14] *Y.*, 18777, fol. 52.

excellent chances to sabotage negotiations. On November 21 the King indicated his willingness to entertain proposals for peace from Parliament. A bloc of fiery spirits opposed sending any. Strode and Haselrig gave reasons for rejecting the King's offer.[15] Young Vane said that whatever propositions Parliament sent might "be returned again with scorn," and Martin reported a rumor, which he probably invented on the spur of the moment, that the Cavaliers threatened to shoot anybody caught bringing propositions from the Houses.[16] But Pym sat silent, and by a very slender majority the House voted to continue debate on the King's message next morning.[17] Again in December Vane, Strode, and Martin tried to tie up negotiations, again Pym made no move to encourage them,[18] and again their scheme fell through.[19] It seems almost certain that Pym smothered both these attempts to stop a treaty with the King under heavy blankets of silence. As leader of a war party he was certainly conducting himself most deplorably.

In view of the evidence adduced above how can we account for the accepted tradition which writes Pym down as leader of the war party? Either the evidence is misleading, or the tradition is wrong. The tradition is not a recent confection; it is of venerable antiquity. It goes back at least as far as Clarendon; and the great Gardiner has put the seal of his approval on it.[20] Yet those two names, justly revered as they are by historians, should nevertheless warn us to caution. After he joined Charles I, Clarendon, except on rare occasions, had to trust rumor and his vivid imagination for his account of affairs in London. Gardiner in describing those affairs relied

[15] *Y.*, 18777, fol. 64*v*.
[16] *Y.*, 18777, fols. 64, 65.
[17] For continuing the debate — 67 (tellers: Holles and Pierpont); against — 66 (tellers: Vane jr. and Mildmay). *C. J.*, II, 858.
[18] *D.*, 164, fols. 270*v*, 273; *Y.*, 18777, fol. 101.
[19] Of course the failure of either Dewes or Yonge to implicate Pym in these proceedings is not proof positive that he was not implicated. Their failure to mention him twice in a month (and in affairs where they both name names) lends a strong presumption to the theory that he was silent.
[20] *C. W.*, I, 61–62.

in the main on the letters of the Venetian ambassador and the Venetian secretary and on the diary of Sir Simond Dewes.[21] In other words, the contemporary account of the period of Pym's ascendancy most familiar to us is that of a Royalist, the King's Chancellor of the Exchequer; and the standard modern account is based on the letters of two foreigners with Cavalier sympathies,[22] and the writings of an extreme member of the peace party in the House, a man who would rather that Parliament should lose a town than break a law. To compensate for the weighting of Clarendon, Dewes, and the Venetians to the right there are no sources of equivalent importance or scope on the left. The *Journal* of the House of Commons attains effortlessly that fine impartiality for which historians strive so hard in vain, and Walter Yonge, if he has any prepossessions, does not let them appear in his diary.[23] Moreover, these neutral sources have not played the part in forming the current conception of Pym's policy that Clarendon, the Venetians, and particularly Dewes have played. Three out of five of the major sources on the Long Parliament stand far to the right of the "middle group" in the House of Commons, and those three have had nine-tenths of the influence in making the historical tradition on Civil War politics. In using these sources we must then take special care to allow for the phenomenon of political foreshortening.

[21] Gardiner, with his wonted perspicuity, takes Dewes with a grain of salt (see *C. W.*, i, 62, n. 2). A grain of salt is, however, not enough. Before he can be used safely on questions of party, Dewes must be figuratively pickled in brine.

[22] Giustinian, Venetian ambassador until his transfer in December 1643, and Agostini, Venetian secretary until his death in February 1645 (*C. S. P. Venetian*, XXVI, 214; XXVII, 176). During the early years of the Civil War the letters of Salvetti, the Florentine resident, add little to the information collected by the Venetians. There are transcripts of the Salvetti correspondence in the British Museum, Additional MSS, 27962.

[23] Only once do we get even a hint about Yonge's political sympathies. On February 16, 1643, in great bold print contrasting sharply with his wonted microscopic script, Yonge sets down, "Some say *Mr. Holles* shall be Secretary of State"; that is, he will be in high favor with the King in case of peace. This kind of rumor was likely to be circulating in anti-peace groups. It is the only clue (if it be a clue) that we have to Yonge's own politics. *Y.*, 18777, fol. 157.

With foreshortening in the physical world we are familiar enough. To an observer at one end of a long corridor an object actually in the middle distance will nevertheless seem much closer to the far end than to the point where the observer stands. In like manner, to a conservative in politics a politician of the center will seem much closer to the radicals than he really is. This is most likely to be true when the conservative lacks both the knowledge and the past experience necessary to correct the present distortion of his political vision. A recent presidential campaign in the United States [24] conveniently illustrates our point. Rugged individualists accused Mr. Roosevelt of being a socialist and a communist. This shot of the individualists was surprisingly far from the mark — but it was not a random shot. It was typical of the marksmanship of a painfully nearsighted man with a nervous twitch aiming and firing as well as his handicaps allow. The rugged individualists realized that a great distance separated Mr. Roosevelt's ideas from their own; they could not understand that an even greater distance lay between his ideas and those of the communists. Their confusion was firmly founded on a paradisaic innocence as to what the doctrines of Communism are. And yet a historian three hundred years hence could study a conservative reporter's account of the presidential campaign of 1936; and if that reporter conscientiously stated most of the facts, the historian, despite the distortion of his source, could reconstruct a fairly accurate picture of the issues and men in the campaign. He could do so by using the observations of fact made by his conservative reporter and compensating for the reporter's bias on value judgments. In writing the history of the Civil War Parliament the historian of today has to make a like use of his sources. His fullest authorities tend to ascribe to all who were not Royalists or defeatists a mere desire to bring everything to confusion and anarchy, or "to make themselves masters of the goods and lives of all." [25]

[24] Campaign of 1936.
[25] *C. S. P. Venetian*, xxvi, 286.

The conspicuous inadequacy of such an analysis is really an
aid to the historian; it simplifies the process of discounting.
He can take, let us say, the diary of Sir Simond Dewes, sub-
tract the part that is pure Dewes from the total narrative, and
get a remainder that roughly approximates one aspect of the
story of the Civil War Parliament *wie es ist eigentlich gewesen.*[26]

A peace-party man of Dewes's temper could not help hating
Pym. Such a man naturally recoiled in horror from the intricate
measures of defense necessary to make the forces of Parliament effective in the field. Because Pym was the prime con-
triver of those measures, Dewes singles him out for special
condemnation. Other proponents of a strong defense policy
Dewes describes simply as "fiery spirits." Pym's prominence
in the political maneuvering that eventually equipped Parliament with a reasonably adequate military machine won him
two extra adjectives; he is an "insolent proud fiery spirit." [27]
Underlying the divergences between Pym and the peace party
over particular policies were two fundamental differences in
attitude. Once in a while and grudgingly Dewes recognized
that the fine fabric of the common law was not proof against
the fury of civil war; [28] but convinced against his will, he was
of the same opinion still. Pym on the other hand might go
through the motions of respect for the law that the general
sentiment demanded of him; [29] but if his actions bear any
testimony to his thoughts, he believed that nice customs curtsy
to great causes. To Dewes the appeal from law to necessity
smacked of the sin against the Holy Ghost; to Pym the
appeal against necessity to the law was willful myopia and

[26] In trying to find Pym's true place among the groups in Parliament I have
employed Dewes's narrative alone, not from any desire to achieve a historical
tour de force, but because the most impressive assertion of Pym's connection
with the "war party" is by Gardiner out of Dewes. There is no surer way of
refuting a man's opinion than by the words of his own mouth or facts of
his own recording.

[27] *D.*, 164, fol. 324.

[28] *D.*, 165, fol. 93.

[29] He once made a great speech in defense of the common law (*Rushworth*,
VIII, 661–670).

black-letter pedantry. There was a war to win, and it must
be won. There was the law to save, and it must be saved.
The purpose of the peaceful admirer of the common law and
the purpose of the politician intensely preoccupied with present
necessities — each noble in its own way — frequently seemed
incompatible. Every time their purposes crossed, the peace
party and Pym naturally found themselves on opposite
sides.[30]

The peace party also differed from Pym in their estimate
of the King. In the face of the most harrowing demonstrations
of his duplicity, they retained a serene and lamblike faith in
the good will of Charles I. Dewes spurns the doubts cast upon
the King's sincerity in the Oxford treaty as "very false and
groundless." [31] Such a triumph of faith over mountains of facts,
evidence, and reason has in it something of the sublime. Yet
Dewes had to believe as he did. If the King could not be trusted,
then Parliament must demand such securities and guarantees for
their liberties as he would never grant except after a defeat in
the field. And if a safe peace could come only through Parliament's victory in the field, then Pym's whole program of illegal
defense measures was perfectly justifiable. Rather than accept
this logical consequence of Charles's duplicity, the peace party
rejected the assumption. Regardless of evidence to the contrary,
they clung to their faith in the King's good will. Pym refused to
perform such an *auto-da-fé*, of which the Parliamentary cause
itself would be the first victim. He needed no psalmist to warn
him against putting his faith in princes. He knew Charles's way
of dealing with Parliament and the way of James, his father,
before him. All Pym needed to remind him of the little love
the Stuarts bore for the highest court of the realm were the
notes he himself had taken in the Parliament of 1621, 1624, and

[30] The best examples of Pym's arguments from necessity are in Yonge (*Y.*,
18777, fol. 91*v*; 18778, fol. 30). So little did such arguments appeal to Dewes
that in the midst of civil war he refused to grant the need for martial law.
"Necessity," he remarks, ". . . was a great reason given in excuse of all the
woes, miseries and oppression brought upon the subject" (*D.*, 165, fol. 164).
[31] *D.*, 164, fol. 292.

1625.[32] Before the Civil War, before the decade of prerogative government without Parliament, in 1626, Pym had heard Charles measure the goodness of Parliaments by the degree of their subservience to him, had heard him declare in effect that only if they conformed to that standard would he use them at all.[33] With the intimate knowledge of a participant Pym knew the history of the King's dealings with his Parliaments, and in all that history a man would find small cause to trust the King. Charles showed no inclination to grant the security that Parliament now demanded for the subjects' liberties and its own privileges. Someday perhaps the King might change his mind; but Pym knew that until that day prudence required preparedness and unremitting wariness.

Pym's attitude toward the King and his indifference to legality often set him at odds with the peace party. It also led him on certain occasions into collaboration with the most violent members of the House. A cursory examination of the diary of Sir Simond Dewes indicates that Pym and the violent members frequently worked together. Again and again we find Pym acting with Martin, Wentworth, Strode, and young Sir Henry Vane, the leading extremists in the House.[34] If we study the diary carefully, we will note two uniformities in these instances of collaboration between Pym and the extremists. In the first place, the collaboration is frequently successful; when Pym acts with the extremists, the House almost invariably approves their joint proposals.[35] In the second

[32] Debates in the House of Commons in 1625, ed. S. R. Gardiner, Camden Society (1873); Commons Debates, 1621, ed. Wallace Notestein, F. H. Relf, and Hartley Simpson, 6 vols. (1935), IV. Pym's notes for 1624 are as yet unpublished.

[33] Gardiner, History of England, VI, 83.

[34] Instances of Pym's collaboration with the extremists: 13 December 1643, Strode, Martin, Wentworth (D., 164, fols. 248–248v); 11 February 1643, Martin, Strode (D., 164, fol. 296v); 17 February 1643, Martin, Strode, Vane, Wentworth (D., 164, fol. 301v); 28 March 1643, Martin, Strode (D., 164, fol. 1345v); 31 March 1643, Strode (D., 164, fol. 350); 6 April 1643, Martin (D., 164, fol. 348v); 27 April 1643, Vane (D., 164, fol. 380).

[35] Sometimes this approval is not immediate. This is especially true in the case of the Vow and Covenant (D., 164, fols. 380, 381).

place, the matters on which Pym and the violent members coöperate seem to have a common end. With few exceptions [36] they aim to enhance Parliament's military effectiveness.[37] The field of common action of Pym and the extremists was circumscribed by Pym's program of constructive measures for the defense of the parliamentary cause; and in this limited field the collaboration was eminently successful.

The radicals did not spend all their energy in supporting Pym's defense measures. They had other activities, and those activities focused on four points — the peace proposals, the King, the peers, and the Committee of Safety. To proposals for a treaty Pym most of the time was merely inert. He only opposed efforts at appeasement on those occasions when the peace party in their anxiety for a quick settlement endangered his defense program. There was no such inertia among the real war-party men. They fought an incessant guerilla action against each and every move toward peace. They tried to prevent the opening of negotiations with the King,[38] they tried to make the parliamentary propositions so harsh that the King would certainly reject them,[39] and once the treaty began they tried to induce Parliament to break it off.[40] Another portion of their energies the violent members directed toward annoying, harassing, and insulting His Majesty. They moved to prevent his personal servants from attending him [41] and to stop his letters to Scotland; [42] they spoke of him with unrestrained and undisguised contempt,[43] and the boldest of them

[36] The exceptions are the impeachment of the Queen (*D.*, 164, fol. 390*v*), and the opposition to a treaty before disbanding (*D.*, 164, fols. 396*v*, 301*v*).

[37] E.g., imposition of an oath in the first assessment ordinance (*D.*, 164, fols. 248–248*v*); assessment of a twentieth part on the members of both Houses (*D.*, 164, fol. 348*v*); Vow and Covenant (*D.*, 164, fol. 380).

[38] Strode, Martin, Vane, Jr. (*D.*, 164, fols. 270*v*, 273).

[39] "Some were very earnest to have all delinquents left to the censure of Parliament" (*D.*, 164, fol. 275).

[40] Gurdon (*D.*, 164, fol. 291*v*); Martin, Strode (*D.*, 164, fol. 292*v*).

[41] Long, Martin (*C. J.*, II, 862); Rigby (*D.*, 164, fol. 245*v*).

[42] A motion that letters from Oxford to Scotland "that concerned the affairs of that Kingdom might pass without being searched . . . was opposed by many hot spirits" (*D.*, 164, fol. 270).

[43] Martin, Wentworth, Strode, Haselrig, Mildway. The author does not

made a frontal attack on the very principle of monarchy.[44]
The peers were the residuary legatees of such rancor as the
violent men could spare from the King. The war party started
by opposing every change the Lords made in measures sent
up from the lower house. They proceeded from a demand
that the Commons refuse a conference with the Lords on
peace propositions [45] to the more radical demand that the
Commons act independently of the Lords on a legislative
measure.[46] Finally they took the forthright position that
the peers were not to be trusted even on oath.[47] They supple-
mented their direct hostilities against the Lords by oblique
attacks on them through the Committee of Safety. This committee was the nearest thing to a centralized executive organ
that Parliament had during Pym's lifetime.[48] It was over-
loaded, however, with pacific peers, and it gave them a dis-
proportionately large share in the administration of war.[49]

---

have the British Museum foliation for this citation; the original Dewes foliation is 910 and 912*v*.

[44] Martin (*D.*, 164, fol. 381*v*).

[45] Strode (*C. J.*, II, 959); Haselrig (*D.*, 164, fol. 291*v*).

[46] Vane, Jr. (*D.*, 164, fol. 388).

[47] Vane, Jr. (*D.*, 165, fol. 98).

[48] There was not, so far as I know, an ordinance granting specific powers to
the Committee of Safety comparable to the one that established the Committee
of Both Kingdoms. No one has ever compared the activities of the committees.
The journals of the two Houses are full enough to show that the Committee of
Both Kingdoms was by far the more vigorous body.

[49] In December 1642 the House of Lords debated the proposals for peace
submitted to them by the House of Commons. The majority of the Lords
voted to strike from the list several men whom the House of Commons voted
to except from pardon. The minority of the peers protested this excision. The
peers who followed the line set by the House of Commons were obviously associates of Pym. In this instance they were the Earls of Bolingbroke, Manchester,
Peterborough, and Warwick, Viscount Say and Sele, and Barons Brook, Grey
of Wark, Wharton and Willoughby. Other peers present during the week in
which the protest took place were the Earls of Bedford, Clare, Exeter, Holland, Northumberland, Pembroke and Salisbury, and Barons Bruce, Fielding,
Howard, and Lovelace (*L. J.*, v, 496–514). A hasty glance at the letter book
of the Committee of Safety, preserved among the Commonwealth Exchequer
papers at the Public Record Office (State Papers 28), is enough to indicate
the major role of the second group of peers, the peace-party Lords, in the
work of the committee. The importance of this role is enough to account for
the detestation the "fiery spirits" felt for the committee. It is worth noting
that almost every peer associated with Pym in 1643 had by 1648 become an

Consequently, the war party seized every chance to expose the inefficiency of the Committee of Safety and to level withering criticism at it.[50] Once they almost succeeded in permanently crippling the committee — but not quite.[51]

"Almost . . . but not quite" — and sometimes not even "almost" — such is the story, told, retold, and told yet again of the efforts of the war party when they were directed toward any other object than the promotion of Pym's defense program. Their attacks on the peace treaty, on the King, on the Lords, on the Committee of Safety, renewed again and again, failed usually by a large margin, sometimes by a small one; but always they failed.[52] The chronic unsuccess in all other matters of a group that achieved so much when working with Pym on his schemes of taxation and defense cries for explanation.

The explanation lies in the attitude of Pym himself. He openly opposed the war party in all its activities not connected with his own program; and he showed his hostility to them,

---

advocate of peace with the King. Of the second group several soon went over to the King — Bedford, Clare, Holland and Lovelace. Three others sat in the Commonwealth House of Commons after the House of Lords had been destroyed — Pembroke, Salisbury and Howard. The change in alignment of the peers under pressure of circumstances almost demands a platitude on the speed with which allegiance shifts in times of civil war.

[50] C. Holland, Martin (*D.*, 164, fol. 354*v*); C. Holland, Morley, Rigby, Martin (*D.*, 164, fol. 297*v*); Rigby (*D.*, 164, fol. 338*v*); Mildmay (*D.*, 164, fol. 369*v*).

[51] Prideaux, Mildmay (*Y.*, 18777, fol. 161*v*); Martin (*C. J.*, II, 976).

[52] There are two apparent exceptions to the consistent failure of the war party. Eventually the House adopted Vane's proposal that they make a new Great Seal without the consent of the Lords (*D.*, 164, fol. 388; *W.*, fol. 60*v*). But this happened only after the Lords had rejected several applications from the Commons to pass the measure (*C. J.*, III, 112, 127, 129). The war party, probably in coalition with the extreme right — Edmund Waller acted as teller with Martin (*C. J.*, II, 976) — induced the House to cripple the Committee of Safety. Dewes does not even record the event. It seems to have happened early in the morning, before he arrived at Parliament (*D.*, 164, fols. 304*v*–305; *Y.*, 18777, fol. 161*v*). The measure passed in a very thin House, only 85 voting as compared with 169 in a division of the previous week (*C. J.*, II, 969, 976). The passage of the measure early in the morning, the thinness of the House at the time, and the failure of its proponents to revive the bill after the Lords rejected it gives the whole episode the appearance of a half successful coup that did not have the support of a real majority in the Commons (*L.J.*, v, 619).

and they their hostility to him, time and again in debate in the House of Commons. When young Sir Henry Vane tried to set Lords and Commons by the ears by conducting the Commons on a sort of heresy hunt among the members of the upper house, Pym intervened to prevent him and save the honor of the peers.[53] Again, when Rigby accused the Committee of Safety of inefficiency and unnecessary delays, Pym took the floor to defend the committee "with heat and vehemence."[54] In the matter of peace proposals, too, he was attacked by Martin, Wentworth, Baynton, and other violent men for daring to call one of the King's answers a "gracious" message and for seeking to prolong the Oxford treaty.[55] At first Pym tried to silence the attacks of the war party on the monarchy by slighting them and inducing the rest of the House to do likewise.[56] When Henry Martin went beyond bounds, however, and hinted at the advantages that might accrue from the demise of the entire royal family, Pym had him promptly thrown out of the House and into the Tower.[57] We noted before that the war-party offensive had four objectives — the King, the Lords, the proposals of peace, and the Committee of Safety. Across the line of their attack on each of these objectives the violent spirits found John Pym blocking their way. Pym was a hard man to get around. At least the war party never learned how to do it. After every attack they had to retire discomfited.

We have watched Pym beat down the opposition of the peace party to his military program, we have seen him neutralize the violence of the war party; once we catch a glimpse of him playing off one side against the other to effect the com-

---

[53] Pym's handling of the situation that Vane created elicited the praise even of Sir Simond Dewes (*D.*, 164, fol. 334*v*).

[54] *D.*, 164, fol. 338.

[55] *D.*, 164, fol. 308*v*, 363. In one instance Martin moved "that we might put not only ourselves (not) to send any answer to those two messages, but rather treat them with scorn as being unworthy of our further regard."

[56] A war-party motion was "slighted by Pym himself, as tending to the utter subversion of the monarchy" (*D.*, 164, fols. 381*v*–382).

[57] *D.*, 165, fol. 152.

promise he wanted. He had written a preamble to the articles
for a cessation of arms to be sent to the King. The peace lords,
anxious for a settlement, had toned the preamble down. Against
the changes of the unduly pacific peers, Pym turned the majority of the lower house. Then from the other side over-
bellicose Commoners opposed the preamble. Let there be,
they said, none of these soothing hypocritical words about
the graciousness of the King's late message. Let Parliament
rather regard that message as an alarm to action. The majority paid no heed; they hardly gave the violent men a
chance to put their objections into words. Against the opposition of the peace party on one side and of the war party on
the other, the majority of the Commoners passed the preamble
word for word as Pym wrote it.[58]

Oddly enough, Pym's relation to the parties in the House
of Commons receives its most impressive illustration not in
a masterful triumph of his strategy but in a complete and
ridiculous defeat. The treaty at Oxford was approaching the
time limit the Houses had set for it. Pym proposed that the
parliamentary commissioners be empowered to treat on certain
additional propositions.[59] Whatever his motives, he might have
hoped that the Commons would accept his plan, if he had been
acting in concert with either the war party or the peace party.
As it was, he found himself hedged in by walls of conflicting
suspicion. The peace party thought his move a mere trick to
speed the winding up of the treaty, while the war party suspected him of a design to prolong the negotiation. His motion
failed through the unintentional union of the two extremes
against the middle.[60]

[58] D., 164, fol. 308v.
[59] The treaty had hitherto been limited to the King's proposition on forts
and garrisons and the propositions of the House on disbanding the armies
(C. J., II, 969).
[60] "Mr. Pym moved that we might give our committee power to move
some of the other propositions to His Majesty, which motion of Mr. Pym's
some conceived to be made out of a desire to further the peace . . . but others
did conceive he did it to hinder any further time to be given to our committee
at Oxford so as almost all men being jealous of his motion did oppose it, and
it came to nothing" (D., 164, fol. 363).

So time after time Sir Simond Dewes sets down the deviations from the true war-party line of "that insolent proud fiery spirit" John Pym, and yet the conscientious diarist remains oblivious to the implications of the facts he records. We can accept Dewes's facts; we are under no obligation to imitate his blindness as to what they signify. With the data furnished us by a man who feared and despised him we can set Pym in our picture of parties in the Civil War Parliament. Already we have sketched in rough outline a middle group between the war party and the peace party. We can now with certainty place Pym somewhere within the limits of this group, and say that from the midst of it and with its aid he guided the destinies of the Houses in their struggle against the King.

CHAPTER IV

THE STRUCTURE OF THE MIDDLE GROUP

A LITTLE burrowing into documentary sources yields us evidence of the existence of a middle group in the Civil War Parliament. Burrowing somewhat deeper, we find substantial proof of Pym's connection with this group. When we extend our operations further, when we try to gain more precise information about the middle party — how large it was, who its adherents were, and how it was organized — we discover that our lode of information has been pretty well exhausted. The returns on a great deal of poking about in the source material are wretchedly poor. Our troubles are due partly to the nature of what we are looking for, partly to the nature of the places where we have to look for it. The difficulties we face do not present themselves only to one in quest of the middle group. It would be just as hard to pick out the members of the war party, almost as hard to pick out the members of the peace party. Each group had its normal pattern of action; in shifting from one side to the other the middle group was pursuing a policy no less coherent than the policies that the war party and the peace party pursued in standing pat. The *politiques* of an earlier generation in France and the "trimmers" of a later generation in England shifted their alliances frequently without altering their fundamental opinions at all, and the same thing is true of the middle group, the *politiques* and trimmers of the Civil War Parliament. We cannot even say that they were less cohesive, more loose-knit, than the two extreme factions.

The character of our information on the Long Parliament is such that it indicates cleavages in the middle group whenever they occur, but fails almost entirely to register cleavages in the war party and the peace party. This is particularly true of information derived from the Commons' *Journal*. We will understand this curious defect in the record if we ask ourselves what happens when one of the extreme parties split on an issue. If there was disagreement in the peace party over, let us say, the expediency of a weekly assessment, the members who opposed the assessment would find themselves standing alone against the war party, the middle group, and some of their own customary allies. In such a case half a faction found itself opposed by two and a half factions. The little remnant, unable to put up any kind of show against a majority so overwhelming, went down to defeat, leaving no mark of its opposition in the *Journal*. Parliamentary custom in the seventeenth century did not encourage small minorities to display their intransigence by demanding a poll of the Houses on every measure they opposed. Nor did little factions have to force divisions they knew they could not carry in order to show their constituents that, although most of the members were rogues, there was still a handful of pure-hearted men in the House. Members only demanded a division when there was a reasonable doubt which side had a majority; and when either extreme party split, no such doubt existed.[1] It was otherwise with a difference of opinion in the middle group. Then one moiety sided with the peace party, another moiety with the war party. A party and a fraction stood against a party and a fraction, with no clear preponderance on either side. A disagreement within the middle group thus involved the House of Commons in a division and left a conspicuous mark in the *Journal*.

So it is no inherently elusive quality of the middle group that thwarts our effort to get precise knowledge about it. What defeats the attempt to achieve fuller knowledge of any party in the Civil War Parliament is the simplest and most insuper-

[1] The *Journal* gives us no inkling of the existence of opposition to most of Pym's war measures. If Dewes had not devoted so much space to condemning those measures, we could hardly surmise that there had been opposition to them. On the custom of the House with respect to divisions, see Thomas E. May, *A Treatise on the Law . . . of Parliament*, 12th ed. (1917), pp. 324–327, and Josef Redlich, *The Procedure of the House of Commons*, 3 vols. (1908), II, 233–239.

able of all difficulties — inadequate and insufficient information. If we knew the stand of every member of the House on twenty selected issues we could with some certainty fix the limits of each party. Such information does not exist and probably never did exist. Our knowledge of the politics of the individual members of the Civil War House of Commons is like a pyramid — at the top a little sector of members about whom we know a good deal, at the bottom an extensive base of members about whose politics we know almost nothing. We know the position of a mere handful of the Commons on twenty issues; about the political position of two score members we can make a reasonable conjecture. But it is out of an anonymous mass of some two hundred members that the leaders draw their following; and of the opinions of individuals among the two hundred we can never hope to know anything.

We can draw a somewhat clearer line between the party of appeasement and the middle group than we can between the middle group and the firebrands. We are able to do this not because the cleavage between peace party and middle group was sharper than that between middle group and war party, but merely because Sir Simond Dewes was a bitter partisan. If Sir Simond had stuck to his work of recording debates, we should know less than we do now about the personnel of the peace party. Because he mixed occasional editorial comment with his reporting we can, for example, say with assurance, as we could not otherwise, that Sir William Lewis was one of the peace party. The reader may remember that we caught Sir William Lewis at one time supporting Pym's sequestration ordinance, at another favoring a policy of appeasement with Charles I.[2] On this evidence we might very tentatively put Lewis somewhere in the middle group. But Dewes tells us that Lewis was one of the intended victims of a plot to kidnap the leading members of the peace party.[3] So we know that Sir William was not of the middle group, merely a peace party leader who once strayed off the reservation; but

[2] See, above, p. 39.   [3] *D.*, 165, fol. 145*v*.

we know this only because Dewes is a gossip, not a mere unofficial clerk of the Commons. On the negative side it is safe
to say of anyone Dewes calls a fiery spirit that he is not of
the peace party. To make finer distinctions on the basis of
Dewes's statements is to put an unwarranted faith in his judgment of political tendencies outside his own group.[4] The lack
of a war party or middle group equivalent of Dewes does not
obliterate the distinction between those two factions; but it
prevents us from clearly discerning the boundary that separated them.

Even if we did know the vote of every member on twenty
issues, it is safe to assume that there would be still a considerable number of men whose position would not lend itself
to strict classification. Several elements characteristic of the
later development of Parliamentary parties did not exist in
this period of their birth. There was no organization in the
counties and boroughs, no elaborate system of patronage, no
ministry dependent on a continuous majority in the lower
house, and no party discipline. The sole bond of parties was
community of sentiment — common fears, common hopes,
common interests. Community of sentiment is a matter of
degree; it has none of the binding force of party discipline.
When they went into the House during the Civil War, the
members did not have to leave their brains outside and vote
just as their leaders told them to. A situation which according
to Private Willis no man could bear with equanimity actually
existed in England's legislature in the middle of the seventeenth century. The Civil War Parliament was in fact

> A lot of dull M.P.'s in close proximity
> All thinking for themselves. . . .

They could vote as they deemed best on each issue as it emerged
without being bound in advance to common action with any

---

[4] To include in the war party all those Dewes at one time or another labeled
"fiery spirits" would be like using *The Red Network* as an authoritative source
for a list of American Communists. The method Dewes and Mrs. Dilling use
in classifying people they do not like is amusing but not edifying.

of the dominant groups. Consequently, Parliament was not divided into three sharply separated parties, but into three clusters, shading off from the cluster in the center to the two clusters at the extremes. To state arbitrarily the size of any party is to define the indefinite. We can point out typical members of peace, middle, and war party — Maynard, Clotworthy, Martin; but as we move out from Clotworthy in the middle or in from Maynard and Martin at the extremes we come to areas of shadow and uncertainty, where we hesitate to say of a member he is this, or he is that. Knowing full well that what we can hope to find is not a compact, solid, easily ponderable body, but rather a vague, shifting, unstable mass, we may nevertheless make a try at measuring the middle party.

Perhaps the best place to look for this group would be in a series of divisions of the House sufficiently diversified to bring out shades of political difference, and yet occurring within so brief an interval that throughout it the composition of the House remained unchanged. As we glance through the Commons' *Journal* we find one set of divisions peculiarly suitable for our purpose. Between February 8 and February 11, 1643, the House of Commons considered the King's counter proposals to the propositions the Houses had sent to Oxford, and tried to decide what to do about them. So difficult was the problem and so various the proposed solutions that in four days the Commons divided eight times. Between the eighth of February and the eleventh no Sabbath intervened. For this reason and because of the importance of the issues in debate attendance in the House fluctuated very little.[5] It reached 190 each day, and exceeded 200 only once. Such an attendance is not

---

[5] February 8, 1643, came on Wednesday; February 11 on Saturday. The House had not yet attained or claimed its fourth great privilege, "freedom of week end." The largest number recorded in each day's division (including four tellers):

Wednesday, Feb. 8	199
Thursday, Feb. 9	201
Friday, Feb. 10	190
Saturday, Feb. 11	190

(*C. J.*, II, 959–962.)

only remarkably stable, it is extraordinarily large — the largest
between the outbreak of the war and the recruiting of the
House.[6] Many members who had left London, disgusted with
the conduct of affairs, had been induced by the peace Lords to
come up for the debates on the King's answer. The more militant Commoners countered by taking advantage of a lull in
army operations to call back the members who were serving as
officers under Essex.[7] A mélange of bellicose petitions against
the royal proposals and apprentice riots for peace enables us
to factor out the direct influence of popular pressure.[8]

On February 8 the war party tried to head off a treaty by
oblique strategy. They presented resolutions that indirectly
but effectively would have prevented further negotiations,
moving first that the King's answer was no answer, then that
it was negative, and finally that it was unsatisfactory.[9] Proceeding by indirection, they were defeated by indirection. The
House turned off the first resolution without a division, the
second by ten, and the third by twenty-one votes.[10] The majority did not actually vote down the war-party resolutions.
They knew as well as the war party did that the King's answer
was both negative and unsatisfactory. So, quite sensibly, instead of passing on such embarrassing motions, they voted that
the questions should not be put, and laid them aside.[11] Next
day, without a division, the Commons agreed with the Lords
that all armies should disband speedily, and then by a majority of thirty-one voted to send commissioners to treat with

[6] On December 17, 1644, a hundred and ninety-seven members voted on a
motion exempting the Earl of Essex from the Self Denying Ordinance. In a
division two days later, however, only a hundred and twenty-five members
took part. (*C. J.*, III, 726, 729.)
[7] *C. S. P. Venetian*, XXVI, 242.
[8] Portland MSS, I, *H. M. C. Report XIII*, app. i, pp. 94–95; Hastings MSS,
II, *H. M. C. Report*, p. 92; *C. S. P. Venetian*, XXVI, 242; *C. J.*, II, 950.
[9] *D.*, 164, fol. 292.
[10] *C. J.*, II, 959.
[11] *C. J.*, II, 959. Whitelock, who offered the motion for setting the resolutions aside (*D.*, 164, fol. 292v), had already admitted that the King's answer
was not positive (*Y.*, 18777, fol. 146). On the significance of the vote against
putting the question see Redlich, *Procedure*, III, 226–227.

the King on the manner of disbanding.[12] Intoxicated by an
altogether unusual success, having carried five successive divisions in two sittings, the peace party next day made a further
gesture toward a speedy settlement. They proposed an armistice
for negotiations before disbanding the armies. At once they
got a sharp lesson on the limitations of their strength, when
on the question the division went against them by forty-one
votes.[13] Finally, somewhat chastened, they tried a new variation on the peace theme: a treaty without cessation and without disbanding. On this proposal they regained only sixteen
of the votes they had lost the previous day.[14] From this jumble
of divisions two polls of the House taken on successive days
stand out — the first, whether Parliament should treat with
the King about disbanding the armies, the second, whether
Parliament should treat on peace propositions before disbanding the armies. Between these two proposals there is no very
great difference. Neither involves an outrageous demand on
the King; neither involves an implicit surrender to him. Both
assume that a way is to be left open for a treaty with His
Majesty. The problem is one of expediency, of the safe method
of treating, of how much Parliament dares risk to get a treaty
started. A majority of thirty-one deemed it safe to treat with
the King about disbanding the armies as a preliminary to
further negotiations. A majority of forty-one deemed it dangerous to treat on other proposals with the King before disbanding. Roughly, thirty-six men, almost a fifth of the members
present, changed sides on this fine point of policy.[15]

[12] *C. J.*, II, 960. Gardiner thinks that, in all probability, Pym and Hampden
voted with the peace group on the ninth (*C. W.*, I, 92). As far as Pym is
concerned the conjecture is reasonable (*Y.*, 18777, fol. 148); but the only
reference to Hampden prior to the ninth seems to indicate a rooted hostility to
a treaty under the existing circumstances (*C. J.*, II, 959, division on granting
the Lords a conference).

[13] *C. J.*, II, 961.

[14] *C. J.*, II, 962.

[15] Computation here is made difficult by a loss of sixteen votes in the totals:
total votes, February 9 — 201, February 10 — 185. Maximum possible shift
(assuming that all the absentees on the tenth would have voted for a cessation
for a treaty), 44; minimum possible shift (assuming that all the absentees

Here then we have a band of some thirty-six men so deli-
cately adjusted to the middle way that when the question
concerns a treaty about disbanding they are all on one side;
when the axis shifts ever so slightly to an armistice for a treaty
without disbanding, they are all on the other side. Despite a
sore rebuff from the King, these members are not so enamored
of war as to abandon all hope of peace, nor yet so anxious for
peace as to jeopardize the cause in a panicky scramble for it.
It may be objected that, after all, the group thus isolated is
not very large, hardly one-fifth of the number that voted in the
February divisions. Yet one-fifth of the House can be a very
effective balancing force between two nearly equal groups, a
fact quite obvious in the particular case in point. A somewhat
coherent fifth of the Commons with Pym for a leader and a
viable policy might have more political force than a greater
number led by Holles with no practical policy at all, or a
greater number under Martin, Vane, and Wentworth with a
policy so violent that the tongue dare not speak it nor the
leaders admit its existence.

There is really no reason to believe that the thirty-six members who changed sides in February constituted the whole of
the loose federation of the middle. The divisions themselves
cannot reveal the full strength of the middle group, because,
as we pointed out before, in the seventeenth century the House
divided only when there was some doubt as to which side had
a majority. When the whole middle group acted with either
extreme party there could be no such doubt, and consequently
no need for a division. Polls of the House and difference of
opinion among the middle group usually happen at the same
time. When we find eight polls of the House in four days over
the negotiations with the King, we can assume a split within
the middle group on that issue. From the names of the tellers

---

would have voted against a cessation), 28. Median point (assuming the loss
was divided evenly between the two groups), 36. There is no evidence one
way or the other as to what the sympathies of the departing members were,
and no possible basis for conjecture.

who acted for the less conciliatory members we may surmise the cause of the split in the middle party.

One class of Commoners, regardless of their party allegiances, had good cause to dislike the idea of a long drawn out treaty for peace. Among the tellers against prolonging negotiations was a disproportionate number of army men — important officers like Purefoy,[16] Stapleton,[17] and Hampden,[18] and the treasurer of the army, Sir Gilbert Gerard.[19] The opposition of the officers does not mean that as a class they were "against peace." Not many men in England believed in war for war's sake; even the profiteers might have favored peace if they thought that it could be made as lucrative as war. But more than that, the opposition of the officers does not mean that they disapproved of Parliament's proposals for the Oxford treaty. On the contrary, Hampden in the midst of the peace debates admitted that "there be divers things in our propositions which are things we need not insist upon"; and a few moments later, "The propositions beside the proposition of religion, privileges, etc., are not such as we will insist upon." [20] That this was not mere talk designed to conceal an ingrained hostility to peace, or to the Oxford proposals, Hampden and Stapleton proved a few months later when they joined in a secret peace negotiation with the Queen on the basis of those very proposals.[21] They were willing to treat secretly on the Oxford proposals; but because they were army men they disliked the idea of an open negotiation on any terms. To them the most immediate and pressing reality was the impending spring campaign. To fight that campaign the army needed supplies and recruits. Already there were disquieting rumors of men, once ready to lend much-needed financial aid to Parliament, who now "would not do anything

[16] C. J., II, 960.
[17] C. J., II, 959, 960, 961, 962.
[18] C. J., II, 959, 960, 961.
[19] C. J., II, 962.
[20] Y., 18777, fol. 162.
[21] M. A. E. Green, Letters of Queen Henrietta Maria, pp. 193–194.

. . . before they knew what would become of this business"
of a peace parley.[22] The army men feared that a long negotiation would jeopardize the military position of the army and its
ability to command necessary supplies. And so the military
members of the middle group opposed every suggestion for
bringing about a treaty that they rightly suspected the King
would use as an excuse for strategic stalling.

In contrast to the soldiers some of Pym's regular followers
were sure that the King could not in the long run reject a
settlement so reasonable as that contained in the Oxford proposals. More tenaciously than their military friends they clung
to hopes of peace. John Glynn never opposed any part of
Pym's defense program. Yet, a fundamentally conservative
common lawyer, he could but realize that a failure to find
the way to peace would force Parliament to plunge ever further along illegal courses. Being a civilian, not a soldier, he
may have realized this more intensely than he realized the
military danger of a long negotiation. In any case, when thirty-
six of his political allies changed sides, Glynn in opposition to
them and in accord with the peace party advocated a treaty
without disbanding the armies.[23] So at either end of the group
of thirty-six who hedged and trimmed in February was an in-
determinate number of members who did not change sides but
consistently favored or consistently opposed the various expedients for bringing about a treaty and yet who, on other
evidence, must be included in the middle group. Although we
are sure that thirty-six trimmers are only the solid core of
the middle group, sharply distinguished by their part in a
unique array of divisions, yet we cannot estimate the number
of peripheral members of the group, because in trying to do
so we find ourselves in those boundary areas where all is vague
and indefinable.

Some members of Parliament no doubt lent their support to
Pym's middle group because they believed it represented the

[22] *Y.*, 18777, fol. 149*v*; *D.*, 164, fol. 294*v*.
[23] *D.*, 164, fol. 295*v*.

righteous way. Others perhaps gave their adherence from motives of interest — hope of political power and advancement, hope of financial gain. But with most of the middle group, as with most men always and everywhere, principle and interest had become so interwoven and tangled that the members themselves could hardly tell in any instance what force impelled their action. Besides the bond of principle and the bond of interest, there was another tie among the men of the middle group that may have operated to give it coherence — the tie of blood relationship. The middle group was covered with a net of kinships, and rare was the member unable to find among his allies a half dozen near relatives — fathers, brothers, sons, uncles, first cousins, nephews.

It is easy to underestimate, easier to overestimate, the importance of the blood bond in Civil War politics. Family relationship has a way of being most conspicuous among men fighting and voting on the same side. We find Smith and Jones standing shoulder to shoulder in battle, and we say, "Why, of course! Smith's aunt married Jones's second cousin. Quite natural." We do not notice Brown and Robinson on the other side, loving what Smith and Jones hate, hating what they love — Robinson, the brother of Smith's wife, and Brown, the husband of Jones's daughter. During the Civil War family connection seldom absolutely determined political affiliation, but there were perhaps times and situations where it might exercise a real influence. Within the enormous latitude allowed for in such a statement the political effectiveness of great family groups varied with changing external conditions.

Family politics in the Long Parliament could not develop as amply as it did in the eighteenth century, because during the Civil War issues emerged which, involving men's most vital convictions, had a corrosive effect on the strongest family ties. The blood bond was not a constant factor in the Long Parliament; its influence varied inversely as the importance of the problems under consideration in the Houses. In the time of the breaking up of the nation when men faced the simple and terrible alternative of fighting for the King against Parliament or for Parliament against the King, family connections were disrupted and broken quite to pieces. The story of the Verney family is well known and well recorded.[24] It is a homely and tragic epitome of the meaning of civil war — the rupture of the ties of kinship and comradeship, with brother against brother, friend against friend, son against father. But the Verneys were only one of many families that saw the bonds of natural affection and love burst by the impact of a revolutionary force. Some kinship groups were mainly Royalist, others mainly Parliamentarian, but there was hardly a man, Cavalier or Roundhead, in all England, who did not have a brother or brother-in-law, a near cousin, a nephew, or a son fighting on the opposite side.

A few years after the outbreak of the war a new crisis split the members who remained at Westminster, and families now found themselves divided between the "Independents" and the army on one side and the "Presbyterians" on the other.[25] Between the two periods of high crisis in which the force of the issues destroyed the influence of family connections there was an interval of lower intensity in political affairs. The power of immediate circumstances further to loosen family ties diminished sharply from the beginning of the Civil War to the time of Pym's death and then gradually increased to the next crisis in 1647.

The crucial decision of the men at Westminster to resist Charles I by force at first left them only the time and the need to work out the manner, the means, and the limits of resistance. To Pym it was of real consequence that the period of his ascendancy should coincide with the period at which the pressure of emergent issues on kinship groups was at its lowest. It meant that in the absence of powerful incentives

[24] F. P. and M. M. Verney, *Memoirs of the Verney Family during the Civil War*, 2 vols. (1892–94).

[25] Anthony Nicholls and Sir William Waller of the Hampden-Barrington connection were impeached in 1647 by the Independents and the army led by Oliver St. John and Oliver Cromwell of the Hampden-Barrington connection.

to differences of opinion he could rely in part on old bonds of kinship to hold his party together.

Superimposed on kinship in Civil War politics, partly including it, partly transcending it, partly nullifying its effect, was a greater entity — the connection. Connection in the Long Parliament was not the intricate mechanism that it became in the eighteenth century; but all the essentials of connectional politics were there. The big men, the magnates, were there, and the kin of the magnates were there, and the lawyers and the estate agents, and the old neighbors and friends, and the old business associates. Yet when we try to trace the lines of connection in the middle group, we at once come up against serious difficulties. Eighteenth-century connections thrived on an abundance of controlled patronage and a dearth of issues; during the Civil War there was a dearth of controlled patronage and an abundance of issues. Mr. Namier can follow the vicissitudes of the Duke of Bedford and his Bloomsbury boys for a well-documented twenty years. The middle group lasted about half twenty months and disappeared leaving scarce a mark behind.

If we are to find the connectional basis of the middle group at all, we must look not to the first year of the Civil War, where our evidence thins down to a barely perceptible trickle, but to the decade or so before the Long Parliament. The objection to such a procedure is only too obvious. We will be looking for the middle group at a time when there is no middle group to look for. The middle group as a political unit was the response of certain members of Parliament to a unique set of circumstances produced by civil war. The most perspicuous of those members could not have foreseen the events that gave the middle group its *raison d'être*. We must adapt our inquiry to the limitations that the brief and unpremeditated career of the middle group imposes on us. The limitations are serious, but we must do the best we can with what we have.

Now although the middle group was the product of civil war, it was in a sense part of a larger entity, far older than the

Civil War. Puritanism had a hundred years' history in England before Parliament took arms against Charles I, and in one of its aspects the Civil War was the climax of an old struggle of the Puritans against the Catholic element in the English Church. Most of the men in the Civil War Parliament were Puritans, and among those Puritans adherents of the middle group stood out conspicuously. Perhaps we had best forget the smaller unit, the middle group, for a time, and seek out the larger unit, the Puritan connection, in the years before the war broke out.

We may first ask ourselves in what kinds of enterprise we may find the Puritans acting together, or, better, in what activities they collaborated *as Puritans*. After the death of Archbishop Bancroft in 1610, primacy in the English Church fell to George Abbott. As long as Abbott controlled the machinery of ecclesiastical discipline, the Puritans found room enough in the Church for their way of worship. The Archbishop did not seek to check them; probably in all questions except that of episcopal government his heart was with them.[26] More than a decade of salutary neglect gave the Puritans a sense of security from which they but slowly aroused themselves when the hour of disaster overtook them. Gradually the influence of the Primate waned; gradually William Laud and his friends found favor at court for their catholicizing ideals.[27]

When Laud, first as Bishop of London and then as Abbott's successor at Canterbury, set his hand to extirpating the Puritan element (he might have said the "Puritan excrescences") in the Church, men to whom that element was the food of life

[26] It is likely that even here there was no sharp difference. The renewed hostility of the mass of Puritans to episcopacy dates from the Laudian regime, and even the Laudian bishops did not convince all Puritans that bishops were against God's ordinance. See the debates on the episcopal clause of the Solemn League and Covenant (*Y.*, 18778, fols. 26*v*–30*v*).

[27] When we speak of Laud's catholicizing ideals, we mean "Anglo-Catholicizing," not "Roman Catholicizing." Without involving ourselves in any doctrinal subtilities we may epitomize the divergencies between Laud and the Puritans. Laud would have liked the Pope to regard the English Church as merely schismatical; the Puritans could not be happy in an English Church that their bogey, the papal Antichrist, deemed anything less than heretical.

and the light of salvation had to bestir themselves. Laud's policy left two ways open to them: they could fight or they could flee; but they could only fight as the conquered fight, secretly and by craft. For the King had disarmed them, had taken from them their only effective weapon of open resistance, by ruling without Parliament for eleven years.

So the Puritans planned for flight, for a mass exodus, in a series of colonizing schemes. Of these schemes the projected Puritan refuge on the little Isle of Providence in the West Indies makes the best starting place for our investigation.[28] The project is closely associated with the Civil War Parliament. Indeed, one contemporary will have us believe it was the very seed from which that Parliament grew. This earliest and most naïve exponent of the *complot* conception of the Puritan uprising tells us that the whole affair was concocted in the rooms of Providence Island Company in Gray's Inn Lane.[29] Without subscribing to this neat and simple theory of revolution, we may admit that an uncommonly large number of men later prominent on the Roundhead side wasted time and money on the Providence Island scheme. The company for the plantation of the Island of Providence was chartered in 1630. Heading the list of adventurers are three of the greatest Puritan peers — William, Viscount Say and Sele, whose bailiwick of Banbury was said to be the most Puritan town in England; Robert, Baron Brook, confirmed in Puritanism by his education in Calvinist Holland; and Robert, Earl of Warwick, who used a private fleet he inherited from his father in profitable anti-Spanish piracy of a more or less high-minded Puritan kind.[30] No less important in Roundhead affairs than

---

[28] What follows is not intended to be an exhaustive study of Puritan activities before the Civil War. Such a study might be worth a monograph. Worth it or not, it would require one to be exhaustive.

[29] "Letter from Mercurius Civicus to Mercurius Rusticus," in *Somers Tracts*, ed. Walter Scott, 13 vols. (1809–15), IV, 582.

[30] The above analysis of "connection" in the Puritan colonial enterprises has no pretensions to completeness. The author has relied heavily on A. P. Newton, *Colonizing Activity*, esp. pp. 34, 60–75, 126–127, on Charles M. Andrews' great work, *The Colonial Period in American History*, I (1934), esp. chaps.

the three lords were three commoners among the Providence
Island adventurers — Sir Thomas Barrington, intimate of Warwick and his deputy lieutenant in Essex, head of the Puritan
Barrington family, and related one way or another to most of
the big Puritan families in the eastern counties; Oliver St.
John, counsel for John Hampden in the ship-money case, and
in 1640 one of the authors of the petition of the twelve peers
for calling a Parliament; and, finally, St. John's collaborator
on the peers' petition, John Pym himself. Excepting two London merchants, who dropped out early in the history of the
Providence Island Company, there were altogether twenty-six
adventurers. Of the twenty-six almost two-thirds sat in the
upper or lower house of the Long Parliament, and there was
not a single Royalist in the lot.[31]

Saybrook, an earlier projected Puritan colony, was not a
costly failure, but it was not a ravishing success either. It
took its name from two of the grandees of the Providence Island
Company. Other participants in the West Indian venture had
joined Lords Say and Brook in planning a settlement on the
Connecticut shore of Long Island Sound: Sir Nathaniel Rich,
Henry Darley, and again the Earl of Warwick and John Pym.
Besides these in the list of patentees for Saybrook we find
three other names that were to loom large in the era of the
Puritan Revolution: Henry Lawrence, elected to the Civil
War Parliament in 1646, and later president of Cromwell's
Council of State;[32] Arthur Haselrig, the regicide republican,
executed at the Restoration for his part in the trial of Charles I,

xvii and xviii, and on Frances Rose-Troup's *John White, the Patriarch of Dorchester* (1930), and *The Massachusetts Bay Company and Its Predecessors*
(1930). F. W. Craven has thrown interesting light on the curious Puritan
piracy of the Earl of Warwick, "The Earl of Warwick, a Speculator in Piracy,"
Hispanic-American Historical Review (1930), x, 457–479.

[31] Earl of Holland, Earl of Warwick, Viscount Say and Sele, Lord Brook,
Lord Robarts, Sir Thomas Barrington, Sir Thomas Cheke, Sir Gilbert Gerard,
Sir Edward Moundeford, Sir Benjamin Rudyerd, Henry Darley, James Fiennes,
John Gurdon, John Pym, Oliver St. John. Holland was not a very good
Roundhead, but he was not a good Royalist either.

[32] *D. N. B.*, under Lawrence, Henry.

and the patriot John Hampden, the champion of English liberty every schoolboy knows.

The Providence Island and Saybrook ventures were anything but brilliant triumphs of colonizing activity. One Puritan attempt at colonization succeeded beyond the fondest dream of the most sanguine of its backers. Several patentees of Saybrook and adventurers for the Providence Plantation had earlier subscribed to the stock of the Massachusetts Bay Company, the pathetic little enterprise that grew into the greatest of all the colonies of England.[33] Also in the list of original subscribers we find the names of almost a dozen members of the Long Parliament, among them John White, family lawyer to the Winthrops[34] and legal guide of the Bay Company. Again all these members were Roundheads in the Civil War.[35]

The overlapping lists of adventurers, patentees, and subscribers interested in colonizing schemes in the New World tell us part of the story of a close-knit Puritan connection before the Civil War, but they do not tell the whole story. For another chapter we may turn to the correspondence of John Winthrop, to whom more than to any other man the Massachusetts Bay Company owed its success. Winthrop maintained contact between the Bay Company and the Saybrook patentees by regular correspondence with George Fenwick, the American agent for the Connecticut venture;[36] but the connection between the Lincolnshire squire and the Puritan magnates antedates the founding of the New England colonies, and in part followed channels independent of the immediate business problems of the New World settlements. Sir Nathaniel

[33] Henry Darley, Charles Fiennes, John Humphrey, Herbert Pelham, Sir Richard Saltonstall. The list of subscribers to the stock of the Massachusetts Bay Company will be found in "Records of the Company of the Massachusetts Bay," *Archaeologia Americana*, III (1857), cxxxiv–cxxxvi.

[34] *M. H. S. Winthrop*, I, 144. Other M.P.'s among the subscribers: Sir William Brereton, Matthew Craddock, Sir Robert Crane, William Crowther, Henry Darley, Samuel Vassal, John Venn, Sir John Yonge.

[35] Sir Robert Crane is a possible exception. He stayed in Parliament until late in 1643, when he went over to the King.

[36] *M. H. S. Collections*, ser. 5, I, 92, 224.

Rich, Sir Arthur Haselrig, Henry Darley, and Herbert Pelham,
all Saybrook patentees, appear as old friends in Winthrop's
letters.[37] Darley and Pelham had both been to New England,
the latter serving as first treasurer to Harvard College. Another
old New Englander and old friend to the Winthrops was John
Gurdon of the Providence Island Adventurers.[38] The lords
who gave their names to Saybrook also knew Winthrop well;
and although some coldness grew between them,[39] in 1637 the
Massachusetts governor received a brotherly letter from his
"loving friend, R. Brooke." [40]

English Puritans not active in colonial affairs were still
deeply interested in the fate of the experiment in New England. They rejoiced in its triumphs, and mourned its mis-
fortunes, and felt it to be, in a way, a thing of their own. They
exchange letters with Winthrop or appear in his correspondence
as old associates and friends. Among them is the Puritan
peer, the Earl of Lincoln. Sir Henry Vane the younger crops
up in Winthrop's letter, as he did in Winthrop's life and in
the early life of the Bay Colony, a disturbing, enigmatic force.[41]
Three Puritans who followed curiously divergent paths in
the Civil War Parliament find a common starting place in the
Winthrop correspondence. Alexander Rigby, a hard-bitten
Commonwealthman, distinguished by his early claim of the
right to tax for the two Houses,[42] appears in the Winthrop
papers, tangled with Sir Ferdinando Gorges in a fight over the
Maine patent.[43] Our old friend Sir Simond Dewes, the peace-
loving diarist, knew Winthrop in the days before the exodus to
Massachusetts.[44] And Sir John Clotworthy, a fiery spirit
to Dewes, to republican Rigby a dangerous Royalist, wrote to

[37] *M. H. S. Collections*, ser. 4, VI, 125; ser. 5, I, 373; ser. 4, VII, 139, 163.
[38] *M. H. S. Collections*, ser. 4, VI, 551. *M. H. S. Winthrop*, I, 317.
[39] See Lord Say's bitter letter to Winthrop, *M. H. S. Collections*, ser. 5, I,
297–303.
[40] *M. H. S. Collections*, ser. 5, I, 240.
[41] *M. H. S. Collections*, ser. 4, VI, 582.
[42] See, above, p. 9.
[43] *M. H. S. Collections*, ser. 4, VII, 537–554.
[44] *M. H. S. Winthrop*, I, 328–329.

Winthrop in the days of Laud of the worship of God now "pompous in the outward but penurious in the inward part." [45] But of all the letters Winthrop received, the one from Henry Lawrence — Saybrook patentee, member of the Civil War Parliament, president of the Protectorate Council of State — best shows how profoundly the hope of a New World refuge moved the English Puritans. "My faith makes me willing to outrun my intelligence in congratulating your safe arrival in New England. For God hath already showed Himself so gracious in conducting those who have gone your way, as we may . . . venture to trust without any farther trial." [46]

We have said that the Puritans had to flee from the Laudian regime or fight it, but that after 1629 they could make no frontal attack on the new ecclesiastical order because they had lost their only offensive weapon, Parliament. They waged a losing guerilla war against Laud, but we cannot pause to follow the history of that war. To do so would take us into every parish in England where a Puritan had the right of presentation,[47] to every parish where the local gentry showed their dislike of the new practices of the new priesthood, to every parish where a Puritan mob tore down an altar screen or heaved rocks at an idolatrous picture-glass window. We can only glance in passing at one of the curious episodes in this resistance, the work of the feoffees of impropriations and its adjunct the "seminary" at St. Anthony's in London. After going through one of the properly Puritan colleges at Oxford or Cambridge, promising young preachers would get practical training in a lectureship at Puritan-controlled St. Anthony's. In the meantime a group of zealous men gathered contributions to buy up lay impropriations, that is, the ecclesiastical income of tithes that had fallen into the hands of laymen, especially at the time of the Reformation. To the disgust of the Laudian faction, the feoffees did not use the purchased tithes to restore

---

[45] *M. H. S. Collections*, ser. 5, I, 208.
[46] *M. H. S. Collections*, ser. 5, I, 214.
[47] Nathaniel Ward, before he went to New England, had been presented the benefice of Standon Massey, Essex, by Sir Nathaniel Rich.

full livings to the ministers in the impropriated parishes. Instead they employed the income from the tithes to establish lectureships and buy benefices for "godly ministers," that is, for bright young Puritans.[48] Before the feoffees had got very far in their work, Laud took alarm and suppressed them. Before the suppression there had been seventeen feoffees.[49] Seven of the seventeen were interested in colonizing schemes, including Christopher Sherland of the Providence Island Company and John White, whom we met just a while back.[50]

Richard Baxter remarks somewhere that the opposition to Charles I ran in two separate streams, religious and political, and that in the Long Parliament the King had to face two sorts of enemies — church enemies and state enemies. Such a distinction, on the face of it, seems dubious; if there are fifteen possible reasons for disliking a man, we most probably will dislike him not for one reason but for all fifteen. To confirm our doubt of Baxter's classification we need not rely on the *cause célèbre* against the King's arbitrary power, the case of ship money, when opposition to taxation without consent found its leaders in two great Puritans — Lord Say and Sele and John Hampden. We need not even point out how happily (or how unpleasantly) black-letter legalism blended with blue-Sunday Puritanism in a William Prynne. We may look back beyond the later Puritan attacks on prerogative government and examine briefly the first attempt to resist the arbitrary policy of Charles I. The matter at issue had nothing to do with purity of religious doctrine or simplicity of religious worship; it had to do with the forced loan of 1627. Resisting ecclesiastical innovation was a complicated and touchy business. Resisting a forced loan was the easiest thing in the world; one merely refused to pay — and went to prison.

A glance down the list of resisters for names of Long Par-

[48] Henry A. Parker, "The Feoffees of Impropriations," *Publications of the Colonial Society of Massachusetts: Transactions* (1906–1907), XI, 263–277.
[49] Five died and were replaced.
[50] There were also George Harwood, Richard Davies, John Davenport, Thomas Goffe and Charles Offspring.

liament men brings us up with a start. The first name that strikes us is that of Thomas Wentworth. For a few days he sat in the upper house of the Long Parliament. Then as Earl of Strafford, councillor to Charles I in all evil things, he died on the block, attainted of treason, forsaken by the King he served so well. Yet Wentworth's refusal to pay need not make us despair of establishing the essentially Puritan character of the resistance to the forced loan. He was but one of twenty Long Parliament men among the resisters. Without exception the other nineteen were Roundheads,[51] from the moderate Sir Harbottle Grimston to the regicide Sir John Danvers. Future members of all three Puritan colonizing companies are represented among the men who refused to lend in 1627: Samuel Vassal of the Massachusetts Bay Company, Sir Thomas Barrington and Sir Gilbert Gerard of the Providence Island Adventurers, and Richard Knightly and John Hampden of the Saybrook patentees. There are other distinguished Puritan names on the list: Sir William Masham, Sir Harbottle Grimston, Sir Nathaniel Barnardiston, all future elders of the Presbyterian Church established by the Civil War Parliament. Barnardiston was an old friend of John Winthrop.[52] So was Sir Francis Barrington, head of the Puritan Barrington family in 1627. While Barrington was in jail for refusing the loan, the elder Winthrop sent young John to him with remembrances of love.[53] Thus in the vanguard of the first attack on the King's secular policy we find the Puritans. And this is only natural. The state policy of Charles I and his church policy are too much

[51] Long Parliament men among the resisters: Nathaniel Stephens (*C. S. P. Domestic*, Charles I, II, 59), Sir Nathaniel Barnardiston (*ibid.*, II, 66), Sir John Wray, Sir Edward Ayscough, Sir William Armyne (*ibid.*, II, 81), Sir Thomas Wentworth, Sir Oliver Luke (*ibid.*, II, 246), Sir John Jennings (*Acts of the Privy Council, 1627*, p. 5), Sir Gilbert Gerard (*ibid.*, pp. 53–54), Sir John Danvers, Richard Knightly (*ibid.*, p. 25), Sir Thomas Hutchinson, Sir Beauchamp St. John (*ibid.*, p. 74), Sir Anthony Irby (*ibid.*, p. 142), Sir Walter Earle, Sir William Masham (*ibid.*, p. 395), Samuel Vassal (*ibid.*, p. 422), Sir Thomas Barrington (*ibid.*, p. 315), Sir Harbottle Grimston, John Hampden (*ibid.*, p. 449).

[52] *M. H. S. Collections*, ser. 4, VI, 552. *M. H. S. Winthrop*, I, 325, 371 n.

[53] *M. H. S. Winthrop*, I, 337.

of a piece to box off into separate compartments. Opposition
to the latter almost inevitably entailed opposition to the
former.[54]

We have traced the activities of the Puritans before the
Civil War in colonization and in resistance to Charles's
churchmanship and statesmanship. We have seen that many
leaders of Puritan colonization and resistance sat in the Long
Parliament. We have seen, too, that the Puritan enterprises
were not each the work of a different group. A number of the
leaders had their fingers in several Puritan pies. The analogy
that immediately suggests itself to us is ultramodern. The
active Puritan groups remind us of nothing so much as a
congeries of independent corporations with directorates conveniently interlocking. If we focus our attention on the Puritan
enterprises from another angle, a new pattern emerges. Instead of seeing a crisscross of interlocking directorates, we see
a family party. Not an exclusive party for just one family,
but a big affair for several families that have known each other
for a long, long time and have asked a few old friends and a
few godly ministers to join them.

The men later destined to leadership in the Civil War Parliament are most heavily concentrated in the Providence Island
and Saybrook enterprises before 1640. For purposes of tracing
family ties we may regard the two projects as one.[55] From
the family point of view the Providence-Saybrook entrepreneurs
fall into six groups, or, better, into three pairs of groups. We
may call them the Bedford-Western Gentry connection, the
Fiennes-Eastern Gentry connection, and the Rich-Eastern
Gentry connection. The bent of Francis, third Earl of Bedford,
was for estate management, fen-draining, and water supply;
he did not take much interest in colonial enterprise. His
daughter's husband, Robert, Lord Brook, did; so, too, Brook's

[54] The converse of the above proposition is not always true. Hyde, who
approved of Charles's religious policy, did not like the eleven years of prerogative government.

[55] For the close connection between the two enterprises, see Newton,
Colonizing Activity, pp. 172–186.

brother-in-law, Sir Arthur Haselrig, and the manager of Bedford's legal business, Oliver St. John. Saybrook occupied Haselrig's attention; St. John owned a share in the Providence Island Company; and Brook was interested in both. Sir Anthony Rous took care of the Bedford property interests along the Devon-Cornwall border. His son-in-law, Upton, was one of the Providence Island Adventurers, and the secretary and moving spirit of the West Indian enterprise was his stepson, John Pym. If Bedford did not concern himself with colonies, Theophilus Clinton-Fiennes, fourth Earl of Lincoln, did. He concerned himself with anything that would help the Puritans. He did not play an active role in the Saybrook-Providence venture; but most of his near-relatives and best friends did — his wife's father and her brother, William, Lord Say and Sele, and James Fiennes; his sister's husband, John Humphrey; and his nephew's brother, Richard Knightly. The Earl's castle at Sempringham was the meeting place of all the Puritans in the neighborhood. Among them was John Gurdon of the Providence Island Company. Gurdon's brother-in-law, Sir Richard Saltonstall, and his uncle, Herbert Pelham, were Saybrook patentees.

Robert Rich, Earl of Warwick, for forty years had a hand in every important overseas enterprise, Puritan or not, legitimate or not; if the purpose was to establish a New Jerusalem around Massachusetts Bay or to establish a suitable base for piracy in the West Indies, so long as it was a trans-Atlantic affair Warwick was in on it, and he carried his kin with him for the ride or for whatever profit to righteousness or the family fortune the project might promise. On behalf of the New England Council, which by 1630 was for all practical purposes Warwick himself, he made the grant to the Saybrook people. Among them were his son and heir, Lord Rich, and Sir Nathaniel Rich, the result, one generation removed, of an indiscreet interval in the life of Warwick's grandfather. Sir Nathaniel and Warwick, of course, had shares in the Providence Island venture. So did Sir Nathaniel's cousin, John Michell; Warwick's brother,

Henry, Earl of Holland; his brother-in-law, Sir Thomas Cheeke; and his two sons-in-law, John, Lord Robartes, and Edward, Lord Mandeville, the Earl of Manchester of Civil War days. The political alliance of the Riches and the Barringtons in Essex was almost as old as the Earl of Warwick and Sir Thomas Barrington were, antedating any possible common interest of the two in anything more grown-up than applefilching and bird's-nesting. Already in 1603 in the elections for King James's first Parliament, Lord Robert Rich, Warwick's father, was exerting all his influence to secure the return of his old friend Sir Francis Barrington, Sir Thomas' father, for the county of Essex.[56] So Sir Thomas, in 1640 deputy lieutenant to Warwick, the lord-lieutenant of the county, naturally came into the Providence Island venture. So did his brother-in-law, Sir Gilbert Gerard, while his first cousin, John Hampden, was a Saybrook patentee. Richard Knightly, Hampden's brother-in-law and, as we have seen, also connected with the Fienneses, was active in both enterprises. Finally, Oliver St. John, whom we met a while ago among the Bedfords, was related by marriage to Sir Thomas at least three different ways, at once a second cousin, a first cousin, and a nephew.[57]

The family ties between the Saybrook–Providence Island men and the early members of the Massachusetts Bay Company were not so close. The former were the cream of the Puritan aristocracy, the latter something a good deal less than that. It seemed that almost anybody could get in on the scheme, and a lot of people who really weren't anybody did. The only great connection well represented in the Massachusetts Bay Company was the Fiennes family and friends. Besides Charles Fiennes, Sir Richard Staltonstall, John Humphrey, and Herbert Pelham, Isaac Johnston, brother-in-law of the Earl and Charles, joined the company. So did Pelham's step-

[56] Lowndes MSS, *H. M. C. Report VII*, app. i, pp. 542–543.

[57] St. John was a second cousin to Sir Thomas' wife, Judith, through the St. Johns of Bletisho, a nephew to Sir Thomas by his first marriage to Sir Thomas' sister's child, Joan Altham, and a first cousin by his second marriage to Elizabeth Cromwell, the daughter of Sir Thomas' uncle.

uncle, the Reverend Edward Clark, and his brother-in-law, Richard Bellingham. Both Johnston and Bellingham had enough faith in the idea of the Puritan exodus to migrate themselves. The former died in the first terrible winter in New England; the latter was one of the early governors of the Bay Colony. Other men, close to Lincoln, had their place in the project: Simon Bradstreet, and, towering above them all, John Winthrop. Besides this group, there was a scattering of other offshoots of the big Puritan families: Thomas Southcote and Sir John Young, related to Pym through Sir Anthony Rous, and Francis Flyer, the nephew of Mandeville's stepmother.

The list of loan-resisters brings us back to the top-crust Puritans, the connections that sent their menfolk to Parliament in large numbers. The Fiennes connection now drops into the background. The only prominent member of the family in trouble for refusing money to Charles in 1627 was Sir Walter Earle, whose son married a daughter of Lord Say and Sele. The part of the Bedford group in resisting the loan was equally negligible. The brunt of the battle fell on the Warwick-Barrington connection. The Barringtons and the Hampdens put up an obviously concerted resistance to the loan, and suffered the consequences. Gerard, Knightly, John Hampden, and Sir Thomas went to jail for refusing to pay. So did the head of the family, Sir Francis Barrington, and his son-in-law, Sir William Masham. Also connected with the group in resistance, and tenuously by family ties, were Sir Edmund Hampden, Sir Beauchamp St. John, Sir Harbottle Grimston, and a group related to Knightly through his cousin Sir Richard: Sir Oliver Luke, Sir Nathaniel Barnardiston, and Sir William Armyne. Sir William probably fits better with another group resisting the loan — the Lincolnshire knights. Three of them were connected with Warwick. Sir Anthony Irby's daughter married the brother of Warwick's son-in-law, Lord Mandeville. Sir John Wray, another of the Lincolnshire resisters, was doubly linked with the Rich connection. His aunt married the first Earl of Warwick, thus becoming the stepmother of the second earl, and his own mother, a Montagu, was first cousin to Lord Mandeville. Sir Thomas Grantham, Sir Thomas Darnell, William Anderson, and Sir Edward Ayscough, a connection of the Wray family, round out the number of Lincoln gentry suffering for rejecting what they considered the illegal demands of the King.

So we end our incomplete sketch of Puritan activity before 1640. Its justification lies in the lack of more than a few shreds of direct evidence about the activities of the middle-group connection in 1642–43. If we view what the Puritans did before the war with a little common sense, we will see that it constitutes strong presumptive evidence for an effective middle-group connection during the first year of the war. The leaders of the Puritans sat in the Long Parliament, and sat there as leaders of the middle group: the Earl of Warwick, Viscount Say and Sele, Lords Brook and Mandeville, Barrington, Hampden, and Pym. Moreover, they brought their relatives, old associates, and friends with them in force. The Rich-Eastern Gentry connection, for example, did not need to go beyond second cousins of their chief men — Hampden, Barrington, Warwick, and Mandeville (now Earl of Manchester) — in order to pick up two dozen members of the Civil War Parliament. And the Fiennes and Russell connections could do at least half as well. Now it simply stands to reason that men who have associated with one another, have conferred and acted together for more than a decade, do not stop conferring and acting and associating just because they have become members of Parliament. By that very event both the facilities and the need for coöperation have multiplied a hundredfold. If men like Pym and Barrington and Warwick felt that they must act together in the uneventful days of prerogative rule, when there was scarcely a new problem each year, how much more pressing was the necessity for common action in the midst of civil war with a fresh crisis every week, almost every day. And how much easier common counsel had become! Pym did not have to cross England to talk matters over with Lord

Say or Warwick. About all he had to do was cross the street. Almost everyone that counted was in London in the winter of 1642–43, and anybody who was not there would probably turn up in a day or so.

Fortunately for Pym and his allies, everyone was in London — unfortunately for us. A man living in Devon might write letters to a friend and ally dwelling in Essex; but a man residing in Gray's Inn Lane did not have to write to a friend in Covent Garden; he could walk over there in a quarter of an hour. Because men could talk their plans over they did not write to one another about them, and, because they did not write, we have little record of the workings of the connections in the middle group. Dewes and the Venetian ambassador toss accusations of conspiracy around with a fine abandon, but they are too indiscriminate to be of any use. We catch a fitful glimpse of the workings of the middle-party men in John Pickering's letters from Scotland. The letters show how Pym and Clotworthy worked together and imply the existence of a more extensive group of insiders. But the series is incomplete, and serves to whet our appetite, not to satisfy it.

One reasonably large batch of the papers of a prominent middle-group man has come down to us. Sir Thomas Barrington spent a good part of the early months of 1643 in Essex and the other eastern countries. Consequently he received many letters from London, and some of them have survived. From these letters we can get a few hints, not of the operations of the connections in the middle group in London, but of Pym's way of using his connections in the counties. He employed them, for one thing, in a primitive kind of pressure politics. When he wanted the House to pass a favorite measure, he could get an influential man from the county to write the House, telling how necessary that measure was for the preservation of the parliamentary party in his county.[58] And when Pym needed information on the needs and temper of a par-

---

[58] Thomas Barrington to the speaker of the House of Commons (*B.*, 2646, fol. 86).

ticular locality he could avail himself of the judgment of friends
he trusted instead of depending on the official letters of ineffec-
tual faction-ridden county committees.

Pym was the preëminent Parliament man of his generation,
but he knew that the greatest forum of free discussion in
Europe was not the ideal place for making the spot decisions
and taking the immediate action which the crises of war sometimes demand. He was not subject to the illusion that God
was against everything that Parliament did not have a chance
to vote on. Occasionally the need arose for a quick move in
the counties. Parliament might refuse to issue the necessary
instructions or might be dilatory about it. Even if Parliament
did eventually get around to the instructions, it was always
an open question whether the county committee would bother
to execute the command of the Houses. The committees were
especially undependable in any affair with a party tinge to it.
The local leaders were themselves split into factions parallel-
ing the factions in Parliament, and polite sabotage was very
simple. It was a much surer way in an emergency to sidestep
Parliament and to write to an influential friend or so in the
county, "This is to be done posthaste. Do it!" So it was when
Pym wanted to gag some critics of the Lord General in Essex.
At the moment the Lord General stood low in the esteem of the
House of Commons. The members might even have refused to
gag his critics, a blow to the general that Pym would be anxious
to ward off. So Pym did not consult Parliament. He wrote
directly to his friend Barrington, asking him to get to work
on the mischief-makers in his county.[59]

But when all is said about the use Pym made of his connections to link the middle group in the Houses to the middle
group in the country, we have not touched the main function
of the connection in his scheme of things. Connection gave
Pym a clue to the opinions of the only men whose opinions
mattered to him. He could always gauge the attitude of the
extremists of peace party and war party to his plans, and

[59] Pym to Barrington (Lowndes MSS, *H. M. C. Report VII*, app. i, p. 551).

discount its effect in advance. It was less easy to be sure in what direction and how far the middle group would go, and the general character of Pym's ideas made it necessary for him not merely to swing enough of the group to make a majority but to win the whole party to his policy. By sounding out the grandees of the middle group connections before proposing a measure, he could assure himself both of their support and of the support of lesser men who followed their lead. If this crude procedure has little in common with the carefully calculated lining up of votes that became matter of course in the next century, it was nevertheless a more effective way of securing Parliamentary action than the old hit-and-hope method. In one of the few cases in which Pym certainly hit and hoped, improvising a policy from the floor of the House instead of preparing his friends for it in advance, he suffered a speedy and thorough defeat.[60] The ultimate adoption of all the constructive policies Pym advocated was due at least in part to his rough foreknowledge of the sentiment toward those policies in the great middle-group connections.

Three men of the middle-group connections brought the party something more than a pendant string of brothers, cousins, and uncles. John Pym, John Hampden, and the Earl of Essex exercised an influence that extended beyond the bounds of their respective families. Had the influence of each been exerted for different ends, had they not worked in closest harmony with one another, the mere bonds of family would not have been enough to hold the middle group together for long. They were the very heart of it; the death of Hampden in June 1643 caused a violent convulsion in the party; the death of Pym half a year later resulted in its total disintegration. It would be hard to find three men further apart in background, temperament, and character than Essex, the haughty, self-willed, frequently foolish peer, Hampden, the quiet, ascetic Puritan country gentleman, and Pym, the busy, high-pressure, energetic man of affairs; yet during six months

[60] See ,above, p. 61.

of civil war Essex and Hampden and Pym united their efforts and wills and influence for a common end, and by their unity kept safe the unity of the middle group.

The Earl of Essex was not at all a great military leader; but on the raw levies at his disposal the talents of a great military leader would have been wasted anyhow, and he had qualities that in the time and the place were more essential than tactical genius. A year after the whole Parliament had resolved to live and die with him,[61] he was held fair game for any fanatic, in the House or out of it, who felt the urge to blame a series of dismal military failures on something further from home than the inefficiency, incompetence, and corruption of Parliament itself. He was libeled, caricatured, abused, and derided, and after Pym's death disregarded, neglected, and betrayed; yet until he felt sure that the attacks of his enemies were due not to misplaced zeal for the cause, as he and Pym had seen it, but to concealed and dangerous schemes, he refused to use against his opponents the underhand tactics they employed against him with systematic pitilessness. Men might justly doubt his talent for generalship; only the willfully blind and the willfully deaf could doubt his loyalty to the cause he had sworn to maintain. Moreover, even in the worst times, even after the collapse of the middle group, when the dominant faction in the House was obviously trying to undermine him and he was a lost cause, his officers remained faithful to him.[62] The *esprit de corps* of the army, so conspicuous in the New Model, was not entirely lacking in the army of the Earl of Essex; what was lacking was a man with the will to make political capital out of it. The middle group needed a general who, regardless of his defects, could inspire the loyalty of others and who was himself perfectly loyal. Essex was not merely a general, however; he was commander-in-chief of all the forces of Parliament. He had accepted a trust which men less resolute

[61] Gardiner, *Constitutional Documents*, p. 261.
[62] When he began to concert action with Holles and the old peace party after Pym's death, many of the army group in Parliament — men like Gerard and Stapleton — followed his lead.

than himself would have shirked; he was the only man Parliament was willing to put in charge of an army. As a commander-in-chief without the slightest aspiration to become a military dictator, he was not only valuable to the middle group, he was indispensable to it. Pym did strenuous work in keeping Essex within the limits of the middle group and in restraining his tendency to stray toward the peace party.

In this labor Pym was ably seconded by Colonel John Hampden, and under their guidance Essex behaved himself. Hampden did not play a conspicuous part in Parliament after the outbreak of the war; he spent most of his time in the army. Nevertheless from the day that the King went down to impeach the five members, Hampden held his place in the royal proclamations as one of the Parliamentarians who must be excepted from pardon, and both Clarendon and Dewes considered him the subtle deviser of many of the plans Pym executed.[63] Of this we know nothing. We do know that qualities other than subtlety won him the place he held in the middle group and in the hearts of his friends. Better than the stolid Essex and the pliant, temporizing Pym he embodied the aspirations of the militant Puritan country gentlemen. Indeed the description of him by Philip Warwick, a thorough Royalist, does not read like the portrait of a flesh-and-blood man; it sounds like an abstract idealization. It might have appeared as a chapter in a character book, under the heading, "The Character of a Puritan Hero."

He was the person of the greatest abilities of any of that party. He had a great knowledge both in scholarship and in law. He was of a concise and significant language — the mildest yet subtlest speaker of any man in the House. . . . He was very well read in history. . . . He was a man of great and plentiful estate and of great interest in his country, and of a regular life.[64]

His trial for refusing ship money suddenly exalted him into a symbol of the resistance of the gentry to the arbitrary acts of

[63] *Clar. H. R.*, bk. VII, par. 411; *D.*, 164, fols. 277–277v, 296v, 301v, 303v.
[64] Philip Warwick, *Memoires of the Reign of Charles I* (1702), p. 265.

the King. "He grew the argument of all tongues, every man inquiring who and what he was that durst at his own charge support the liberty and property of the Kingdom and rescue his country from being made a prey to the Court." [65] The intimate confidant of the future Lord Protector, Oliver Cromwell,[66] he was lamented in death by men who were to follow very different roads from the one Oliver trod. Pym's nephew, Anthony Nicholls, who in 1647 was impeached by Cromwell's army, writes, "Poor Hampden is dead. . . . I have scarce strength to pronounce that word. Never Kingdom received a greater loss in one subject. Never man a truer and faithfuller friend." Robert Goodwyn, future councillor of state to the Commonwealth Cromwell destroyed, bewails the "sad tidings of Colonel Hampden's death . . . a cause to all honest men of much reluctation and sorrow." [67] To Sir John Coke, a somewhat bewildered moderate, Hampden's death was ill news,[68] and the semiliterate Puritan Countess of Sussex, who did not even know Hampden, sorrowed that he was lost to the cause.[69] The taciturn gentleman from Buckinghamshire had acted as a sort of moral cement for the parliamentary cause. Concentrated in him was the best of what was good in the Puritan opposition to Charles. He bound the conservative legalist party against the King to the radical religious group. What he bound, his death loosed; and it could never be bound permanently again, although Pym despite almost insuperable difficulty achieved a temporary restoration of the unity of the middle group.

It was, of course, his unmatched ability to get big results out of a little material that constituted Pym's greatest contribution to the middle group. He also helped to bring the

[65] *Clar. H. R.*, bk. VII, par. 82.

[66] Thomas Carlyle, *Letters and Speeches of Oliver Cromwell*, ed. S. C. Lomas, 3 vols. (1904), III, 164–166.

[67] Anthony Nicholls to Sir Thomas Barrington (Lowndes MSS, *H. M. C. Report VII*, app. i, p. 553); Robert Goodwyn to Sir Thomas Barrington (*B.*, 2646, fol. 293).

[68] Cowper MSS, *H. M. C. Report XII*, app. ii, p. 335.

[69] F. P. and M. M. Verney, *Memoirs of the Verney Family*, II, 159.

group one follower without whose aid the Houses could not have kept an army in the field for a week. The City of London was a difficult and dangerous ally, with an awkward tendency to hearken to the hasty counsels of hotheaded Puritan preachers. For a time, however, during the critical months when he was working out the first measures in his defense program, Pym was able to control the political action of the metropolis. Although we can only gauge the extent of his power on the basis of external evidence, the concurrences between what Pym wanted and what the City asked for are so frequent as to imply a close connection. When he needed an unconditional offer of aid,[70] or a conditional offer of aid,[71] the offer was always forthcoming from the City. When he wanted external pressure on Parliament for an assessment ordinance [72] or a vow and covenant,[73] the City or "divers well-affected citizens" were sure to demand an assessment and a covenant. Sir Simond Dewes testifies bitterly to Pym's ability to make the City produce,[74] but he gives us no clue as to how Pym did it. And what Dewes does not tell us we have been unable to learn elsewhere. We have a hazy notion that Pym's long residence in London before the Long Parliament, as treasurer for the Providence Island Company, may have familiarized him with the ins and outs of metropolitan politics and given him useful connections in the City.[75] We know nothing of the nature of Pym's hold on the City government or on the politically active unofficial group of citizens. We know nothing of the schemes of London financiers or of their method of controlling the pressure of the City money bags on the House. We know little of the mechanism and operation of mass petitioning. We do not know who the men were that could pour a mob into Westminster easily and on demand, as a bar maid pours ale into a mug. The historians have explored and explained none of these matters.[76] We do not even know how or exactly why Pym lost

---

[70] *C. J.*, II, 847.
[71] *D.*, 164, fol. 381.
[72] *C. J.*, II, 858.
[73] *C. J.*, II, 976; *D.*, 164, fol. 381.
[74] *D.*, 164, fol. 303.
[75] *C. S. P. Colonial*, I, *passim*.
[76] Any writer on the politics of the Long Parliament will eventually feel the

control of the City. We only know that sometime in the late spring or early summer of 1643 the City got out of hand and turned on Pym's friend Essex.[77] In general we may say that the City was like an avalanche in that it was easy to start and very hard to stop once it got going, and that it was also like a gas attack in that a change in the political wind might send it rolling back on the men who used it. But that is merely in general and does not explain specifically why the City kicked back on Pym in the summer of 1643. Whatever the explanation may be, it is probably now buried in unthumbed volumes of the municipal records.[78]

One interesting point in connection with the middle group remains to be discussed. Because it omits one very important element our analysis of the structure of this group may seem to lack depth. The historian of the Civil War and the Long Parliament is likely to put a high estimate on the importance of religion during the period and to regard it as the master key to many a hard problem. Yet in all that has been said here about the middle group there is hardly a word about religion — about Anglicans and Puritans, about Presbyterians and Independents. The middle group has been traced back to the Puritans of pre-war days, and a Puritan party line in that period has been suggested. But of the Puritanism of the middle group, once the war began, nothing has been said.

Now it is impossible to write anything significant about the politics of the first year of the Long Parliament without examining the relation of Anglican to Puritan. It is equally impossible to write of the Civil War Parliament from 1645 on

lack of a reputable and thorough study of London during the Rebellion. One political problem after another remains insoluble because of our ignorance of what actually went on in the councils of the City. Neither R. R. Sharpe's *London and the Kingdom* (3 vols. [1894–95], II, 132–353) nor C. H. Firth's article, "London during the Civil War" (*History*, XI [1926], 25–36), even approach the problems.

[77] See, below, pp. 107–112.

[78] It is not enough to say that the City was reacting to military failures. Under the circumstances it might have either rallied to Essex or turned against him. The question is who induced it to take the latter course.

without trying to unscramble Presbyterian and Independent.[79]
It is only natural that one should try to apply the religious
standard — so useful before and after — to the years between,
including the year of Pym's ascendancy. But it will not work.
During Pym's hegemony in the House of Commons the religious issue emerged in Parliament but twice, and both times
it only demonstrated the insignificance of religion in the
determination of party divisions in 1643. In both cases the
religious question took the same form: Shall Parliament immediately abolish episcopacy, or shall it bide its time and try
to reform the bishops? And in both cases instead of consolidat-
ing the factions internally and widening the gulfs that separated
them one from another, the religious question split the factions
internally. In December in the debates on the Oxford treaty
propositions, Holles and Dewes, consistent peace-party men,
wanted to include in the proposals a provision for abolishing
episcopacy.[80] Maynard, an equally consistent peace-party man,
argued against the inclusion of such a proposition.[81] When the
House came to pass on the Solemn League and Covenant with
the Scots, the same sort of intramural division showed itself
in the middle group. John Glynn opposed the portion of the
Covenant which bound the Houses to the utter extirpation of
the bishops.[82] John Pym on the other hand upheld the anti-
episcopal clause; [83] and, as in December most of the House
stood with Dewes and Holles against Maynard and the bishops,
so in September it stood with Pym against Glynn and the
bishops. So we find no coincidence between the old Anglican-
Puritan division of Parliament and the grouping of parties in
1643. If instead of looking back we look forward and try to
judge the religious complexion of parties in Pym's time from
what their adherents became at a later day, we get another

[79] For a general approach to the problem of the relation of religion to
politics in the later years of the Civil War, see J. H. Hexter, "The Problem
of the Presbyterian Independents," *American Historical Review* (1938), XLIV,
29–49.

[80] D., 164, fols. 279, 280.   [82] Y., 18778, fols. 29–29v.
[81] D., 164, fol. 279.   [83] Y., 18778, fol. 30.

unintelligible pattern. In each faction — peace party, middle group, and war party — we find men who, having the opportunity, affiliated themselves with the Presbyterian Church established by Parliament in 1645–47 and other men who, having the same opportunity, did not.[84]

The close-knit Hampden-Barrington connection of the middle group included in 1643 men later known as "Independents," others later known as "Presbyterians," and yet others who were surely Erastians. Sir William Masham sat in the "Independent" Rump Parliament and in the Republican Council of State.[85] Oliver St. John was the Lord Chief Justice of the "Independent" Commonwealth. Masham was Barrington's brother-in-law, St. John his nephew and cousin. In 1647 the army impeached Anthony Nicholls, one of the eleven "Presbyterian" grandees, and in 1648 in Pride's Purge the army jailed Richard Knightly,[86] another "Presbyterian." Nicholls was Barrington's son-in-law, Knightly the second cousin of Barrington and St. John. Samuel Brown's religious thought was strictly Erastian,[87] although in politics he acted with the Independents until 1648. He was St. John's first cousin and Barrington's second cousin. By the time men got around to calling their legitimate King "that man of blood," ties of kinship had not the power to hold together even the closest family connection, and near relatives went divers ways — some by a devious route to worldly success, some to prison, some up a short path of glory that stopped abruptly at the headsman's block.

[84] Members associated with presbyteries, 1645–47: peace party — Sir Simond Dewes (W. A. Shaw, *A History of the English Church during the Civil War and under the Commonwealth* (2 vols. [1900], II, 428), Harbottle Grimston (*ibid.*, II, 391); middle group — Sir John Corbett (*ibid.*, II, 410), Sir William Masham (*ibid.*, II, 380); war party — John Gurdon (*ibid.*, II, 423), Alexander Rigby (*ibid.*, II, 397). Members not associated with presbyteries: peace party — Sir Robert Parkhurst, Sir Poynings Moore; middle group — Sir John Clotworthy, Sir Gilbert Gerard; war party — John Venn, Isaac Pennington.

[85] *A. O. I.*, II, 2, 64.

[86] Son of the Richard Knightly mentioned above (d. 1639), and husband of Hampden's daughter.

[87] *Minutes of the Proceedings of the Assembly of Divines*, ed. A. F. Mitchell and J. Struthers (1874), pp. 452–455.

So fails our attempt to find an Anglican-Puritan division, or a Presbyterian-Independent cleavage in the House of Commons under Pym, that will coincide with the political pattern of peace party, middle group, and war party. Nor is the reason for our failure far to seek. By and large, the men who stayed at Westminster when the Civil War broke out were Puritans. Regardless of how they might differ as to the ideal church of the future, they all agreed on the necessity of a drastic change in the church of the past.[88] The Anglican-Puritan issue was already settled in 1643; the Presbyterian-Independent issue had not yet emerged. Until the House had to determine the form of the new church, there was no real religious problem before them. The members had enough troubles without agitating themselves over an evil that was dead and one that was not yet vigorous enough to do any damage. So between the time they smote the Anglican sons of Baal and the time strife began between Presbyterian Israel and Independent Judea, the Chosen of the Lord did not quarrel over religion. Not that each man sat under his own vine and each under his own fig-tree at peace with his brethren. They fought about who should control the army, and whether there should be peace with the King and on what terms, and they wrangled over each successive defense measure that Pym proposed. But while they were at each other over questions of political and military policy, and as long as the issue was not forced on their attention, they did not get around to effective fratricidal strife over religion. Some men said that Pym and the other leaders purposely buried the question of church reform in the Westminster Assembly of Divines to avert or postpone an inconvenient conflict.[89] Be that as it may, the religious question did stay buried in the Assembly until long after Pym's death; and so he was able to build his middle group regardless of the incongruities in the religious beliefs of his allies.

[88] Even Glynn would have had no scruples against an oath to extirpate the "present" episcopal government of the Church, "for," he said, "the present government is abominable" (*Y.*, 18778, fol. 30).

[89] *C. S. P. Venetian*, XXVI, 301–302.

PART TWO

PYM AND ESSEX

CHAPTER V

OMENS OF WOE

Pym's delicate technique for controlling Parliament could not forever remain effective. In fact, its effectiveness did not survive the death of the only man who really mastered it. Two months after Pym died the struggle for control of the Committee of Both Kingdoms uncovered a schism in Parliament so wide that it was years before the members on either side found common ground again.[1] The affair of the Committee of Both Kingdoms was only the natural result of internal changes in the House of Commons that had their tangible beginning in a foolish act of the Lord General, the Earl of Essex, in July 1643. The rate of change increased as Pym's illness weakened his hold over the various sections of his unruly coalition, and soon after he died it terminated in an open split within the middle group.

Although the Lord General's letter of July 9 precipitated the first serious crisis in the middle group, a discerning observer might earlier have had forebodings of the impending doom of Pym's scheme of parliamentary control. The danger did not come from the men favoring appeasement. They could always be relied on to support any proposal for peace and to help brake the headlong haste of the violent men. On the other hand, the line of treason determined how far a man could go in

---

[1] See Professor Notestein's excellent article "The Establishment of the Committee of Both Kingdoms," *American Historical Review* (1912), XVII, 477–495. On one point only is there much doubt about Professor Notestein's thesis. His distinction between Presbyterians and Independents was important in Parliament in 1645. But religious issues apparently had no influence in the immediate controversy over the committee, in which, indeed, the stauncher Presbyterians, following the lead of the Scots, were aligned with Vane and St. John against Holles, the future leader of the "Presbyterian" party. The immediate issue in February 1644 was a personal one between the friends of Essex and the enemies of Essex.

quest of peace, and the reluctance of Charles to see reason as even the peaceful members at Westminster saw it acted as a continuous repellent force on those who veered too far toward accommodation with him. The would-be peace makers were shunted like shuttles from Charles to the war party and so ever back and forth as the fear of the despotism of the one or the extremism of the other took ascendancy in their minds.[2]

The real threat to a middle-group policy came from the other side. Firebrands of all sorts regularly supported any war measures Pym might want, and some that he did not want at all.[3] But for the support of hotheaded, violent, doctrinaire men one must pay a price. The best men available to make Parliament move fast, the radicals often sought to determine the direction it should take. Then it was as if the black horse of Plato's parable had taken the bit in his teeth. They plunged on, uncontrollable, and the very vigor and determination that made them so great an asset in the prosecution of the war strained to the breaking point the fragile lines that held them in harness with the rest of the house.

We have already seen how the violence of the war party went beyond the bounds Pym wanted to set for it. We have seen the fiery spirits attacking the King against Pym's better judgment, insulting the Lords when he would have salved them, and directly seeking to thwart him by assaults on the Committee of Safety. Soon they went further and, turning their fire inward, took every opportunity to threaten, embarrass, and intimidate the peace party in the House of Commons with accusations of lukewarmness to the cause and even of treachery.[4]

---

[2] Those few who did not swing back from the King, despite his opposition to what the Houses professed to be fighting for, simply deserted. Their number was on the whole remarkably small. Despite their love of peace, not a single member of the peace party in the House of Commons was implicated in the Waller plot, save its protagonist.

[3] See, above, pp. 56–60.

[4] Attacks on individual members: Gurdon on Sir Thomas Jermyn (*D.*, 164, fols. 274–274*v*), Sir Henry Mildmay on Sir Thomas Bendish (*D.*, 164, fols. 282–282*v*), William Strode on Sir Simond Dewes (*D.*, 164, fol. 292*v*), Miles

In Parliament the intransigent hotheads were a small though vociferous minority. Had they confined their activities within the walls of the House of Commons, they might have annoyed Pym without endangering the operation of his political organization. Their ardor allowed of no such limitation. It spilled over and infected a vital section of Pym's extra-Parliamentary support — the City of London and the men who shaped London opinion, the Puritan clergy of the City.[5] Rumor had it that certain ministers from the pulpits recommended devout prayers to God for a zealous youth who proposed to assassinate the King *pro bono publico*,[6] and that the Reverend Hugh Peters, late returned from the New Jerusalem of Massachusetts Bay, was circulating a petition to depose Charles I.[7] Thomas Case, chaplain to Lord Mayor Pennington, offered the sacrament to all who had contributed to Parliament, but "denounced damnation to such as should presume to receive it" without giving to the cause.[8] Another minister, Edward Bowles, said that it was "more necessary to the welfare of the Kingdom" that the honor of Parliament be maintained "than of any particular person whatsoever." [9] Everyone knew that the "particular person" whose honor Bowles would subordinate to that of Parliament was Charles I of England. As the clergy went, so went the City. In the twenty years of the Puritan Revolution there was never a serious difference of opinion between the ministers of London and the bulk of the citizens of London. If the blackcoats

Corbett on Sir William Playters (*D.*, 164, fol. 232), Dennis Bond on William Whitaker (*D.*, 164, fols. 232–232*v*), William Strode on Sir Edward Hales, Sir Humphrey Tufton, Sir Norton Knatchbull, and Sir Edward Partridge (*D.*, 164, fols. 356*v*–357). The general character of the attacks on the peace party may be gauged by William Strode's "There are some members of the House that are unfit materials" (*D.*, 164, fol. 293).

[5] In the twenty years of the Interregnum there was not, to the best of my knowledge, a serious difference of opinion between the mass of the London clergy and the bulk of the City.

[6] *C. S. P. Venetian*, XXVI, 249.

[7] *Mercurius Aulicus*, April 2–8, 1643.

[8] *Mercurius Aulicus*, February 19–25, 1643.

[9] Edward Bowles, *Plaine Englishe* (1643), p. 11.

raised a cry after the royal family the people of the City were sure to chime in. Especially they hated the Queen, the tainted child of the Red Woman of Rome; [10] but the King did not escape their wrath. Among them, too, the idea of deposing him had taken root; and when Parliament seized the regalia, a man watching in the crowd had remarked that the crown had best be saved to put on the head of the Duke of Glouces-ter.[11]

Lèse majesté and treason are not safe commodities even when respectable people avoid them; but soon dangerous notions about monarchy received quasi-official and official sanction in the City of London. We have seen to what extremes the Lord Mayor's chaplain went. Report accused the Lord Mayor himself of refusing to act against a man who expressed the hope of washing his hands in the King's blood, and of delaying action against one who had said if he could come at the King he would stick him with a dagger.[12] Edward Bowles spoke the mind of many when he scoffed at the pretense, carefully maintained by Parliament, that the King was not personally responsible for the deeds which made peace impossible, that in such matters he was misled by evil councillors. Bowles's logic cut straight through this nonsense. The King himself denied that anyone misled him; he accepted full responsibility for the deeds the Houses tried to palm off on hidden forces of darkness. All Parliament's talk about evil councillors was patently a silly fiction.[13]

It is a risky and an unwise thing to tear away the comforting sophistries tender-minded men use to veil the naked acts of force that revolution demands of them. If the fiction of the responsibility of bad ministers for Charles's perverse policy was to be thrust aside, what became of the legal justification of Parliamentary resistance? Always the Houses maintained that the war was not for Parliament against the King, but of

[10] *Mercurius Aulicus*, February 26–March 4, 1643.
[11] *Mercurius Aulicus*, June 4–11, 1643.
[12] *Mercurius Aulicus*, January 22–28, 1643.
[13] Edward Bowles, *op. cit.*, p. 11.

Parliament for the King against the men who beguiled him into error. To weaken that fiction was to weaken the last support of the wavering consciences of moderate men, already sorely tried to justify the deeds they had done. But men with untroubled consciences rarely understand or sympathize with the spiritual torment of their less whole-souled brethren. Thus without compunction some of the leading aldermen of the City in a petition to the Common Council laid the blame for the troubles of the kingdom directly on Charles, and even dared to contend that decisions of the Houses for the safety of the country were binding on the King, whether he assented to them or no.[14] This thinly veiled republicanism got a hearing in the Common Council, a body so powerful in its influence that jesting Royalists called it the third House of Parliament.

No more in the City than in the Commons did the fiery spirits restrict their attacks to the royal family. In London, too, a cry went up against the Lords, and some of the most violent citizens held "several secret meetings . . . in which they . . . discussed at length the means of having arrested five members of the Upper House more venturesome than the others in speaking in favor of peace." [15] So long as the violence of the *enragés* spent itself in outbursts against the King and Queen, so long, even, as it ended in petty harassing of and ill-concealed plots against the peace party in Parliament, though it might be potentially troublesome, it was not immediately and acutely menacing. When the *enragés* turned against the members of the middle group that Pym led, when they concentrated their attack on one of the key men of that group, they became a dangerous force, the more to be feared because Pym needed their support for his war measures.

Overt distrust of the Lord General of the parliamentary forces, the Earl of Essex, cropped out early in the Civil War. It began with doubts, not altogether unjustified, of his ability as a commander; and soon men who disliked his religious con-

[14] *Mercurius Aulicus*, April 2–8, 1643.
[15] *C. S. P. Venetian*, XXVI, 251.

victions and his political principles were using those doubts
to bring about his downfall. For anybody with a grievance
the Lord General made a fine target to shoot at. He was never
an inspiring or even a very successful military leader. Until
the march on Gloucester he showed no sign of tactical skill.
His generalship was as sober, dull, and stodgy as his personal
appearance. For ten months after Edgehill he engaged the
King in no major battle, and occasional success in skirmishes
never balanced the victories of the Royalists in similar minor
encounters. Men led to expect a quick decisive victory got
little satisfaction from hearing once in a while of the capture
of thirty of the King's infantry in some unheard-of corner of
Berkshire. They had hoped for greater things.

The newspaper press poured out hitherto unparalleled masses
of fiction about the condition of the army. Journalism was in
its lusty infancy, but here as elsewhere the child is father of
the man. Lacking present-day facilities for gathering news,
the writers of the Diurnals and Intelligences and Messengers
of the seventeenth century did not have to face the modern editorial problem of distorting information; they just made it up.
With no previous experience at discounting war news at
seventy-five per cent, the Londoner who read in the *Kingdom's Weekly Intelligencer* that Essex had thirty thousand
men in his army probably believed what he read.[16] And he
naturally wondered why with such a force Essex did not fight.
He could not know that when the *Intelligencer* published its
figures there were really about eight thousand men in the
Lord General's army, of whom almost one-half were too
sick to fight.[17]

Even those who might have known better, the members of
Parliament, found complaining of Essex's failures a more congenial and less trying occupation than analyzing the causes
of his unsuccess and applying remedies. The low and sordid
problem of military supply and finance did not fascinate the

[16] *Kingdomes Weekly Intelligencer*, June 13–June 20, 1643.
[17] *C. J.*, III, 189.

average Parliament man. He might admit that the Lord
General's army frequently had no shoes to march on, no food
to eat, no clothes to wear, and no guns to shoot; but he did not
therefore conclude that a naked, starving, unarmed force faced
slaughter if exposed to the onset of Rupert's fast-riding cavalry.
It was unfortunate, too, that pestilence scourged the ranks of
the army and that some of the soldiers, discovering that one
engaged in war with hazard of life and limb, tended to slip
away when battle seemed imminent. This was indeed too bad;
but admitting all of it from a well-warmed seat in the House
of Commons, the fact remained that Essex had won no battles,
and after all what was a lord general for but to win battles? [18]

Discontent with the Lord General first showed itself in the
City. The London men were very much aware of their importance to Parliament, as the cornucopia from which all fiscal
blessings flowed. Many of them did not like the way the army
they paid for was being run; and the Corporation did not
hesitate to try a bit of meddling, bruise whom it might. Distrustful of Essex's power and wanting to make themselves
"independent of the arbitrament of a single individual," [19]
the City men schemed to pull the control of the London militia
out from under the Lord General and get it into their own
hands. This, as the Venetian ambassador observed, was "a

---

[18] Sir Simond Dewes gives a fine demonstration of wisdom after the event.
On June 26, 1643, he enters in his diary a criticism of the Earl of Essex's failure
to proceed immediately from Reading to Oxford in April. Had the Lord General
acted at once "the King's army would have disbanded before they had come
up to them" (*D.*, 164, fols. 233–233*v*). By June 26 Dewes had managed to
forget a number of unpleasant facts. After taking Reading, Essex had warned
the House he could not move until his army was paid (*C. W.*, I, 131). From
the time he asked for the money to the time he got it three weeks elapsed
(*ibid.*, I, 134), and in that time ammunition had come through to the King
and disease had broken out in the parliamentary army, a concurrence of events
that crippled Essex until the Houses gave him effective support for the relief of
Gloucester. The whole story of the Lord General's army in those dark days
has been told by Professor Godfrey Davies in "The Parliamentary Army under
the Earl of Essex, 1642–1645," *English Historical Review* (1934), XLIX, 32–54.
Professor Davies absolves Essex of any major fault in the failure of his army
in the spring and summer campaign of 1643.

[19] *C. S. P. Venetian*, XXVI, 203.

shrewd blow at General Essex" and one that he resented.[20]
A touch of lordly resentment did not feaze the Londoners or
put a stop to their interfering. They soon began to poke into
abuses of the muster rolls,[21] and in February, by a petition
to Parliament demanding the reform of the army, they im-
pugned Essex's management of the war.[22]

The cry without the walls found echoes in the House of
Commons, as some of the fiery spirits began to cry down the
Lord General. Martin attacked him openly, contrasting the
military successes in the north and west with the Earl's immobility near London in December. "It is summer in Devonshire, summer in Yorkshire and only winter at Windsor,"
where the General was in quarters. Hoyle seconded Martin,
hinting that Essex's slowness and carelessness would ruin the
kingdom.[23] Suspicions of the Earl's integrity, groundless as
they were, "had already taken birth," and they proliferated
when he balked at attacking Reading, which the Commons
wanted him to besiege, after six lords, favorable to peace, had
conferred with him in camp.[24] Consequently the violent men
in the House took over the City's scheme, and tried to set
up a volunteer army under a commander whose spirit, martial
and political, would be akin to their own. The hour had not
struck for such a move, however, and for the time being nothing
came of the project.[25]

These early forays against the Lord General produced no
immediate results. In the months that followed the opening
of the treaty at Oxford, the opposition to Essex from the firebrands died down. Indeed when we find Blakiston and John

[20] C. S. P. Venetian, XXVI, 206–207.
[21] C. J., II, 884.
[22] C. J., II, 976.
[23] D., 164, fol. 243.
[24] C. S. P. Venetian, XXVI, 216–217, 219.
[25] A committee heavily weighted with violent Commoners was appointed to
consider the formation of a volunteer army. Of its eighteen members three
were dead in 1648, and all the rest were active in the government after Charles's
execution. Twelve of them immediately took their seats in the Commonwealth
Rump, ten were appointed to the High Court of Justice, and three were regicides (C. J., II, 943).

Gurdon, wild-eyed radicals, rising in the House to defend the
Earl against the criticism of the peace party,[26] we are almost
inclined to believe that the fiery spirits had undergone a change
of heart. What really had changed was not the hearts of the
fiery ones, but circumstances, which notoriously alter cases.
Negotiations with the King had started. The great stumbling
block to peace was the question of disbanding the armies and
disposing of ships, forts, and garrisons. Should Essex wish,
he might carry enough men with him to make a majority for
whatever settlement he thought best. If he conceded too much
to the King, the violent men and their aims and measures
faced irretrievable ruin. They knew they had given the Lord
General little reason to love them; but now at whatever cost
he must be kept on their side. Inescapable necessity drove the
violent men to speak gently and tread lightly in matters of
interest to Essex. When the necessity vanished, so did the
gentleness; the termination of the Oxford treaty was a signal
for a new drive against the Earl.

The newspapers, hitherto friendly to or neutral toward the
Lord General,[27] reflected the change. Acidulous criticism of
his generalship and his dealing with his troops began to be
heard. The love of his soldiers for loot, it was said, transcended
their love of the cause. When they should have been fighting
they were pillaging. "Such indiscreet covetousness hath here-
tofore lost many glorious victories." [28] Failure to follow up
an advantage was a weakness that the Lord General shared
with his men. He captured Reading, but, the Londoners
grumbled, "the glory of the action . . . seems to be eclipsed
by our staying there so long without advancing, contrary to
our declarations . . . and the expectations of the Parliament
and City." Men might make excuses for the delay, but, wrote
one pamphleteer bluntly, those excuses are "contrary to my
own judgment." [29] Louder and louder the complaints rose, until

[26] *D.*, 164, fols. 349v–350.
[27] See Appendix A for a discussion of London newsbooks.
[28] *Certaine Informations*, April 24–May 1, 1643.
[29] *Kingdomes Weekly Intelligencer*, May 2–9, 1643.

they reached a crescendo: the Lord General's soldiers lie wholly idle, they have put the kingdom to an immense charge and done little or nothing for it, they are "fay neants." [30] And, of course, by implication the Lord General is the worst *fainéant* of all.

Throughout the spring of 1643 news of disaster to the armies of Parliament and treachery to the cause of Parliament was coming in from all corners of the kingdom. Between terror of visible enemies without the gates and dread of secret enemies within, panic prevailed in London. With each new piece of bad news resentment at Essex's inactivity increased. The Earl, bogged down at Thame without food or pay or recruits, his army decimated by disease and desertion, was smoldering with rage at the injustice of the obloquy and insult heaped on him. In the west, doing great things with small means, Sir William Waller appeared as a new hero to receive the praise that Essex forfeited, and perhaps to take the place he might lose. Events were heading toward catastrophe. Yet the explosion was a long time delayed, and, when it came, it only endangered but did not destroy the position of the Lord General. Quietly and unobtrusively, certain influences were working in his favor.

In some men no whit more inclined to submit to a recreant's peace than the most fiery of fiery spirits the Lord General inspired both trust and devotion. Walter Strickland was Parliament's resident in the Netherlands. Time and the shifting force of factional politics separated him from moderate men of Essex's stamp; and within ten years, as ambassador of the Commonwealth of England to the United Provinces, he was keeping a suspicious eye on many of the Earl's friends in exile there. In December 1642, however, in the midst of the earliest attack on Essex, Strickland wrote Pym, begging leave to return from Holland "to add one more sword to those that wait on the Lord General." [31] Edward Bowles, proponent

---

[30] *Certaine Informations*, May 22–29, 1643.
[31] Bouverie MSS, *H. M. C. Report X*, app. vi, p. 94.

of the oath of association, opponent of the useful make-believe
that absolved the King from responsibility for his own acts, in
every respect a warlike clergyman, vigorously upheld the army,
which, he said, in all its imperfections only reflected the imperfections of Parliament itself. It was among themselves, he
went on, in their own lack of resolution, in their own self-
seeking, that the members would find the source of their military failures, not in the army, especially not in the conduct of
"the truly noble and valiant Earl of Essex." [32]

The confidence he inspired in men like Bowles and Strickland made Essex indispensable to Pym. His great rank, his
dogged integrity, and the unique way in which he embodied
everything that stood for respectability and conservatism in a
cause some of whose supporters were not very respectable, and
many of whose supporters were not at all conservative, were
essential assets of the middle group. To alienate him was to
encourage a division in Parliament in the midst of the middle
group, which might become wider than that which separated
many of the members from the King. Men would then tend
to recede from the center toward the extremes, with the possible result that not one but both groups in Parliament might
find a private settlement with Charles I a less disagreeable
course than continued coöperation with one another. And,
indeed, the treacherous negotiations with the Royalists and
the underhand dealings of the factions in the four years following Pym's death were the effect of the schism in Parliament
when it finally did come.

Pym for the time being sought to prevent or at worst to
postpone such a disaster, getting supplies for the Lord General,
smoothing his ruffled temper, and preventing irresponsible or
hostile members of the House from ruffling it further. In
matters of little moment, as in large affairs, the great commoner placed himself at the disposal of the commander of
Parliament's army. So when the Roundheads in their peren-
nial quest for cavalry mounts appropriated the Countess Rivers'

[32] Edward Bowles, *op. cit.*, pp. 24, 27.

coach horses and Essex chivalrously insisted that this wrong
to her be righted, Pym introduced into the House of Commons the order for returning the horses.[33]   In more essential
matters Pym nursed the Lord General along as one would a
temperamental prima donna.   Fearing that Essex might hearken
to the guileful urgings of the peace party [34] and deviate from
the middle-group line on the question of cessation, in February
Pym made a special trip to the army to confirm the Earl in
the true faith.[35]   After Essex proved his fidelity to the middle
group by repudiating the peace policy of the upper house,
Pym, besides looking out for the permanent necessities of the
army, took much care for the immediate needs of the Lord
General.   He secured marching orders for the army from the
Commons.[36]   He defended Essex from opponents who said
he was levying exorbitant taxes in the counties.[37]   He squeezed
army loans out of City financiers increasingly disinclined to
let their zeal inflict further punishment on their pocketbooks
in behalf of a commander they distrusted.[38]   In the campaign
of 1643, with his nephew Nicholls [39] acting as liaison officer
between the army and the Houses,[40] Pym had access to "spot
news" in army matters.   The rising tide of criticism against
the Lord General disturbed him; but Pym was not a man
quickly to run with the tide against his better judgment.   Instead he set himself to thwart the "subtle practices . . . set
afoot . . . to disaffect the people . . . to my Lord General" of
whose "dangerous consequence" he was acutely aware.   He
begged his influential friends to stamp out the ugly and disruptive whispering campaign against the Earl.[41]

[33] *Mercurius Aulicus*, May 21–28, 1643.   [36] *D*., 164, fol. 318.
[34] *C. S. P. Venetian*, XXVI, 249.   [37] *D*., 164, fol. 350.
[35] *C. J.*, II, 975; *C. S. P. Venetian*, XXVI, 249.   [38] *D*., 164, fol. 324.
      [39] Really a half-nephew, Nicholls was the son of Pym's half-sister, Philippa
Rous.
      [40] *D*., 164, fol. 376*v*.
      [41] John Pym to Sir Thomas Barrington: "I do rather write . . . to you,
who I know to have an honest heart, because I hear some subtle practices are
set afoot in your country to disaffect the people to the Parliament and to my
Lord General, both which of what dangerous consequence they are is not unknown to you" (Lowndes MSS, *H. M. C. Report VII*, app. i, p. 551.

Regardless of Pym's disapproval of their activities and despite his efforts to thwart them, the enemies of Essex turned the screws tighter and tighter. And just at the moment he needed every available aid to hold the middle group together against the powerful pull to the left, Pym suffered a sudden, tragic, and irreparable loss. The bullet that lodged in Hampden's shoulder at Chalgrove Field carried off something more vital than a "most discreet good man." [42] Discreet good men were "good-cheap" in London during the Civil War. They lived and died, and few marked the day or the hour. When Hampden died the day was marked by all who loved or hated him; and that meant almost everyone actively concerned in the Civil War.

He was one of the three key men in the middle group. For months he had helped the second key man, Pym, control the third key man, Essex, concerting schemes with the former,[43] guiding the latter in the management of the army [44] and of his tongue. The Lord General's tongue was perhaps more untractable than his army, which is saying a great deal. With Hampden at headquarters Essex had little chance to commit blunders or indiscretions commensurate with his real talent for them. But now Hampden was dead, and only God knew what Essex would do next, although one did not need divine prescience to guess that it would be something embarrassing to his friend Pym. In Hampden's death Pym lost something even more valuable than immediate control over a splenetic commander-in-chief; he lost the only remaining link between Essex and the fiery spirits. As the Lord General stood near the point where the middle group merged insensibly into the

---

[42] "i am very sory for mr. hamdon; i do not know him . . . but i have harde he is a most discrite good man"; Lady Sussex to Sir Ralph Verney (F. P. and M. M. Verney, *Memoirs of the Verney Family*, II, 159).

[43] *D.*, 164, fols. 277–277v, 296v, 301v, 303v.

[44] Hampden was "wiser than any of the others . . . acting as colonel . . . with the direction of the whole army of Essex" (*C. S. P. Venetian*, XXVI, 294–295). This was probably the substantial fact behind the rumor spread at Oxford that Hampden was to take over the command of the army (*Mercurius Aulicus*, July 2–9, 1643).

peace party, so Hampden was close to the shadowy ground between the middle group and the war party. He was the living, talking, worshipping, fighting image of militant Puritanism, the ideal radical country gentleman. The best of the fiery spirits loved him; even the worst pretended to admire him. Yet, militant as he was, to the day of his death Hampden did not waver in his fidelity to the Earl of Essex. In the last letter he wrote before he died he employed his deep religious spirit in the service of his commander, pleading that the county of Essex, "the place of most life of religion in the land," come forward to help the Lord General and his army.[45]

Hampden wrote this last letter to a man who was also godly according to his lights; but if that man responded to his friend's plea, it was the last time that he turned his hand for the Lord General; for Oliver Cromwell was one of those who felt that he owed allegiance to Essex only through Hampden. When Hampden died, the bond of homage was undone, and the fiery spirits were not slow to take advantage of their new-won liberty. A brief and cruelly candid item in a London newsbook revealed the way to military ruin open by one man's death: "The loss of Colonel Hampden . . . makes some conceive little content to be at the army now that he is gone." [46] In the City as well as in the army and especially in the House of Commons men felt old inhibitions give place to a new freedom. While Hampden lived and faithfully served his commander, it was almost impossible to throw mud at the Lord General without spattering the colonel, and many hesitated to risk besmirching the hero whom God and his countrymen honored. Now death had taken a hand, the bond was loosened; the check was gone; mud was king.

[45] *C. W.*, I, 153, n. 2.
[46] *Kingdomes Weekly Intelligencer*, June 27–July 4, 1643.

CHAPTER VI

THE DARKEST HOURS, JULY–AUGUST, 1643

THE enemies of the Lord General, who were waiting for him to put himself at their mercy, did not have their patience seriously strained. Essex did not stay for trouble to come to him; but with the terrifying myopia of persons overconscious of their own rectitude he stalked into it head on. He was tired of waiting for supplies that came too late or never came at all; tired of worrying about new levies that gobbled up what little supply there was and then deserted, if pestilence did not strike them down first; tired of trying to protect a slow-moving bogged-down army of foot from the lightning forays of Rupert's fast-riding horsemen. His thin skin smarted under the ceaseless castigation, ridicule, and libel of brilliant second-guessers and fiery pothouse strategists in London. Fighting Royalists, disease, desertion, malnutrition, and distrust all at once was a thankless, hopeless job. His slow mind had not yet grasped the danger that lay in the designs of the more violent Roundheads. Once he did understand the danger, he stuck to his job of commander with such conviction and dogged stubbornness that it took something like *force majeur* to pry him loose. In July 1643, however, he was only an unsuccessful general, weary of warlike doing, groping for a way out of the bloody morass he was stuck in.

In his gropings he hit on a wondrous scheme which a few weeks before would have died a-borning, Hampden taking care to put it painlessly out of the way. Now Essex revealed it in its naked *naïveté* in a letter to the Houses. He started out with the simple admission that his infantry could not protect the countryside from the pillage of the Royalist cavalry. He went on to insist that the time had come to send peace proposals to the King again. If that failed, let Charles draw away from his forces so that "it might be tried by a battle" between the Royalist and parliamentary armies, "in which case," Essex concluded, "he would do his duty." [1] Of such earth-shaking, well-intentioned ineptitude, rolling three big blunders all together, only the Lord General was capable. Every part of the letter could be misconstrued. The Earl's admission of the superiority of the King's army might be twisted into a confession of his own incompetence, his suggestion of a treaty into an attempt to overawe the Houses, and his proposal of a seventeenth-century mass version of a medieval trial by battle "in which case he would do his duty" into anything from treachery to sheer madness.[2]

As the news of Essex's letter spread through London all the voices that had been sporadically raised against him joined in one magnificent chorus of vituperation. The Lord Mayor's chaplain preached a sermon against the Earl, and the Reverend Thomas Hill with elaborate indirection castigated the "carnal self-love" which in military undertakings made "too many Judas-like sell Christ for some few pieces of silver." [3] The Puritan clergy no longer had to rely on individual action. Assembled at Westminster to reform the English Church was the pick of the Puritan ministry of England. The men of the Westminster Assembly on ordinary occasions meddled only with ecclesiastical things and kept clear of secular politics; but in the crisis that Essex had precipitated they saw, or thought they saw, their duty; and they did it. They petitioned the Houses for a public fast and a purge of the army.[4] The

---

[1] *D.*, 165, fol. 122.

[2] Oddly enough, the romantic dream of a trial by battle probably originated not with Essex but with Sir Philip Stapleton. At least, Stapleton had already suggested something of the sort in November 1642. "Sir Philip Stapleton . . . would have us desire the King to withdraw himself from his army and they that persuade him to such courses to meet us at Hampstead Heath and we will fight with them" (*Y.*, 18777, fol. 65).

[3] *The Earle of Essex his Letter to Mister Speaker* (1643); Thomas Hill, *The Militant Church Triumphant over the Dragon* (1643), p. 28.

[4] John Lightfoot, "The Journal . . . of the Assembly of Divines," *The Whole Works of the Rev. John Lightfoot*, ed. Rev. J. R. Pitman, 14 vols. (1842), XIII, 6–7.

Lord General's letter aroused the wrath of the laity of the
City no less than that of the clergy.[5] Early and hostile action
on it was expected from the London militia committee. The
newspapers sneered at Essex's plaints of the immobility of
his army; let him get a flying army in place of it. If he means
to do nothing, let him stop wasting the City's good money.
"There is come to him lately a good round sum and would go
a great way were there fewer officers and more common men." [6]
The Lord General was "abused in pictures, censured in pulpits, dishonored in the table talk of the common people." On
those sensitive but sadly perishable registers of the sentiments
of the masses, the chalkings on walls, popular distrust of the
Earl of Essex made itself felt.[7] He was caricatured, sitting in
an easy chair, a glass of wine in one hand, a pipe in the other,
an English Nero bibbing while London burned, or at least
might burn any minute. The firebrands in the House were
no less disgruntled than the violent men in the City at the
Lord General's confession of weakness and plea for peace. At
the reading of the letter, "Mr. Strode, Sir Peter Wentworth
and some other violent spirits were observed to pluck their
hats over their eyes." [8] Next day the most brilliant radical
of them all, young Sir Henry Vane, made a virulent speech
scoffing at the Earl's presumption in proposing a treaty, and
remarking that apparently he would do his duty only if the
Houses assented to his proposals.[9] It was a most unkind cut.

Rumors of the Lord General's contemplated treachery were
rife in the City. The Venetian secretary heard that Essex
had ready a proclamation declaring that an evil faction was
misleading Parliament and ruining the people. But, says the
judicious secretary, "there is nothing to show that he has made
any arrangement with the King." [10] Few men in London were

[5] *Mercurius Aulicus*, July 9–16, 1643.
[6] *Parliament Scout*, July 6–13, 1643.
[7] *Mercurius Aulicus*, August 6–13, 1643; *C. W.*, I, 180.
[8] *D.*, 164, fol. 228.
[9] *D.*, 165, fol. 123v.
[10] *C. S. P. Venetian*, xxvii, 2.

willing to wait around to find out whether Essex intended to
betray the cause or not. Their instinct, like that of all panic-
stricken or rash people, was to act first and ask questions
afterwards; their instant impulse was to attack the danger at
its source. They wanted to get rid of the Lord General, to
replace him by someone in whose military ability and god-
liness they had more faith.[11] A few months earlier such a
scheme, however desirable in the abstract, would have been
practically impossible for lack of a suitable substitute for
Essex. Lately, in the midst of blackest disaster to the parliamentary cause, with dark news coming from all quarters, a
gleam of new hope had appeared in the west.

It was Sir William Waller's peculiar good fortune that since
the outbreak of the war he had been too busy fighting to make
many enemies. His professional skill in generalship stood out
sharply from the average bumbling incompetence of the parliamentary commanders. With superior numbers they crumpled
under Royalist attacks; with a mere handful of men he achieved
much. In him rigorous personal piety went hand in hand with
high soldier-like qualities, and won equal praise from all parties.
Even the peace-loving Dewes had nothing but praise for Waller, "a man of extraordinary valor and integrity." [12] For several weeks the groups who were crying Essex down were equally
assiduous in crying Waller up, urging "all that desire a speedy
end of their troubles to give him all the aid they can both of
money and addition of power." Because of his masterful conduct of the campaign in the west "they at Oxford are terrible
afraid of Sir William Waller." [13] While Essex in his letters
destroyed what little faith the London zealots still had in
him, Sir William won new glory in his defense at Lansdowne
against three Royalist armies under Hopton, Hertford, and

[11] *Whitelock*, p. 67; *C. S. P. Venetian*, XXVI, 300; William Waller, "Recollections," *The Poetry of Anna Matilda* (1788), p. 131n.
[12] *D.*, 164, fol. 368; see also Anthony Nicholls to Judith Barrington (*B.*,
2646, fol. 297); Countess of Sussex to Sir Ralph Verney, July 19, 1643 (Verney
MSS at Claydon, Bucks.).
[13] *Parliament Scout*, June 23–June 30, 1643.

Prince Maurice. In a single issue the weekly news sheets recorded the fainthearted despair of the Lord General and the splendid achievement of the valiant knight. The City declared the glory of Waller, and the western parts showed his handiwork. So the war party, turning to their new champion, "William the Conqueror," plotted to put him in Essex's place as commander-in-chief. Waller himself knew of the scheme,[14] and the rumor of it spread in Parliament, in the City, to Oxford, everywhere.[15]

Sir William was not the first nor the last to discover the fickleness of the fortunes of war; but few men have suffered a sadder shift from good luck to bad at a more inopportune moment. Less than a fortnight after his heroic stand at Lansdowne, before Parliament had recovered from the shock of the Lord General's letter, Sir William was decisively defeated at Roundway Down by Hopton, and fled from the battle with the remnant of his cavalry, leaving his foot soldiers on the field to be cut down or captured. To this overthrow in the west Waller later attributed his failure to become commander-in-chief. "The zealous . . . moved that the command of their army might be bestowed on me; but the news of this defeat arrived while they were deliberating on my advancement, and it was to me a double defeat." [16] No doubt his flight did diminish his prestige; [17] but even before the news of that disaster reached London, his sponsors had run into insuperable obstacles to their original plan. The majority in Parliament did not take easily to the idea of a sudden shift in commanders while the enemy was literally almost at the gate, and the officers of the army displayed an unexpected loyalty to the Earl of Essex and a strong opposition against attempts to discard or even malign him.[18]

[14] Waller, *op. cit.*, pp. 131, 138.
[15] After Essex's letter was read "some intimated the promoting of Waller to his place" (*Whitelock*, p. 70). See also *C. S. P. Venetian*, xxvi, 300; *Mercurius Aulicus*, July 9–July 16, 1643.
[16] Waller, *op. cit.*, p. 131.
[17] *Whitelock*, p. 70.
[18] *C. S. P. Venetian*, xxvi, 300. Colonel Stapleton and Goodwyn forced

The determined and unforeseen resistance to their original scheme forced the opponents of the Lord General to take up a new position, or, rather, fall back on an old one long since abandoned. In the previous winter a faction already dissatisfied with Essex's leadership tried to set up an army independent of him.[19] Early in July, even before Essex had written his foolish letter, discontented groups began to experiment with a new version of this scheme. They wanted to get authority from the Houses and the Earl to raise an army of ten thousand volunteers "who are godly . . . and that the commander-in-chief may be some godly nobleman . . . and all other commanders and officers may be godly." [20] The Lord General's letter confirmed his antagonists in their belief that they needed a strong independent military force to counterbalance his power. There were stirrings ominous of impending action at Guildhall and at the headquarters of the London Militia Committee at Grocers' Hall,[21] and rumors spread that the City would demand the raising of an army of twelve thousand, "to be maintained at their expense during the war, and commanded by a general independent of the Earl" of Essex.[22]

Then in a short time these diffuse movements came into focus, or rather to two foci. On July 18 the lord mayor, aldermen, and Common Council of the City petitioned for an ordinance putting "all the forces raised and to be raised" in the City and its environs "under the sole command of the Committee for the militia of the City under the direction of both

---

young Vane to apologize twice over for his slurs on Essex in the House (*D.*, 165, fols. 123*v*–124).

[19] See, above, pp. 109–110.

[20] *Instructions and Propositions Drawn and Agreed on by Divers Well-Affected Persons* (1643), pp. 1–2. This pamphlet is dated July 8 by Thomason (*Catalogue of the Pamphlets . . . Collected by George Thomason*, ed. G. K. Fortescue, 2 vols. [1908], I, 272–273). It is possible that Thomason's dating is inaccurate, and that the pamphlet was not published until after July 10, but there is no evidence in the pamphlet to justify this assumption.

[21] *Mecurius Aulicus*, July 9–July 16, 1643; Cowper MSS, II, *H. M. C. Report XII*, app. ii, p. 335.

[22] Salvetti Correspondence, x, British Museum, Additional MSS, 27962K, fol. 129*v*.

Houses of Parliament." [23] This apparently innocuous request concealed an implied threat: that unless the Houses removed the Earl of Essex from all part in control of the London forces they could not hope for support from the City in this hour of adversity. On the twentieth, "divers inhabitants" of the City brought in a second petition, proposing a general rising, a *levée en masse* of the citizens, in defense of the cause. A committee of the House of Commons was to supervise the project, with power to raise money, arms, and horse and to appoint the officers of the new army; [24] but the House was allowed no voice in choosing the members to exercise these high and arbitrary powers. In flagrant violation of the privileges of the Commons the petitioners in advance had hand-picked the Committee of the House that they would accept, and they had chosen some rather wild specimens, including among the thirteen committee members ten future Commonwealthmen, seven future nominees to the High Court of Justice that tried the King, and two future regicides.[25] The Commons were in no condition to stand on their privilege; in the evil days the cause had fallen on they had to take help where they could get it, and be not overnice about the amenities. So they mildly reproved the petitioners for their breach of privilege, as a timid father would reprove a rambunctious son twice as big and thrice as strong as himself, and then complied with the ultimatum and appointed the desired committee.

In three days the House had been forced to take two decisive steps toward reducing Essex to a mere paper commander. The citizens' petition called for an army of ten thousand men, while the Lord General's force, cut off from all hope of recruiting if the projects set out in two petitions were carried through, numbered eighty-five hundred men, of whom three

[23] House of Lords MSS, *H. M. C. Report V*, app. i, p. 96.
[24] *Y.*, 18778, fols. 6–6v; *C. J.*, III, 175–176.
[25] The Committee: John Blakiston, Thomas Hoyle, Sir William Masham, William Strode, Henry Heyman, Denis Bond, John Gurdon, Herbert Morley, Alexander Rigby, William Ashurst, Edward Baynton, Henry Martin, Isaac Pennington (*C. J.*, III, 176).

thousand were disabled by sickness. Over neither of the new armies, both larger than his, would the Lord General have any control. These arrangements, as the Florentine resident remarked, struck deeply at the reputation of the Earl.[26] The House of Commons, still irked at the letter of July 9, added to his humiliation. In reply to his request for military directions, they curtly told him to do as he pleased.[27]

Yet more wormwood was in store for the unhappy man. The projectors for the two new armies had not at first specified who was to command the fresh levies; but soon after they had gained authorization for their schemes both groups independently nominated the same commander, Sir William Waller, who had just received a thorough and not too creditable drubbing in the west, and now rushed toward London to blame Essex for his downfall,[28] a task already efficiently taken in hand there by Lady Waller acting as her husband's proxy.[29] So the Lord General's most potent rival, a "man who concurred . . . in all those councils that were most violent," [30] had in prospect a force twice the size of Essex's own and independent of his control. The fiery spirits could hardly have asked for more. They had sped from triumph to triumph over their antagonist, the Earl. So far, however, their successes were of the paper variety — accepted petitions and orders of the Houses. It remained to translate them into the essential reality of glistening pikes, men on horseback, marching men.

From the twenty-seventh to the twenty-ninth of July there were great festivities in London. Salutes were fired and there was much speechmaking, for the City had turned out to greet its hero, Sir William Waller, returning from his defeat in the west, his head unbowed and, somewhat to his discredit, not

---

[26] Salvetti Correspondence, x, British Museum, Additional MSS, 27962K, fol. 132*v*.

[27] *D.*, 165, fol. 128*v*.

[28] Henry Percy to Prince Rupert, "Waller is gone as fast as he can to London to complain of my Lord of Essex for betraying him" (*Pythouse Papers*, ed. W. A. Day [1879], p. 54).

[29] *C. S. P. Venetian*, XXVI, 304–305.

[30] *Clar. H. R.*, bk. VII, par. 100.

even bloody.[31] On the day of his triumphant entry into the City the Commons ratified his appointment as general of the new volunteer army; [32] and at a meeting at the Merchant Taylors' Hall, where the committee for the general rising sat, he gratefully accepted his nomination. On the twenty-ninth the selection of Sir William by the City militia committee to command their forces again loosened the tongues of the godly, producing a veritable effluxion of oratory. The radicals undeniably talked a fine victory. At a Common Hall, Henry Martin made a grandiose speech in the old Roman style, full of the very best bombast about going forth all to meet the enemy, not as slaves with ropes about their necks, but as "men with swords in their hands." [33]

A fate with a twisted sense of humor must have chosen Henry Martin to be the expounder of the scheme of the godly men and the panegyrist of their Christian hero, Sir William Waller. Colonel Henry Martin himself was no hero, and for that matter no Christian either, godly or otherwise. He was distinguished in the Long Parliament, an assembly aggressively pure in principle, by his disregard of marriage, the respectable way of attaining what he most ardently sought. Oliver Cromwell put the case more succinctly when he called Colonel Henry a whoremaster. Martin's right to the colonelcy was rather more equivocal than his claim to the other title. True, he had spent several months early in 1643 kidnapping horses with the ostensible purpose of raising a troop of cavalry. But the troop never materialized; and when he was commanded to join the Lord General for the summer campaign, Martin refused to go. All this lends a certain piquancy to his enthusiasm for dying with his sword in his hand. Besides his indifference to marital propriety two other characteristics set Martin apart from the godly folk he led. His religious principles were unorthodox in the extreme (he was of "the natural religion" and believed in

[31] See accounts in *Mercurius Civicus*, July 20–28; *A Declaration of the Proceedings . . . at Merchant Taylors Hall* (1643), pp. 3–5.
[32] *C. J.*, III, 183.
[33] *Three Speeches Delivered at a Common Hall* (1643), p. 18.

toleration even for Catholics) and he possessed a sense of humor. And yet the apotheosis of Sir William Waller by a notorious freethinker and loose-liver was in a way an appropriate climax to a celebration that behind its brave front concealed a scheme already crumbling from its inherent weaknesses and from the incompetence and jealousies of those engaged in carrying it out.[34]

The fiery spirits soon showed themselves totally incapable of making the important transition from loud talk and fine phrases to effective action. Martin's first report to the House from the committee on the general rising was so inadequate and muddled that the Commons refused even to discuss it.[35] The members' lack of enthusiasm for the report was as nothing compared with the citizens' lack of enthusiasm for the project itself. The proponents of the scheme in a moment of indiscreet enthusiasm had predicted a stampede of twenty-two thousand men to Waller's standard. The Florentine resident remarked that "people did not rush on the wing with that alacrity . . . that was expected." This is a little gem of understatement.[36] The projectors of the general rising were plagued by the generality's manifest disinclination to rise. Upon Waller's "endeavoring to raise the said army, there were not yet in near upon a week's space about 300 that he could get to list themselves." So runs the epitaph that Dewes prepared for the scheme.[37]

[34] The stories of Martin's unconventional fondness for pretty girls find a place in several of the better-known books of the seventeenth century: Anthony à Wood, *Athenae Oxoniensis*, ed. P. Bliss, 4 vols. (1813–20), III, 1237; John Aubrey, *Letters Written by Eminent Persons*, 2 vols. (1813), II, 434–437. There are less famous references to his loose morals in Dewes (*D.*, 164, fol. 326) and in the newsletters of the Duke of Sutherland MSS (*H. M. C. Report V*, app. i, p. 192). In 1647 he voted with Selden to extend toleration even to Catholics (*C. W.*, III, 212). For his horse-snatching activities and his refusal to join Essex's army see *Mercurius Aulicus, passim, D.*, 164, fols. 233*v* and 329, and *C. S. P. Venetian*, XXVI, 286–287. There is an excellent sketch of his life by Firth in the *D. N. B.*, under Marten, Henry or Harry (1602–1680).

[35] *W.*, fol. 65.

[36] Salvetti Correspondence x, British Museum, Additional MSS, 27962K, fol. 140.

[37] *D.*, 165, fols. 135–135*v*.

As things went from bad to worse the committee for the general rising got into a squabble with the London militia committee. On the face of it the two groups seem to be natural allies. They were both hostile to the Earl of Essex, both raising troops for armies that would overshadow his. They had both chosen Waller to command their new armies. But the committee for the general rising had a real grievance against the London people. When men came to enlist with Martin's committee at the Merchant Taylors' Hall, agents from Grocers' Hall seduced them to join up under the banner of the militia committee instead.[38] This was not hard to do. The committee for a general rising stood or fell on the voluntary principle — voluntary enlistment, voluntary contributions. When the scheme verged on failure there was some talk that "if contrary to their expectations" the zeal for contributing and enlisting "should prove defective," the committee "did not doubt but in such case to be supplied by a coercive power from the House." [39] This was mere whistling in the dark. The House of Commons gave no sign that it intended to vest any coercive power in the committee. Besides, such power would have to come as a grant from both Houses, and the Lords would make short work of a bill to give carte blanche to a gang of notorious peer-baiters. The upshot was that the militia committee, relying for support on the City money bags, could offer more attractive terms to volunteers than Martin's committee, with no visible means of support.

Under the volunteer-stealing lay a more deep-seated difference; although Waller had command of both forces, the militia committee and Martin's radicals did not see eye to eye on policy. Martin wanted Waller to take the field and do great deeds while Essex rotted near London. With three Royalist armies converging on the metropolis, the City fathers insisted that Waller should protect London and let Essex go against the King. All this friction ended in a flare-up in the House of

[38] *Y.*, 18778, fol. 8.
[39] *Proceedings . . . at Merchant Taylors Hall*, p. 6.

Commons, Martin demanding that Waller be free to march
where he pleased with all the soldiers under his command,
Glynn, the recorder of London, insisting that Waller should
lead only the forces of the militia committee, which meant
that he should march nowhere at all.[40] Sir William, caught
between the contending groups, and noticing the disparity between the magnificent promises and meager performance of his
sponsors,[41] began to wrangle with them. As the net result of
all the sound and fury of the fiery spirits Parliament had to
show at the beginning of August only confusion and anarchy,
disgruntled generals bickering with one another, with the
Houses and with the City, and not a single considerable army
ready to take the field against the King. In the midst of this
hurly-burly news came to London that Colonel Fiennes had
surrendered Parliament's great western garrison at Bristol to
Prince Rupert.

The fall of Bristol was only the latest of the series of disas-
ters that had dogged the cause since Essex took Reading. The
west — the populous counties of Devon, Dorset, Gloucester,
Somerset, and Wiltshire, with large parts of Hampshire and
Berkshire — had fallen into Royalist hands. In the north
Parliament lost the West Riding of Yorkshire and Derbyshire;
and with the advent of the Earl of Newcastle's white coats
Lincoln, too, was engulfed by the rising Royalist tide. To set
against these losses Parliament had to show only the capture
of the barren north of Lancashire and some mean acres in
Staffordshire. Save for the solid block of counties south and
east of London and a narrow, insecurely held strip running
northwest into Lancashire, the Roundheads were reduced to
a few garrisons. In the north the Royalists had laid siege to
Hull, in the Severn estuary to Gloucester; Plymouth on the
Channel was still safe, but Exeter was doomed to fall to Prince
Maurice as Bristol had to his brother Rupert. While Parliament lost control of county after county its armies were being

wiped out one by one in the field. In the west Hopton over-
whelmed the superior force of the Earl of Stamford at Stratton. In the north the Earl of Newcastle rolled over the army
of the Fairfaxes at Adwalton Moor. With the bedraggled remnant of their army the Fairfaxes now stood siege at Hull.
After a promising start Waller, out to regain the west, had lost
his whole army at Roundway Down. Two forces remained
undefeated. Cromwell had marched his horse into Lincolnshire and, realizing the futility of trying to withstand Newcastle there, had marched them out again. Essex squatted
immobile in the upper valley of the Thames nursing grievances
and sick soldiers.

Soon the rats began to desert an apparently sinking ship.
In March, before the Roundhead cause began to decline, Sir
Hugh Cholmley, moved more by conscience than by coward-
ice, delivered Scarborough to the Royalists. Chudleigh, disgusted with his poltroon soldiers and his poltroon superior
officer, Stamford, at Stratton, joined up with the Royalist
Hopton. The Hothams did their best to sell out Hull to the
King, and paid with their lives the price of treachery that fails.
In the very heart of the Roundhead domain the men of Kent
took arms against the Houses, and in London, Edmund Waller
reared his plot on the known disaffection of many of the inhabitants of the Puritan metropolis.

Unrelieved mishap rubbed raw the nerves of Parliamentary
commanders, and, lacking victories to boast of, they betook
themselves to the congenial work of blame-tossing and self-
justification. The Fairfaxes accused the Hothams and Colonel
Boynton of failing to support them in the north.[42] Wray, Ais-
cough, and Cromwell fell foul of Lord Grey of Groby for
trying to protect the ancestral estates at Leicester instead of
campaigning,[43] while Essex lumped Cromwell with Grey and
Sir John Gell as the parties responsible for letting the Queen's
convoy get through to Oxford.[44] The disease spread to Par-

---

[42] D., 164, fol. 377v.   [43] D., 164, fol. 384v.
[44] Rossetti Correspondence, Public Record Office Transcripts, 9:23, fol. 250.

liament, where interested parties edged Sir John Corbett out
of his command in Shropshire,[45] and Martin and Morley refused to go to the Lord General's army, where they held commissions.[46] All these skirmishes were insignificant prelim-
inaries to the battle royal between Essex and Waller, each
seeking to thrust the blame for Sir William's defeat on the
other.[47]

Discord, desertion, defeat, disaster were the daily fare of
Londoners during the summer of 1643, and such a diet produced its inevitable consequence — gloom, fear, and despair.
As catastrophe followed catastrophe negative gloom became
something like positive panic. It was not only chronic nay-
sayers like Dewes that fell prey to dark forebodings. He
rather fancied himself as the voice in the wilderness, clad in
wild beasts' skins, crying, "Repent, repent!" [48] Men who
found such a role not at all to their liking still could not
blind themselves to the evil trend of events. Week after week
good Roundheads like Robert Goodwin and Sir William
Masham had to write in the same strain: "There is no good
news." This army has been defeated, this town has been
lost, this garrison has surrendered — no good news.[49] The
mere report of ill-tidings gave way after a while to dispirited
prophecies of a bitter hour near at hand. "There is reason for
. . . earnestness. I fear we shall see sorrowful times." [50] "It
is well for us to be prepared, for many expect the storm ere
long to come upon us." [51] Finally we see the transition from
foreboding to outright hysterical panic in Masham's terrified

---

[45] *D.*, 165, fols. 143–143*v*.

[46] *D.*, 164, fols. 241, 233*v*.

[47] *C. J.*, III, 191, and see, above, p. 124.

[48] "An higher providence hath been justly irritated . . . for God is a God
of Peace, and a God of Unity" (*D.*, 165, fol. 139*v*).

[49] R. Goodwin to Sir Thomas Barrington, June 26 (*B.*, 2646, fol. 293).
Richard Harman to the Norwich Committee, August 1: "This week hath pro-
duced no good news, the City of Bristol is lost to our great grief" (MSS.
Collections Relating to Norwich, I, British Museum Additional MSS, 22619).

[50] Harbottle Grimston to Sir Thomas Barrington, July 19 (*B.*, 2647, fol.
38*v*).

[51] Sir William Masham to Sir Thomas Barrington, July 17 (*B.*, 2647, fol. 34).

postscript to a perfectly innocuous newsletter: "When you have read this, burn it." [52]

An embittered Royalist lady ruthlessly pointed the moral to a man who had sacrificed much that was dear to him in giving his allegiance to Parliament. Dorothy Leake wrote to Sir Ralph Verney,

God hath blessed [the King] above all your expectations, and he is now in so good a condition that he need not fear the Parliament, though they have gone all the ways in the world to destroy him. They have neither wanted men, money nor towns until now, yet you see how they have prospered. . . . Look upon the King from the beginning, and think with yourself if God's blessing had not gone with him, whether it had been possible he could have been in such a condition as he is now.[53]

In our skeptical age we do not regard such an argument as decisive; but the seventeenth century was not a skeptical age. A series of victories in those days was good prima facie evidence that Deity in the background was in unseen ways smoothing the path of the victor; and God's wrath explained as nothing else could a long succession of defeats. So in August 1643 it seemed that God must be very angry with His people, deeply displeased with the Saints. How else explain the dissensions among them, the victories of their enemies, the converging of three Royalist hosts on London, against which the godly folk could oppose only the rags and tatters of an old army and the incomplete skeleton of a new one? With the hand of the Lord heavy on the metropolis of the Saints, who knew what the end might be? Perhaps quick overthrow, the sack of the City, and the slaughter of God's people; perhaps the rise of another John of Leyden to make of London another, a greater, a bloodier Münster. Only a special providence, only a miracle, it seemed, could save the cause from impending doom. And yet a month after Bristol fell the most promising candidate for John of Leyden's crown lay prisoner in the Tower, the shops of the

[52] Sir William Masham to Sir Thomas Barrington (*B.*, 2647, fol. 59).
[53] *C. W.*, I, 200.

City were closed, not for fear of sack but because so many apprentices were marching to save Gloucester in the largest array yet gathered during the war, the dissensions among the Parliamentary generals had been smoothed over, and two new armies were forming, this time no mere paper battalions but flesh and blood fighting men who in a few weeks would go into the field of battle. Far to the north across the Humber, the Tyne, and the Tweed, another host made ready to take arms for Parliament. The army of the Covenant of the Scottish nation with God prepared to march to the aid of their English brethren. All these things came to pass in a month; and yet there was no miracle, unless a cool head in times of peril, an unerring eye for the main chance, painstaking unremitting toil, and rare persistence, patience, and tact are a miracle. If they are, then we must turn to John Pym to learn how it was performed.

CHAPTER VII

DAWN

HAMPDEN'S death and the unopposed plundering of Wycombe by Rupert took Pym off balance. Surrounded by fear and panic, threatened with disaster, his control of the House imperiled by the death of his friend, for a moment he got out of control himself, and struck out at Essex, whom he had hitherto so assiduously defended. At the behest of the House he wrote the Lord General a letter criticizing his inactivity, saying people now felt "more safe to be under the command of the King's army than under his." [1] Whereupon the Lord General offered his resignation. Meantime Pym had recovered his balance. The fiery spirits were probably quite ready to take Essex at his word, and Martin objected to any show of submissiveness by the House.[2] Pym had other ideas, and, as Dewes puts it, having "broken my Lord General's head with his former indiscreet letter was now employed to prepare a plaster for it." [3] With almost flamboyant submissiveness, he acknowledged on behalf of the House the "great worth and fidelity" of the Earl, and denied that "the former letter had been written with . . . any intent to reflect upon his Lordship's honor." [4] For the rest of his parliamentary career Pym showed nothing but solicitude for the Lord General, and when for a little while men hostile to Essex took from Pym the immediate management of affairs, he simply turned his back on events of the day and concentrated on his old program of defense measures.

Essex's peace letter wrenched control of the House from Pym and put it in the hands of the fiery spirits; but it left him with one task requiring prompt attention. For the first

---

[1] D., 165, fol. 100v.
[2] D., 165, fol. 101.

[3] D., 165, fol. 100v.
[4] D., 165, fol. 101.

time since the outbreak of the war the officer group in the
Lord General's army had aligned themselves with the peace
party. Their shift was the natural consequence of being left
for three months to rot with sick soldiers on a riverbank, but
it could hardly have come at a worse time. Charles had just
declared Parliament an illegal assembly, and in the field he
was everywhere successful. He would greet offers of a treaty
with a demand for unconditional surrender or with an ill-concealed jeer. Pym sought to woo the officers away from their
advocacy of a treaty; but in doing so he carefully dissociated
himself from the faction that was heaping criticism on Essex's
head. He praised the noble intentions of the Lord General's
proposals, but showed that his plan was impractical.[5] For the
rest, other men had taken the reins from him, and the counsels
of new leaders prevailed in a terrified House. On the list of
members chosen by these leaders to carry out their pet scheme
of a general rising, Pym's name was conspicuously missing.[6]
So he sat back, watched the fiery spirits get tangled in their
own plans, adjusted himself to the change in the political
climate, and saw his last batch of constructive war legislation
through the Houses.

On July 24 the Commons passed a renewal of the assessment
ordinance in two hours with none of the hesitancy and reluctance that beset them when they first considered the measure.[7]
Then they proceeded to make the excise an effective fiscal de-
vice by putting tobacco, beer, and ale on the list of excisable
commodities; and again the speed with which they dispatched
the business showed how far they had veered toward Pym's
opinion that strict legality makes a slender diet for a starved
cause.[8] Another of Pym's projects came to its long-delayed
fruition in the midst of the July panic, when Parliament dis-

[5] *D.*, 165, fol. 123*v*.
[6] *C. J.*, III, 176.
[7] July 24. "This ordinance did cost about two hours to have it read and
passed, and it were a strange thing that no man spake against it" (*D.*, 165,
fol. 129*v*).
[8] *C. J.*, III, 88, 177.

patched to Scotland a committee officially instructed to conclude with the Scots a treaty for mutual military assistance.[9] Finally, as August began, the House of Commons passed the last fundamental war measure of the Civil War period, the ordinance for the impressment of men to military service.[10] For five more years the civil wars desolated England, and in those years Parliament made many new laws. The bill for the Committee of Both Kingdoms and the army ordinances of 1645 had great political significance; the system of compounding for delinquency brought new revenues to Parliament. But the former measures from a military point of view, the latter from a fiscal point of view, were only reshufflings of basic laws all written in the ordinance book several months before Pym died.[11] From November 1642 to August 1643, in hours of high hope and in hours of dark despair, Pym had pressed his program, patient, resilient, undismayed by delays and apparent defeats. He would set a whole batch of defense measures before the House in a few days. Then, slowing the pace, he gave the more scrupulous members a chance to recover from their shock at the enormity of the things they were called upon to do. Timing his thrust carefully, he renewed pressure for one or another of his schemes; and when that had gone through, and the House had adjusted itself to its latest collective assault on the law and custom of England, Pym rallied it for the next forward movement, and the next, and the next. So, always setting his tempo to the mood of the members, he led them on from objective to objective toward his ultimate goal — a powerful Parliament united against the enemy.

[9] *C. J.*, III, 165, 169.
[10] *A. O. I.*, I, 241–242.
[11] Careful study has convinced me that no new principle was introduced in the ordinances establishing the New Model Army. There was nothing novel in the idea of an independent standing army regularly paid from a constant source of revenue. The success of the New Model was due to its size, to the long experience of its officers and men, to the relative regularity of its pay and the consequent rarity of desertions, and to the talents of Oliver Cromwell, none of which phenomena come under the category of legislative enactment.

When Pym had finished his job of building the foundation of Parliament's military power, his successors had little left to do but tinker with the superstructure; and they could tinker to their hearts' content perfectly confident that Pym's groundwork would stand any strain. When one considers the sheer bulk of Pym's achievement and realizes how little time he had for his labors, one feels sure that rarely in history has a minister unlearned in the ways of war, with such recalcitrant, shoddy, and mean material to hand, built so rapidly and yet so well. In August 1643 Pym's great constructive work was done; in a year or two it was so much taken for granted that the pain of the building was almost forgotten. The clash of arms at Marston Moor and Naseby, the thundering hoof beats of the Ironside regiments, the clamorous prayer to the Lord of Hosts rising from the ranks of the New Model Army on the eve of battle, all drowned out one quiet little truth: the fact of Parliament's eventual triumph over the King, as distinguished from the manner and the *élan* of it, owed less to Oliver Cromwell than to a pudgy little man whose last year was spent amid tidings of disaster at Westminster, and whose body lay at rest in the Abbey long before Parliament plucked the first fruits of victory. For Parliament owed the substance, though not the form, of its ultimate success to the series of dull ordinances that John Pym wrote on the record in the first year of the Civil War.

With the last of those dull ordinances, the one for the impressment of soldiers, Pym gave notice that he had resumed his rightful place at the helm in the midst of the crisis. After all, one might cajole the Houses into passing the most complete and elegant set of defense measures; yet ordinances would be quite useless if the Royalists marched into London, or if Parliament made peace with Charles I on conditions equivalent to surrender. And one or the other of those eventualities appeared imminent as the disastrous month of July drew toward its close. By that time the failure of the old armies and the inability of the violent Commoners to get new ones into the field seemed to have reduced Parliament to the unattractive alternatives of capitulation or forcible subjugation. Under the circumstances it behooved Pym to drop the role of disinterested spectator and get back into the fray.

Before Martin's committee had time to show its inadequacy to the task it had undertaken, Pym set out to recapture the initiative in the House for himself and for the benefit of the Lord General. The two objectives were in a way one. Whether he willed it so or not, Pym's dominance and prestige in the House depended on the salvage of Essex's forces. The City troops belonged to the London militia committee, and Pym could not control that committee. The volunteer army would be a political asset to the committee that raised it and especially to Henry Martin, Pym's chief enemy in Parliament. The army of the Earl of Essex was in a peculiar sense Pym's army, the military first fruit of the Parliamentary resistance he led, whose chief officers were his friends. Before the committee for the volunteer army and the London militia committee got well under way, Pym had a third committee at work — a committee to investigate the grievances of the Lord General's officers. Of this committee John Pym was chairman.[12] Before Sir William Waller, around whom all the plans of Pym's enemies centered, reached London from the west, Pym had driven through the House six resolutions intended to repair the worst deficiencies in the army of the Earl of Essex.[13]

Pym, as befits a politician in matters of tactics, was about a week ahead of public opinion. Gradually events were dampening the ardor of some of the antagonists of the Earl of Essex. Martin might maintain his attitude of hostility to the Lord General;[14] but after Waller's overthrow at Roundway Down wiser men indulged in a little painful heart-searching. No weekly news sheet had reacted more violently to Essex's letter than the *Parliament Scout*. No sheet lavished more fulsome eulogy on Sir William.[15] Yet after Roundway Down the *Scout*

[12] *C. J.*, III, 178.
[13] *C. J.*, III, 180.
[14] *D.*, 165, fols. 134v, 149.
[15] *Parliament Scout*, July 6–July 13, 1643.

changed its tactics. To Waller it remained friendly, albeit
in a manner a little more aloof and subdued. Toward Essex
it dropped its wonted fishwife tone for a more-to-be-pitied-
than-censured, even a more-to-be-praised-than-pitied, attitude.[16] This change of feeling, let it be noted, began even
before the committee for the *levée en masse* had a chance to
exhibit its incompetence to deal with the military situation.
Making a bold transition from the *Parliament Scout* to the
group whose opinion it seems to reflect, we may surmise that
the men who had adhered to the middle group through Hampden rather than through Pym or Essex were finding little
satisfaction in their ill-considered alliance with Martin and his
gang, and were veering around to their old association with
Pym. And, whether they knew it or not, veering around to
Pym meant veering around to Essex. Prompt action by the
Earl's subordinates furnished an impetus to the shift. Their
fidelity to their general in an evil hour helped Pym force the
first move toward a rapprochement on a still hesitant House.
The Lord General's most influential officers stood in good
repute — Sir Philip Stapleton, the staunch middle-group man,
rather bellicose than otherwise, and Arthur Goodwyn, the
best-beloved friend of the Puritan hero, Hampden.[17] Commoners who paid no attention to Essex's complaints could not
disregard the report of Stapleton and Goodwyn on the pitiful
plight of the army. That report opened the way to the resolutions of Pym's committee, the first step toward the rehabilitation of Essex and his army. The resentment of Essex's officers
at the Houses' treatment of their chief also thwarted the attempt both of the committee for the *levée en masse* and of
the London militia committee entirely to emancipate the new

[16] Warning against too great haste in casting Essex off, the *Scout* spoke "a
little of that noble lord, . . . who certainly is right to the cause or no man is.
And if he hath been unhappy in a Council of War, must that reflect wholly
upon himself. . . . Winnow but the chaff from him and you will find him as
good wheat as any in England" (*Parliament Scout*, July 13–July 20, 1643).
[17] For Goodwyn's association with Hampden, see H. R. Williamson, *John
Hampden: A Life* (1933), especially Goodwyn's letter on Hampden's death,
pp. 331–332.

armies from the Lord General's control. The bulk of the House showed itself indisposed further to alienate Essex's staff in order to set up two armies that would be practically independent not only of him but of Parliament itself. Parliament gave Waller immediate command of both new forces, but, instead of freezing Essex out, as the backers of the projects had wished, it made Sir William a general subordinate to the Earl.[18]

The majority of the House, which had moved away from Pym when he showed himself unwilling to join in their game of throwing mud and brickbats at the prostrate commander with whom they had lately sworn to live and die, now moved back again. If Waller was to command under Essex, he must get his commission from him; but to ask Essex to commission a man who tried to blame him for the loss of the west was futile unless something should be done to placate the Lord General, and that placating would have to take the form of something more substantial than proclamations of undying affection. Fortunately, for once in his life the Earl did not go out of his way to repel the resurgence of sentiment in his favor. Instead he sent a letter to Parliament reciting his grievances, a letter so mild in tone, so moderate in substance, so reasonable altogether that it is hard to believe that Essex had any hand in composing it. Anyone not blinded by partisanship could see that the Lord General's case was a good one. Out of six thousand foot soldiers in his army only three thousand were in fit

[18] After the rejection by the House of his first report from the committee for the *levée en masse*, a report which had been suspiciously silent on the relation of the committee's army to the other Parliamentary forces (*W.*, fol. 65), Martin brought in a second report according to which Waller was to receive his commission from the Lord General (*D.*, 165, fol. 130*v*). All we know of Martin makes it inconceivable that he should knuckle down to Essex so supinely, if he had any hope of making a successful resistance. The London authorities had explicitly provided in their petition that the commander of the city militia should be responsible to the militia committee and Parliament alone (see, above, p. 122). They seem to have drawn a bill with this provision and presented it through Mr. Recorder Glynn to the House, which at once amended it to provide that Waller should have his commission from and command under the Lord General (*W.*, fol. 66*v*).

condition to march. The rest were sick, without clothing or
pay. The promise of a recruit of horse had come to nothing,
so the cavalry numbered but twenty-five hundred. The men,
desperate for lack of money and provisions, deserted to other
parliamentary armies in hope of better treatment; and what
was worse, their desertion went unpunished. That Parliament
should thus condone the decimation of the army of their chosen
commander-in-chief was an unbearable scandal on the Lord
General and his officers. Moreover all hope of successful
recruiting was cut off by the slanders and libels against the
Earl freely circulated in the City and in the country. To prevent these outrages Parliament did nothing. Essex proposed
specific remedies: a vindication of his conduct by Parliament
and the punishment of his slanderers, immediate recruiting
and regular pay for his army, and no recruiting of other forces
until his army had its full complement of men, restoration to
him of complete control of commissions, and an investigation
of the real cause of the loss of the west, which his libelers
blamed on him.[19]

Parliament could not safely give effect to all these recom-
mendations. To give Essex absolute control of commissions
when he was at swords' points with Waller, the new general of
the London militia, would endanger the whole military structure. To start an investigation into the loss of the west would
rub salt into old wounds, make old rancors indelible.[20] So the
House said nothing about commissions and refused to put itself
in the position of judge between Essex and Waller in the matter
of the west. Considering what the attitude of the House toward
Essex had been but two weeks before, what they refused him
was not nearly so remarkable as what they granted him. To
offset their rejection of the negative part of his plan, they
resolved to raise four thousand men for his army, to send

[19] *L. J.*, vi, 160.

[20] The vote against the inquiry broke party lines. Selden, a very peaceful
man, and Tate, who was probably a fiery spirit, opposed the inquiry. Holles,
the leader of the peace party, and Sir John Corbett, who once stood well to
the left of that group, favored it (*C. J.*, iii, 191).

speedily a month's pay for his soldiers, to grant him what
remained of the assessment of the twentieth part after deduct-
ing the ten thousand pounds earmarked for Waller. They
promised to publish and did publish a vindication of the Lord
General, and ordered the punishment of those who slandered
him.[21]

Between July 27 and July 29, with London celebrating the
advent of Waller and the committee for the volunteer army
drumming up trade, the Lord General's fortunes seemed irrev-
ocably on the downgrade, heading straight for the bottom.
In less than a week the course of things reversed, and Essex
was slowly and steadily climbing to that peak of popularity
he attained by forcing the King to raise the siege of Gloucester.
The change seemed almost a political miracle, so much so, in
fact, that at least one hardheaded observer refused to believe
his eyes. Because of his impartial contempt for all the parties
involved, the Venetian secretary in London often gauged accurately the significance of factional changes in the House of
Commons. When the House voted to recruit four thousand
men for the Lord General's army,[22] the secretary thought it
was a silly attempt to fool Essex with impossible promises.[23]
He could not have been more wrong. The rehabilitation of the
Earl and the reconstruction of his army went on whether people
believed in it or not.

While many members still reeled from the shock of the fall
of Bristol, Pym declined to become hysterical over the loss,
did not waver a moment, but applied all his energy to the
present task of rescuing the cause from the mire.[24] And while
many members groaned in despair of any good thing, Pym's
hopefulness communicated itself to those closest to him. Thus
his nephew Nicholls wrote to a friend with restrained but
steady confidence of the impending recruitment of Essex's

[21] *C. J.*, III, 189–191.
[22] *C. J.*, III, 189.
[23] *C. S. P. Venetian*, XXVII, 5–6.
[24] John Pym to Sir Thomas Barrington, August 2 (Lowndes MSS, *H. M. C. Report VII*, app. i, pp. 557–558).

army, of supplies to be sent and arrears to be paid, of Parliament's strict orders against the defamation of the Lord General and his officers. In the same letter Nicholls records a very significant, almost incredible, alteration in the attitude of the City toward Essex. Following Parliament's cue, the municipal authorities had taken measures against his slanderers "and tomorrow send two of their Aldermen and four of their Common Councilmen with an assurance from the City that they will live and die with him." All these small items added up to something bigger than the sum of them. If but for a moment, Pym had restored to the cause an essence which any witness of the disruptive effect of Essex's letter might have believed forever lost — unity. Fittingly Nicholls closed his chronicle of the week's news, "I have great hopes we shall all be united together again; it is unity that in this exigency of affairs must preserve us." [25] And here, though the hand was the hand of Nicholls, the voice was the voice of Pym.

Although Pym was obviously making progress in healing the breach in the middle group, no one — not even he himself — could know how well or how ill he had succeeded in drawing together again Essex on one side and men who a few weeks earlier had cried for his dismissal on the other. The focus of danger to his work had in the past fortnight shifted from the extreme left to the extreme right. In July it seemed that Martin and the fiery spirits would absorb the militant section of the middle group, leaving impotent Pym and his personal following. Now the tide had turned. Martin had failed as a leader. He might continue to inveigh against the Lord General; [26] but he had lost his audience. The militant part of the middle group deserted him and, like an unscrupulous lady of easy virtue whose discarded lover has unexpectedly come into a fortune, tried to win Essex back again. Now under Pym's skillful guidance they were going through motions calculated to convey their undying affection for the Lord General; but

[25] Anthony Nicholls to Sir Thomas Barrington, August 1 (*B.*, 2647, fol. 97).
[26] *D.*, 165, fol. 149.

since he had witnessed the same exhibition before, there was some doubt how much conviction it carried this time.

The great question mark at the beginning of August was not the power of Martin over part of the middle group but the power of the peace party over Essex, whom they had befriended in his hours of tribulation in July. Only time could reveal the extent of his commitments; but, had he been one-tenth the traitor that rumor a few weeks before had made him out,[27] the militant gentlemen might have spared themselves all their seductive gestures. Fortunately for them, Essex was something more than the poltroon that many thought him, not altogether a fool, and not at all a traitor. To this day we do not know how far he went with the peace party. We can only guess. Probably in the July winter of his discontent Essex cursed his fair weather friends rather often. Probably the Earl of Holland witnessed some of these outbursts. Probably mistaking his own hopes for reality, as he did his life long, he assumed that the Lord General would go the limit out of pique and for revenge.[28] The peace party soon suffered for Holland's overestimate of Essex's complaisance. Hoping to turn to account the panic that followed the fall of Bristol, the peace lords framed a new set of proposals to send to the King. Totally lacking any safeguard against Charles's abuse of the militia, which was to be turned over to him unconditionally, making provision even less satisfactory for the reformation of religion, the propositions were nothing more than a thinly veiled capitulation to the Royalists.[29] Holland did not even wait for the upper house to vote on the proposals but hastened to the army encampment to see that Essex was right to the project. He might have saved himself the trip; Pym had beaten him before he started.

On August 1 Richard Harman, M.P., could confidently write his constituency at Norwich that "Sir William Waller shall

---

[27] *C. S. P. Venetian*, xxvii, 2.
[28] *Clar. H. R.*, bk. vii, par. 187.
[29] House of Lords MSS, *H. M. C. Report V*, app. i, pp. 98-99.

command in chief the City forces that are to be raised to go into the West." [30] Had he written a day later, he would have had a different story to tell. On that day the Commons passed three important resolutions on military affairs. They set up, as a policy-forming body to advise the Commons on military questions, a Council of War with the Lord General's old and faithful friends, Clotworthy, Gerard, and Pym, as its leading members and without a single fiery spirit on it.[31] They also resolved to raise four thousand new foot soldiers and five hundred new cavalrymen for the Lord General's army. But most important they voted that, with the aid of the friendly Council and with almost five thousand recruits, not Sir William Waller but the Lord General the Earl of Essex was to march westward to meet the King's armies.[32] The Earl was to have his chance to vindicate himself from all the aspersions his enemies had cast upon him, to take his rightful place as commander-in-chief of the Parliamentary armies, to become once again what he had been but a year before, the hero and darling of the parliamentary cause. Pym had offered the proud Earl the one bait no proud man humiliated before his peers can resist — the opportunity to put his critics and tormentors to shame.

When the Earl of Holland came to get Essex's blessing on the Lords' bid for peace, he had to deal with a man who no

---

[30] MSS Collections Relating to Norwich, i, British Museum Additional MSS, 22619.

[31] C. J., iii, 191. In some respects the Council of War was an embryonic Committee of Both Kingdoms, especially in its duty to coördinate military plans and in the imposition of an oath of secrecy on its members. It differed from the Committee of Both Kingdoms in being a strictly advisory rather than an executive body, and in its responsibility to the Commons alone rather than to both Houses. There seems to have been some effort made to include on the committee a representative or two from all the parliamentary forces. Thus we have Thomas Stockdale to represent the Fairfaxes, Alexander Popham for the Western garrisons, Crew for the midland county forces, Colonels Harvey and Mainwaring for the London militia, and Waller for his own army. Not all the council were members of the House. They were as follows: members — A. Popham, Pym, Gerard, Clotworthy, Waller, Jephson, Crew; non-members — Stockdale, Harvey, Mainwaring, Sir H. Holcroft, Sir R. King, M. Mazeres.

[32] W., fol. 67.

longer had everything to gain and nothing to lose by a peace at any price.[33] On the other hand, the Lord General had much to lose and nothing to gain from a Parliament distracted from recruiting and supplying his army by a highly controversial set of peace proposals. Just what passed between the lordly first-cousins we do not know.[34] We do know that Essex did not repeat his *faux pas* of July. Throughout the debate in Parliament on the propositions he maintained a position of strict neutrality. No man could rise in either House to say the Lord General willed it thus or so. In the decisive division of the Commons, when five men swung the balance against further considering the peers' proposals, the silence of the Earl of Essex was probably worth a dozen votes to John Pym in thwarting the peace party.[35]

So far the Lord General vindicated Pym's policy of picking him up when he was prostrate instead of kicking him in the face. The Earl's fidelity and Pym's policy were soon again to be tested. As a dissuasive from peace, certain Londoners had more faith in the efficiency of a howling mob than of a silent general.[36] On Sunday, August 6, the militant clergy of London exhorted their congregations to flock to Westminster next day and save the cause from betrayal by the majority in Parliament. The same suggestion was printed in a broadside distributed in the City.[37] The rabble responded magnificently to the incitement to violence and came whooping, five thousand strong, to the Parliament house. In action, however, they limited themselves to shouting and shaking their fists at the peace lords, all of which probably had slight effect on the ultimate decision of the Commoners.[38] To Holland's mind the

---

[33] *D.*, 165, fol. 135.

[34] Essex's aunt, Penelope Devereux, was the Earl of Holland's mother.

[35] A perplexing feature of this crisis is the action of Sir Philip Stapleton, Essex's cavalry commander, in favoring further consideration of the proposals on August 5 (*C. J.*, III, 196). The decisive vote of August 7 was 81 in favor of continuing consideration of the propositions, 88 opposed (*C. J.*, III, 197).

[36] Some had still greater faith in the effectiveness of a bit of judicious, selective kidnapping (*D.*, 165, fol. 145).

[37] *D.*, 165, fol. 145*v*; *Clar. H. R.*, bk. VII, par. 168–170.

[38] *Y.*, 18778, fols. 11*v*–12.

existence of the mob rendered Parliament unfree, so having learned nothing from his first rebuff, he sallied forth to the Lord General with another fine scheme. The menaced members of the peace party were to come off from Parliament and throw themselves into Essex's army. Under his protection they would dictate a peace on terms acceptable to both Royalists and Roundheads. If one side or the other should balk at those terms, the army would apparently be used to make the recalcitrant see reason.[39] Holland had committed the very common human blunder of reckoning without his host. In his career the Lord General very rarely indulged in any act which the most rigorous could call underhanded. He had sworn to support the cause of Parliament, and the Earl of Holland was trying to seduce him into something very like treachery to that cause. Essex did more than refuse to have anything to do with Holland's scheme.

The Earl was too scrupulous and too punctual to that which he called his trust, and this was too barefaced a separation for him to engage in . . . so he did not only reject what was proposed to him, but expressed such a dislike of the Earl of Holland for proposing it that he (Holland) thought it high time to get himself out of his reach.[40]

Twice in two weeks Pym's whole plan of action, nay more, the whole fate of the cause he led, depended on the soundness of the judgment he had made of the character of the Lord General. Twice, without wavering or hesitation, the Lord

[39] It has been said justly that the Earl of Holland's scheme was both puerile and dangerous. On the other hand, a great deal of praise has been lavished on the Heads of the Proposals of the New Model Army of 1647. Yet, the essence, if not the incidental features, of the two schemes was identical. An army supported by a faction in Parliament was to arrogate to itself the function of arbiter between King and Parliament. In neither case was any provision made for the eventuality that actually came to pass in the case of the Heads of the Proposals, of one or both parties to the dispute rejecting arbitration by the military. And it may be doubted whether Holland's scheme, if attempted, would have been any more disastrous than the New Model's was to the peace which both schemes purported to aim at.

[40] *Clar. H. R.*, bk. VII, par. 188. See Appendix A for an analysis of the value of Clarendon's account of this episode.

General had so acted as to justify fully the faith Pym had in him. Thereby he bestowed on Pym's policy the only accolade which all politicians at all times recognize and understand — success. Besides sound judgment one other trait of a great politician Pym had preëminently. With only the normal politician's conscience about overreaching his enemies, a leathery kind of conscience at best, he never deceived, deserted, or tricked his friends. In this alone he was superior to his successor to power, young Sir Henry Vane, who was a far cleverer man than he. Vane used men for his secret purposes and then tossed them aside; Pym never crawled out from under his obligations or found any undertaking too difficult if it was due to a faithful ally as a *quid pro quo*. In the jargon of contemporary American politics, when Pym promised "to deliver the goods," he delivered them.

Now the time had come to reward the Lord General for his fidelity. Pym did not temporize or hedge or balk even for a moment, but delivered promptly and to the full extent of his debt. Hardly had the last unkind obiter dicta been spoken over the dead peace proposals of the Lords before Pym was on his feet demanding immediate action from the House on its promises and commitments to the Earl of Essex.[41] Once more the Houses responded to the magic of Pym's political skill. If there are degrees of deadness, then the fiery spirits' opposition to Essex was even deader than the peace proposals of the Lords. In stony silence the violent men sat while the middle group took over the floor of the House to pronounce eulogies on the Lord General,[42] took over the City money bags to pour twenty thousand pounds into the Lord General's lap,[43] and as a final blow took the London militia away from Waller, the hero of the fiery ones, and sent it marching to the relief of Gloucester under the command of the Lord General, the Earl of Essex.[44]

[41] *Y.*, 18778, fol. 12.
[42] *D.*, 165, fol. 150.
[43] MSS Collections Relating to Norwich, I, British Museum Additional MSS, 22619, fol. 105.
[44] *C. J.*, III, 215.

Pym celebrated his victory over the radicals in a very characteristic way. He used the strength his triumph gave him to pluck from his side — his left side — a thorn that for a long time had bothered him and had once spread a poison that threatened him with political extinction. For months Henry Martin had tried how far he could go in besmirching popular idols and harassing John Pym, and at last he went too far. On August 16, during a debate in the House, Martin remarked that it was better that one family should perish than that the whole kingdom be destroyed. Pressed by Pym's friend Neville Poole to explain himself, he admitted that he referred to the royal family.[45] Pym had probably waited long for the chance Martin's misstep gave him. Now he could settle scores once and for all with the man who had persistently mocked at his losses and thwarted his gains, and at the same time he could reaffirm, so that the world would hear of it, his faith in monarchy and his fidelity to the Stuart dynasty.[46] Just what proportion righteous indignation bore to low cunning in his action the historian can never know. Probably Pym did not know himself, since most successful politicians either assume the sanctity of their own motive or do not give the matter any thought. In any case Pym did not waste time in motive-searching when the main chance came; he simply "fell foul" upon Martin "with a long speech saying he was a man extremely guilty of injustice and lewdness." [47] Without a division the House voted to expel Martin and imprison him in the Tower.[48] Thus Pym achieved his double purpose of taking the edge off Royalist

[45] *Whitelock*, p. 68; *W.*, fols. 70v–71; *D.*, 165, fols. 151–152.

[46] That Pym was a sound judge of politico-dramatic effects is proved by the number of contemporary references to the expulsion of Martin. Members of Parliament who reduced their letters home to the barest bones of news record the event. (Gawdy MSS, II, British Museum Additional MSS, 27395, fol. 172.)

[47] *Mercurius Aulicus*, August 13–August 20, 1643. Dewes corroborates Pym's part in the proceeding: "The true and only cause why he was at this time put out of the House was by reason of his almost constantly opposing and wittily jerking at old Pym, who by the help of his friends . . . took this opportunity to get Martin beside the saddle" (*D.*, 165, fol. 152).

[48] *C. J.*, III, 206.

jibes at the republicanism of Parliament [49] and of ridding himself of a nuisance.

For Pym, throwing Martin into the Tower was merely a pleasant byplay, a semicomic interlude to the main line of work. That work came to a climax when on September 26 the army of the Earl of Essex broke its line of communication with London and set out from Colnebrook on its march through hostile territory to relieve besieged Gloucester. The shutters were down in the shops of the City, for behind the Lord General in bright and varied regimental colors marched the trainbands of the London militia, thousands upon thousands of apprentices following the Earl to save the western garrison. Succeeding where those who would have thrust him aside had failed, Pym had again "delivered the goods." He gave Parliament in its hour of deepest need an army in the field, strong in number and high in morale. The march to Gloucester, a first-rate practical achievement, was also the physical symbol of a thing more important than itself, the outward and visible sign of an inward spiritual change in Parliament and the adherents of Parliament.

Letters written by members of the House late in August and early in September reflect the new spirit. No more do we hear lamentations over ill news, no more do men set down in dark words prophecies of impending disaster. The days of defeat are forgotten — Stratton, and Adwalton Moor, and Roundway Down, and even Bristol. Men write with a new buoyancy of the good things that have happened and of the better things to come.[50] No longer do they wonder why God has forsaken them, no longer does an occasional failure where there was high expectation of success shake their faith in

[49] The strongly Royalist Florentine resident writes of Martin's expulsion, "This sentiment of the Lower House, both just and honorable, will seem to show the world that its intention was always to preserve the kingship and not to take it away as many report" (Salvetti Correspondence, x, British Museum Additional MSS, 27962K).

[50] Sir Roger Burgoyne to Sir Ralph Verney, August 29, 1643 (Verney MSS at Claydon, Bucks.).

God's solicitude for his people or in his intention to "do His own work," [51] which is their work. Every letter has in it some bit of news carrying a note of hope, even the letters of men who formerly knew only the monotone of despair.[52] Better than any other, Anthony Nicholls caught the feeling appropriate to the dawning of the new day.

This gallant City, considering the distress that Gloucester is in, has enabled his Excellency with five new regiments of foot [to march west], so that I believe now he is a more considerable army than ever he was since he was general. His Excellency . . . intends not to stay until such time as he has relieved that City. If God bless us in this design it will give a great turn to our affairs. The Scots have with one consent declared their resolution of coming to our assistance and have sent us a Covenant to unite us the firmer together, which I hope we shall in our House take with a unanimous [53] consent, so that there is no question but that these good brethren of ours will take care of the North. The commission is now come for Sir William Waller, so that his levies will go speedily on to second my Lord General if there be an occasion.[54]

It is not in his lumping together of a batch of news items that Nicholls catches the feeling of the new day. Rather it is that in his hopeful blending of things done and things yet to do we sense the underlying cause of the new state of affairs, a new spirit not created by, but the creator of, the Lord General's army. It was the spirit that made small things easy to Parliament, and great things possible, the driving force that set Essex's regiments on their westward march, singing, cheering, confident of victory. It was a new-old attachment to the cause of Parliament as above the separate aims of momentarily

[51] Warwick (Sir Roger Burgoyne) to Sir Ralph Verney, September 5, 1643: "They come not in to Sir William Waller as I expected and hoped, but it is no matter. God can do His own work with a few as well as with many" (Verney MSS at Claydon, Bucks.).

[52] Richard Harman to the burgesses of Norwich, August 24, 1643 (MSS Collections Relating to Norwich, I, British Museum Additional MSS, 22619, fol. 105).

[53] The MS has "onamouse." Nicholls' attitude toward spelling was heretical even in that day of orthographic latitudinarianism.

[54] Anthony Nicholls to Sir Thomas Barrington, August 28, 1643. (*B.*, 2647, fol. 188.)

dominant factions, a spirit of men of good will freely joined for a common high purpose, a spirit of unity. It is very fitting that Pym's nephew should best express the reborn unity of the cause, for Pym was surely the maker and molder of that unity. To create it he labored against apparently insuperable difficulties; and when he had overcome them, the particular problem of putting an army in the field solved itself. This re-creation of unity in August — however transitory it should prove to be — out of the diversity, hostility, faction, and chaos of July was perhaps the masterwork of the master politician, John Pym.

It was also Pym's last great work. Sick to death, he lived but a few months longer, coming to the House whenever his rotting, pain-racked body would let him. He lived to hear of the relief of Gloucester and the battle of Newbury, and to take the Solemn League and Covenant with the rest of the House. Gloucester, Newbury, and the Covenant were all end points of policies he had begun, yet they were not distinctively his. He had shaped the spirit that made the army that relieved Gloucester and fought at Newbury; but the raising of the siege and the battle both belonged to the Lord General. He had long advocated a Scottish alliance to an indifferent Parliament, and yet the Solemn League and Covenant was not his work. It was the work of young Sir Henry Vane and the Scot, Archibald Johnston of Warriston, men very different from Pym, with different aspirations and different ideas on the best way to their goals. For Vane and Johnston of Warriston were radical men, each after his own fashion, and the slow patient way of Pym was not their way. Nevertheless, while they were still in Edinburgh, Pym guided the Covenant, almost intact as they had sent it, through Parliament. In 1644 the Covenant in the hands of Vane and Johnston became the flaming standard of the "godly party," which sought to destroy and did destroy much that Pym had tried to save. The godly did their best to ruin Essex, whom Pym had protected and defended; and between Essex on one side and Vane on the other, the middle group was hopelessly torn asunder. The policy of slowly moving along in the van of a solid majority — the policy of Pym — gave way to the fitful raids of minority groups on a perplexed neutral mass to secure a temporary preponderance — the policy of Vane. With the triumph of Vane's policy went the destruction of the middle group, and the end of the middle group meant the end of that fragile unity of Parliament and its cause that Pym had struggled so hard to maintain. But before other leaders had their way with the House he once led, ten men dropped into a hole under the floor of Westminster Abbey all that remained mortal of John Pym.

EPILOGUE

CHAPTER VIII

CIVIL WAR GROUPS

TIMES of revolutions are times of mirage. The ordinary day-to-day routine of affairs is distorted, and the packing of great events into brief hours makes the distance between heart's desire and its attainment look deceptively short. To men who think they see the path to heaven on earth open wide and suddenly before them, workaday hopes and limited aspirations seem drab, cheap, and unworthy. The high-spirited and the heroic, the best the time produces, save they have extraordinary prescience and a great fund of common sense, desert the dull rambling road of ordinary political processes to run straight toward the bright light in a dark world, the light that burns at the wicket gate where one enters Earthly Paradise. The light is dazzling, and men have the full range of their imaginative fancy, freed from the grey tinge of reality, wherewith to paint in flaming colors the joys that await them beyond the light. Little wonder then that in times of revolution earnest men, men in ordinary times quite sane, try to reach heaven by a quick spurt over a short cut.

Times of revolution are times of faction. That is one of the cruel ironies of revolutions. The distortion of political perspective in a world turned topsy-turvy makes Heaven shine clear and the way thence seem short to sanguine men; but it does not make all men see the same heaven, and it does not make all men see the same way. This is the very stuff of which faction is made. A man who knows with all his being — his heart and soul and mind — exactly where the New Jerusalem is, and how to get there, cannot listen patiently to those who claim they have discovered another city of light along another road. God does not misguide His saints; there is but one God, one road, one goal. Strait is the way and narrow the gate. As

for the ways and the gates other men see, they are no greater
in number than the wiles of Satan to mislead weak and foolish
mortals. And the light other men follow is no real light; it is
but the "darkness visible" that serves for light in Hell. They
who are not with God are against Him; and it behooves the
pure in spirit to join together and wage relentless war on the
enemies of the Lord, to unite in exposing the false prophets
who would lead innocents down the broad road to the City of
Destruction. So in periods of revolution men join in little
groups, small bands of true believers clustered about the
altar of some exclusive doctrine, ready to defend it against
all enemies, ready to spread its light, should the chance come,
through the world. Each band is powerfully bound together
by the conviction of its members that in a hostile world, full
of knaves and fools marked out by God for destruction, they
alone possess the truth that saves, and that in a day not far
distant the sons of light will triumph over the sons of darkness
and rule in the New Jerusalem.

Times of revolution are times of disillusion — disillusion for
the faiths that fail, disillusion scarcely less painful for the
faiths that triumph for a while. Many of the factions revolution breeds never even touch the reins of power; but without
power they cannot make the world over in the image of their
dream. With the ever-longer postponement of the great day
of triumph, the brethren who are weak in spirit or strong in
sense tend to lose their zeal for a cause that begins to appear
hopeless. Only a small and increasingly fanatical core remains
and abides the day. Even while they wait God's help, the zealot
factions split and subdivide into a myriad of sects, too deeply
engaged in their internecine doctrinal squabbles to see the specter of counter-revolution that menaces them all equally. When
the counter-revolution comes, the sects quickly decline or dis-
appear entirely. Because only a handful of true believers have
found hope in each tight little sectarian Utopia, when the first
generation of the prophets dies or is scattered, the fires die
before the altars of their faith, and men soon forget that such
a hope ever was.

Disillusion comes to the factions that succeed in a revolution as to the factions that fail. In the vision of revolutionary factions there is always a persistent element of eschatology; the day of their triumph must be a new day when men are born anew in truth. Such notions of governance as the factions have presuppose a world peopled with saints or with men of reason and virtue. From this high peak of hope to the real problem of governing a real world peopled with real men, in whom the Old Adam refuses to yield to the New, the descent is steep and painful. Yet successful revolutionaries must make that descent or, refusing to rule such men in such a world, draw back to their dreams to wait again for the true dawn of the true day. The revolutionaries who accept power may for a time cherish the hope of remaking the men they must rule. Soon or late, however, if they are to retain power, they must learn the bitterest lesson of all; they must learn to compromise, to come to terms with a world of men they never made and cannot altogether remake. As the revolutionists become preoccupied with the hard, unfamiliar problems of political control, the time set for attaining the Heavenly City recedes further and further into the future, and the present Kingdom of the Saints takes on more and more the color and the shape of that worldly kingdom the saints once rose to destroy. It is then that the successful revolutionary idealist suffers his deepest humiliation. His old companions in faith, whose fervor has not been damped by disillusioning contact with a real political world, turn on him. He has betrayed all the noble things that they and he aspired to; he has compromised with evil. And in his heart the revolutionary knows a terrible thing: either his old friends are right, or the very dream itself was somehow wrong.

The Puritan Revolution produced its full quota of mirage, faction, and disillusion. Many men set out to remake the world according to the Word of God as they read it in Scripture with the eyes of faith or according to the desires they found in their hearts. But different eyes found different meanings in the Word of God they read; heart's desire differed from heart to heart; and out of this diversity emerged a vast variety of revolutionary Utopias. The first mirage to stir an important faction of Puritans was the Presbyterian Heavenly City, dear to the heart of the old Puritan clergy, wherein all Englishmen, good and evil, saved and damned, would enjoy the somewhat rigorous delights of the godly discipline.[1]

The Presbyterians soon found their way blocked by the Independents,[2] who would have none of the Genevan-Scottish theocracy but found their ideal in the "New England way" of the Massachusetts Bay congregations.[3] Close on the heels of the Independents a more fantastic generation of dreamers came to the fore. The Fifth Monarchy Men, impatient of Presbyterian and Independent palliatives, expected and prepared for the speedy second coming of King Jesus and the millennial reign of the Saints.[4] The men called Levellers took the egalitarian element in the Christian tradition so seriously that they proposed to establish English government on a democratic basis.[5] The Diggers went even further. To the naïve democracy of the Levellers they added an even more naïve communism of their own.[6] Presbyterians, Independents, Fifth Monarchy Men, Levellers, and Diggers were only the more prominent architects of ideal societies who flourished in England during the Puritan revolution. There were a dozen madder and merrier builders of New Jerusalems. The proliferation of Utopias reached an appropriate climax in the pious zany

---

[1] *The Platforme of the Presbyterian Government* (1644); Lightfoot, "The Journal of the Assembly of Divines," *Whole Works of the Rev. John Lightfoot,* vol. xiii, *passim.*

[2] On the conflict between Presbyterians and Independents see Shaw, *English Church,* I, 149–205, 238–297.

[3] *An Apologeticall Narration* (1644); John Cotton, *The Way of the Churches of Christ in New England* (1645).

[4] Louise F. Brown, *Political Activities of the Baptists and Fifth Monarchy Men* (1912).

[5] Theodore C. Pease, *The Leveller Movement* (1916); George P. Gooch, *English Democratic Ideas in the Seventeenth Century* (1898), pp. 118–133, 166–174; *Clarke Papers,* ed. C. H. Firth, 4 vols. (1891–1901), I, 303–305, 317–318.

[6] Lewis Berens, *The Digger Movement* (1906).

who with his wife set out in a rowboat to convert the Pope, and was never heard of again.[7]

So it went. No dream was too weird for some men to dream it, no hope too wild for some to hope it. In the pulpit, in the press, and from tubs on the city streets the hawkers of political and religious panaceas cried up their own wares, cried down the wares of their competitors, and cursed whatever government was in power, while most Englishmen went about their business and said little but began to feel a nostalgia for the good old days when a man could make a rough guess at what was going to happen next. The fanatics bickered and fought and conspired year in, year out, and then the Stuarts came back, and silence was the end of all their noise. They soon forgot their old dreams, or came to doubt them, or by easy stages transported them from this world to a happy land beyond the grave. In a generation or so the only living reminders of ideas that once shook England were the Dissenters, that pale progeny of fathers who had wrought mightily for their God. Republican and democratic and communistic ideas vanished. John Lilburne [8] was the shadow of a half-forgotten name,[9] and Gerald Winstanley's name was altogether forgotten.[10] The Good Old Cause was a bogeyman to scare the politically infantile. Oblivion was the end of mirage and faction and disillusion.

[7] For the story about the Quaker who went to convert the Pope, see William Tindall, *John Bunyan, Mechanick Preacher* (1934).

[8] Prof. William Haller has laid bare the Puritan foundation of Lilburne's political radicalism in *The Rise of Puritanism* (1938), pp. 272–287.

[9] For a sketch of Lilburne's life see *D. N. B.*, article Lilburne, John (1614?–1657).

[10] For a treatment of Winstanley see Gooch, *op. cit.*, pp. 182–191, and Berens, *op. cit.*

CHAPTER IX

THE MIDDLE GROUP

ALTHOUGH some Civil War factions endured through a decade or so of senile decay before expiring, none remained in full vigor for more than a few years, and many disappeared with incredible speed. Of all the short-lived factions of the forties and fifties, Pym's middle party had the shortest career as an organized group. It held together for a year and a half from the outbreak of the war to the beginning of 1644. Then, shortly after Pym's death, it came to grief on the issue of the Committee of Both Kingdoms.[1] The short life and sudden political demise of the middle party raise the question of the place of that party among the Civil War political groups and the more general problem of its ultimate significance in the unfolding of English history.

Two characteristics peculiar to the middle party serve to distinguish it at once from all later Civil War factions. In the first place there was in the rather limited range of middle-party political ideas no room for a Utopia. In the second place the political doctrines of the middle group outlived the party itself not by years but by decades. They finally found a place among the basic principles of both the Whig and the Tory parties.

To isolate the principles of the middle group is not easy. In the early months of the Civil War the Houses set forth declaration after declaration to justify their resistance to the King, but the declarations contain no clear statement of political doctrine. They are inconsistent, incoherent, and confused, and for our purposes utterly useless.[2] In the story of the Long

---

[1] Wallace Notestein, "The Establishment of the Committee of Both Kingdoms," *American Historical Review* (1912), XVII, 477–495.

[2] John W. Allen, *English Political Thought, 1603–1660* (1938), I, 386–412.

Parliament we must go all the way back to the Grand Remonstrance of 1641 before we come to anything we can call
the political program of the middle group. The court party
and the moderate Royalists opposed the Remonstrance. A few
men later connected with the peace party spoke for it. But the
brunt of the work of putting it through fell on our old aquaint-
ances John Glynn and Sir Thomas Barrington and Sir John
Clotworthy, on Richard Knightly, Hampden's son-in-law, and
Arthur Goodwyn, Hampden's closest friend, and especially
on Hampden himself and on John Pym. The Remonstrance
was essentially a middle-group measure.

The Grand Remonstrance was the apologia of the House of
Commons.[3] The members were about to demand that the
King choose as his advisors men who had the confidence of
both Houses.[4] They had to make that extraordinary demand
seem reasonable and just. In the Remonstrance they brought
history to their support. They did so by telling the tale of
Charles I's reign as they understood it. The villains of the
piece are the wicked advisors of the King — false councillors,
bishops, and "Jesuited Papists." [5] The hero is Parliament.
From the account of evil doings of the villains and the pious
works of the hero we can get an insight into the political ideals
of the middle party. According to the Remonstrance the villains aimed to romanize Protestantism, to root out the people
called Puritans, and to transform the English commonwealth
into a despotism where every man's liberty and property would
be at the mercy of the King.[6] In order to gain their ends
Charles's malignant advisors tried to "maintain continual differences and discontents between the King and the people upon

---

[3] Gardiner, *Constitutional Documents*, pp. 202–232. The story of the Grand
Remonstrance is told by John Forster, *The Debates on the Grand Remonstrance*
(1860), pp. 202–371. The defects of the Forster account are dealt with in
Gardiner, *History of England*, IX, 71–79. The names of the tellers in divisions
are in the Commons *Journal* (II, 317, 322, 324). An account of the debates
is in *Verney Papers*, ed. J. Bruce (1845).

[4] Gardiner, *Constitutional Documents*, pp. 205, 231–232.

[5] Gardiner, pp. 206–207.

[6] Gardiner, pp. 215–216.

questions of prerogative and liberty, . . . to suppress the purity and power of religion," to form an alliance of Papists, Arminians, and Libertines against true Protestants, and "to disaffect the King to Parliament." [7]

In all the misdeeds of Charles I during the early years of his reign the Remonstrants saw the hand of the false councillors, the bishops and the Jesuited Papists — in the disastrous foreign adventures, in the forced loan, in the dismissal of Chief Justice Crew, in the abuse of quartering and martial law, in the illegal detention of the five knights, and in the nullification of the Petition of Right. They blamed the same insidious malefactors for the iniquities of the eleven years of prerogative rule — for forest fines, distraint of knighthood and monopolies, for the persecution of the Puritans and the friendly entente with Rome, for the oppressive activities of the High Commission and the Star Chamber, for the collection of tonnage and poundage and ship money without the consent of Parliament, and, worst of all, for the intermission of Parliament itself so that the aggrieved people could find no redress or remedy. The evil advisors continued active even after the summoning of the Long Parliament. They had but lately mixed in the wicked schemes of the Papists, in two army plots against Parliament, and even in the low dealing that provoked a Catholic rebellion in Ireland.[8]

All these things the middle group hated; and what they hated they blamed on Charles's evil advisors. For our understanding of the middle party, what they hated is scarcely less important than what they loved. In a way what they hated is more important than what they loved, since the positive program of the middle party is little more than the measures sponsored by them in Parliament to eradicate the things they hated and prevent them from ever appearing again. The main part of the positive program of the middle party we find in the statute book, imbedded in the Petition of Right and the legislation of

[7] Gardiner, p. 207.
[8] Gardiner, pp. 208–215, 224–228.

1641. A tone of parental pride suffuses the Remonstrance when it describes the positive achievement of the Long Parliament in its first year.[9] The Houses have put down the prerogative courts used by the malefactors around the King for curtailing the liberties of the subject; they have reëstablished the credit of a bankrupt monarchy and at the same time, by outlawing ship money and subjecting the collection of tonnage and pound-age to the consent of Parliament, have made arbitrary exac-tions by the King once and for all illegal; they have partially reformed the Church; they have provided machinery for the regular summoning of Parliament, so henceforth the people may always voice their grievances in the assembly of their chosen representatives; finally they have brought to justice some of the wicked councillors to whom all England's woe is due.

On the middle group program of reform, as we find it in the Grand Remonstrance, stand only two major items of un-finished business, only two really important things left to do. The first is to finish the reform of the Church, root and branch. The second is to remove the false advisors who still have the King's ear and to substitute for them ministers in whom the Houses have confidence. The Remonstrance was constructed with a sound sense of dramatic values to make the strongest possible case for giving the Houses a veto over royal appoint-ments. The Commons set out their plan of reform; they called the history of the whole reign to witness that reform was doomed as long as the King took advice from men who hated all the work the Houses had done. In the Remonstrance the middle party implicitly asked the people to choose between the par-liamentary plan of reform and the King's prerogative of seeking advice wherever he saw fit. In setting out its plan of reform the middle party spoke little of things to do; save in the matter of church reform it spoke mainly of things already done. It pointed not to a goal in the future but to the solid achieve-ment of the recent past, to the great constructive work of the

[9] Gardiner, pp. 221–223.

Long Parliament. That work had aimed at putting the King's prerogative under law to prevent forever the rise of an arbitrary despotism in England. In the early days of the Civil War the Houses insisted that they fought to preserve the King's just prerogative, the privileges of Parliament, and the liberties of the subject. The reforms of 1641 were the citadel of that prerogative, those privileges, and those liberties.

If the Grand Remonstrance is the crucial document for understanding the middle party, if it contains the fundamental program of that party, then between the middle party and later Civil War factions there is a real distinction. The Levellers, for example, demand as ends in themselves changes in the structure of English government and policy that are frankly subversive. In the main they justify their proposals by an appeal to the Law of Nature, interpreted in a revolutionary egalitarian sense. The Leveller program is meaningless apart from demands for abolition of tithes, disestablishment of the Church, religious freedom, and political equality. In the middle-party program the one strictly revolutionary element, parliamentary veto over the royal choice of ministers, is an afterthought. It is justified not as an end in itself, but as the only available guarantee for what Parliament had already done. What Parliament had already done was written into the statute book for all to see, and of what Parliament had written into the statute book in 1641 the overwhelming majority of Englishmen who cared anything about politics approved.

We may call both Levellers and middle party revolutionary factions; but, when we do so, we should realize we are making the word "revolutionary" serve in two very different capacities. The Levellers were revolutionaries consciously and intentionally. The middle party was revolutionary casually, accidentally, almost unconsciously. The one patently radical element in its program, the demand for control over the King's advisors, did not emerge from premises which middle-party men would have regarded as generally valid; it was forced on them by a course of events that none of them foresaw when they began their work of reform. They had become radical through force of circumstance. Even their rather vague desire to reform the Church root and branch was no new thing; Puritanism had a pedigree at least as long as Anglicanism. The rest of the program of the middle party was moderate enough for a Royalist to subscribe to; in fact many Royalists did subscribe to it. That was the trouble with the program of the middle party; for the time at hand it was too moderate. The time at hand was a time of revolution. And times of revolution are times of mirage, when limited objectives and concrete achievement look grey and dull beside heroic dreams and apocalyptic visions. After 1643 politically effective men forgot about the program of the middle party. Indeed, if one wanted to be effective politically in the midst of the violent upsurge of revolution, one had to forget about it.

Yet neither the disintegration of the middle group nor the emergence of Utopian radicalism could destroy forever the work of the party. When the clamor of the doctrinaires died down and the excitement of new ideas began to pall, voices long silent started to speak again. What they said was what the men of the middle party had said in the days before the war: England is a royal commonwealth, not a despotic monarchy; Englishmen are free, not slaves of the state; the will of the ruler of England must be bound by the known law, else no man's property and liberty can be secure.

On January 1657 Mr. Ash rose in the House of Commons to move "that His Highness would be pleased to take upon him the government according to the ancient constitution. . . . Both our liberties and peace and the preservation and privileges of His Highness would be founded upon an old and sure foundation."[10] George Downing seconded Mr. Ash's motion, saying,

[10] Thomas Burton, *Diary of Thomas Burton, Esq.*, ed. J. T. Rutt, 4 vols. (1828), I, 362–363.

Those governments are best which are upon . . . the long experience of our ancestors . . . such whereby the people may understand their liberty and the Lord Protector his privilege. . . . Constitutions never fall. . . . I cannot propound a better expedient for the preserving both of His Highness and the people than by establishing the government upon the old and tried foundation.[11]

Mr. Ash was an old Long Parliament man. George Downing would ride out the Restoration, play an unsavory part in sending some of his old republican colleagues to the scaffold as regicides, and die in 1684 full of riches, years, and dishonor.[12] Thus were the old and the new, the man of the past and the man of the future, conjoined in the first demand in Parliament since the death of Charles I for the reëstablishment of the kingship.

Had Ash and Downing been alone in seeking to press the crown on Oliver Cromwell, their action would have been interesting but not especially significant. They were not alone. A few months later, eight years after the Rump, declaring that the kingship was "unnecessary, burdensome, and dangerous to the liberty, safety, and public interest of the kingdom,"[13] had abolished the office of king in England, a clear majority of a Puritan Parliament petitioned Oliver Cromwell to accept the crown. A committee chosen by the House explained to the Lord Protector the reasons for the petition. One of the committeemen spoke in this wise:

The office of King is a lawful office, and the title, too, approved by the word of God; that is plain. It is plain likewise it is an office that hath been exercised in this nation from the time it hath been a nation, and I think it is true that there never was any quarrel with the office but the mal-administration. . . . The name of king is a name known to the law, and Parliament doth desire that your Highness would assume that title. . . . You are now Lord Protector of three nations by the Instrument (of Government) and there is a clause . . . that you should govern according to law, and your Highness is sworn to that government.

[11] Burton, I, 363–364.
[12] For Downing's career see *D. N. B.*, under Downing, Sir George (1623?–1684). [13] Gardiner, *Constitutional Documents*, pp. 384–387.

Yet, though this is the case, Parliament fears that under the Instrument the people cannot feel safe in their liberties, nor can the Lord Protector exercise his executive office effectively. The existing establishment provides no sure foundation for either government or people. And this is the reason:

A King hath been through so many ages of this nation and hath governed this nation by that title and style, that it is known to the law; for the law of the nation is no otherwise than what hath been accustomed to be practised and hath been approved by the people to be good. That is the law. . . . Now they have been governed by that title and by that minister and by that office. If so be Your Highness should do any act, and one should come and say:

"My Lord Protector, why are you sworn to govern by the law, and you do thus and thus as you are Lord Protector?"

"Do I? Why, how am I bound to do?"

"Why, the King could not do so."

"Why, but I am not King. I am not bound to do as the King. I am Lord Protector. Show me what the law doth require me to do as Protector. If I have not acted as Protector, show me where the law is."

. . . However some may pretend a King's prerogative is so large that we know it not (and that) it is not bounded, . . . the Parliament are not of that opinion. The King's prerogative is known by law. He [Charles I] did expatiate it beyond the duty; that is the evil of the man. But in Westminster Hall the King's prerogative was under the courts of justice, and is bounded as well as any acre of land or anything a man hath. . . . And therefore the office [of King] being lawful in its nature, known to our nation, certain in itself, and confined and regulated by the law, and the other office [of Protector] being not so, that was . . . the reason why Parliament did so much insist upon that office and title, not as circumstantial but as essential.

The speech does not represent the opinion merely of the speaker. "What we speak here is no other but that which we can understand was the sense of the Parliament in justification of that which they have done." [14]

[14] "Monarchy Asserted to be the Best, Most Ancient and Legal Form of Government," *Somers Tracts*, ed. Sir Walter Scott, v, 358–359. Scott erroneously attributes the speech to Glynn.

The speech is a noteworthy presentation of the ideas of the middle party, but more worthy of note than the intrinsic merits of the speech are the extrinsic circumstances — the time of it, the speaker of it, and the man to whom it was spoken. The time was thirteen years after the middle party had disappeared as an active force in politics. Had that party been as later Civil War factions were, the faint echo of its watchwords would have been hardly audible so long after the party itself disappeared. The speech of 1657 was no mere faint echo of the ideals of 1643; it was a resounding reaffirmation of them. The speaker asked for a king, and one might suppose that, after a decade and a half of revolutionary unrest and turmoil, in asking for a king he was asking for a strong man, an arbitrary despot who would bring order out of chaos by a ruthless use of iron hand and iron heel against any opposition. It is not unusual for a time of political ferment and disruption to prepare the way for a time when men are ready to pay the price of peace with the coin of liberty. The speech hints at no willingness to pay such a price for peace; the king the speaker wants is no dictator. Rather he wants a king as a bar to dictatorship, a monarch ruling under the law and regarding the law as the most precious jewel of his crown, a ruler whose right is as clearly bounded as any acre of land in England, a middle-party king.

The speaker was Oliver St. John. He had been Solicitor General to Charles I, and during the first year of the Civil War he stood close to Pym. In 1644 with Sir Henry Vane, the younger, he deliberately set out to undermine the position of the too-moderate Earl of Essex.[15] He finally succeeded; but his success destroyed the unity of the middle party. In his attack on Essex he had used the Scots; but he broke with them on the church issue and guided the efforts of the Inde-

---

[15] The evidence on which is based the statement that St. John and young Sir Henry Vane deliberately set out to ruin Essex is too complex to set forth here. The materials on which the conclusion is based are the sources already used in this volume and Robert Baillie, *Letters and Journals of Robert Baillie,* ed. D. Laing, 3 vols. (1841–42), vols. I–II.

pendents to sabotage the "Godly discipline" in England. In the crisis of 1647–48 he sided with Cromwell and the New Model, and to enemies of army rule and radicalism the two Olivers became the symbol of all iniquity. Although he took office as Chief Justice of the Commonwealth, he was shaken by the execution of the King. But Oliver St. John was a religious zealot, so the complete triumph of the army of the Republic cleared away his misgivings. In that triumph God had declared Himself; and when God speaks, erring mortals must cease questioning and be silent.[16]

The man Oliver St. John, who had so long forsaken moderate courses in politics and religion, was in 1657 an eloquent advocate of the moderate way of the middle party, the way of monarchy under the rule of law. St. John's was a split personality. With him, as with all men who see God's hand in every victory, might establishes a strong presumption of right sanctioned by the divine will. Yet the zealot did not have full sway over Oliver St. John. Living in the same body was a brilliant common-law pleader, the man who had argued Hampden's cause in the case of ship money, the man of precedent and legal lore, the enemy of arbitrary power, who believed that the best guarantee of the liberty of the people was the old established custom of the land. The zealot and the man of the law could never be altogether at peace with one another, and the struggle of the two for supremacy that went on in the heart of Oliver St. John must have taken place in the breast of many another Englishman whose religious enthusiasm consorted ill with his common-law rationalism. While the curve of revolutionary fever rose the religious enthusiast was in the ascendant, drinking deep of intoxicating hopes, dreaming of and striving for a world made new. In England the revolution reached the crest of extremism in 1653 with the summoning of the Assembly of Saints. From that time there was a gradual falling off, a period of awakening and slow painful sobering. Then men like

---

[16] *Original Letters and Papers of State Addressed to Oliver Cromwell*, ed. J. Nickolls (1743), p. 24.

St. John began to look at the world about them less with the
eye of the religious enthusiast and more with the eye of the
lawyer. What they saw, the lawyer in them did not like. They
saw confusion, lawlessness, violence; they saw puppet governments of undefined power, and they saw that the army held the
strings controlling every puppet government; they saw what
to a lawyer must always be an ugly thing — the rule of military
force, of might, where the rule of law, of right, should be.
Looking back over the events of many years — the violent and
lawless dissolution of the Rump, the violent and lawless execution of the King, the violent and lawless purge of Parliament
by Pride's men, the violent and lawless coercion of Parliament
by the army in 1647 — such men finally came to the days when
men were taking up arms not to destroy the law but to defend
it from the violent and lawless will of Charles I. As their hope
of remolding the world grew faint, they came to want with an
insistent longing a settled and lawful way of government;
and in the changed world in which they found themselves they
tried to establish such a government. St. John carried the good
will of many men with him when he spoke before Lord Protector Cromwell.

By arguing that the advantage of kingship lay in the legal
limits it imposed on the power of the ruler, St. John tried to
persuade Oliver Cromwell to accept the crown. Cromwell at
the time was military dictator of England, Scotland, and Ireland, "a person having power over three kingdoms without
bound or limit set." [17] The common law meant little to Cromwell. If he was ever exposed to its mollifying influence, the
effect had long since worn off.[18] Yet St. John tried to persuade
him to accept a kingship as clearly bounded by law "as any
acre of land." One does not usually try to please an autocrat
by prescribing a limitation of his power; but St. John, better
than most men, knew his Cromwell, and knew that the Lord

---

[17] Thomas Carlyle, *Letters and Speeches of Oliver Cromwell*, II, 373.
[18] Wilbur C. Abbott, *The Writings and Speeches of Oliver Cromwell*, I
(1937), 32–34.

Protector, too, had come back to moderate courses and fondly aspired to lead England along them. Less smoothly perhaps than St. John, but no less warmly and no less persuasively, Oliver Cromwell made his plea for a tempered monarchy, for the government of one man and a Parliament, a government under a law so firmly founded that all the winds of doctrine would blast it in vain. He who had torn through many bonds of the law now asked men to stop tearing through the bonds of the law. If England was to be saved from anarchy, it must have a law "fundamental, somewhat like Magna Charta, that should be steady and unalterable." Without such a firm foundation no system of laws, said Cromwell, would be safe from the tampering of each successive legislature. "Would it be lasting? It would be like a rope of sand. It would give no security, for the same men may unbuild what they have built." [19]

During the years of the Protectorate, Cromwell used his great powers to return England to a moderate and civil way of government. He restored a bicameral legislature. He promulgated a set of fundamental laws. He established a broad Puritan Church organization. He gave his ear to civilian councillors of temperate views. But no assiduous display of the velvet glove could hide the unpleasant truth that, under the Protectorate as before it, the real source of Cromwell's power was the iron hand of the army. The civilians knew it, and — what was worse — the army knew it. Not sharing Cromwell's enthusiasm for the resumption of civil government, the army set a limit to the signs he might give of the integrity of his intentions. Such gestures as the army allowed him were not enough to eradicate the deep distrust of moderate men for one who reached his high position only by using military force against the civil power. It was the last irony in the life of the most magnificent failure in English history that Oliver Cromwell should die trying to transform a military dictatorship into a lawful monarchy. The attempt was predestined to frustration because with the best of will he could not shake himself free

[19] Cromwell, *Letters and Speeches*, II, 382.

of his own past. Too late he learned that there is more than a literal meaning in the words, "He who takes the sword shall perish by the sword."

In one sense Cromwell did not fail. Though he himself could not establish a secure legal monarchy in England, he prepared the way for a man with a less dubious political background to achieve what he could only attempt. This, perhaps, rather than his own failure was the ultimate irony of Oliver's career: that, all unknowing, the head of the House of Cromwell planted the seed for the head of the House of Stuart to reap the fruit. Cromwell's measures prepared the minds of Englishmen for the return of their legitimate king; but it was not by measures only that he cleared the way for the Restoration. His conversion from experiments in doctrinaire Utopias to the idea of reconstruction along moderate monarchical lines resulted in and was emphasized by the drift back into politics of Pym's old middle-party followers. They might with some justice have insisted that they did not drift at all, but simply stood still and waited for politics to drift back to them. Whichever way it was, certainly many old middle-group leaders had by choice or compulsion retired from politics in 1649. Most of them stayed out up to 1653. Then after the failure of the effort of Barebones' Parliament to raise up the New Jerusalem on England's broad and sunny fields, Saints began to give way to old Parliament hands in high offices of government.[20] Pym's nephew Nicholls, one of eleven members impeached by Cromwell's army in 1647, took his seat in the Protectorate House of Commons. John Crew and Sir Richard Onslow, arrested in 1648 for their attempt to make peace between King and Parliament, became Lord Crew and Lord Onslow in the Protectorate's "Other House." Gilbert Gerard, who in 1643 faithfully defended the Earl of Essex against war party and peace party, had been purged along with Crew and Onslow by Cromwell's soldiers. He became Lord Gerard of the Cromwellian creation.

[20] No adequate study of the personnel of politics under the Protectorate has ever been made.

Lord Say and Sele's second son Nathaniel, the brightest of the Fiennes tribe, which had found itself unable to stomach the Commonwealth, stepped out of retirement and into the office of Lord Commissioner of the Great Seal under Protector Oliver. Finally there was John Glynn, former recorder of London, the very model of a moderate middle-group man, whose career Cromwell's soldiers had lopped off in 1647. They had him put out of the House and dismissed him from the recordership; and when he did not flee with the rest of the eleven members they clapped him into jail. But under the new Cromwellian dispensation he first edged in, and then up and up, until he became Lord Chief Justice of the Protectorate. So Cromwell by the measures he introduced and by the men he trusted for advice on their administration moved toward a middle way of government. In so doing he unwittingly began to prepare England for the return of Charles II. And it was in part because the men of the middle group had come back into politics under Cromwell to bridge the gap between two eras that the Restoration in England was on the whole the mildest reaction that ever followed an epoch of revolution.

When the shrewdest of the Stuarts came back from his travels, he consigned the Puritan Revolution to legal limbo. He dated his reign not from the bright day in May 1660 when after a long absence he again set foot on English soil at Dover, but from the dark January day, eleven years before, when his father's throat lay bare on the block for the stroke of the executioner's ax. After the Restoration no court in the land could recognize as valid any enactment of any English assembly passed since March 1642. In form and law almost two decades of English history were as if they had never been. Yet it lay not in the power of Charles II or of any man to set the clock all the way back.

When Charles II assumed the crown, he assumed with it all the statutes duly enacted defining the powers the crown gave him. Among those statutes were the measures the Long Parliament had passed before the complete breach with Charles I.[21] The legislation of 1641, which the Stuart of 1661 accepted, outlawed the prerogative jurisdictions — High Commission, Council of the North, Star Chamber — that had enabled his father to circumvent the common law. It specifically denied to the King the right to raise money by any extraordinary means and made the customs duties, one of the principal regular sources of royal revenue, depend on the grant of Parliament. It thus anchored the King to Parliament. He must either finance the government in a parliamentary way or resort to expedients not merely extraordinary but patently illegal. Taken with the Petition of Right, the statutes of 1641 halted the advance of prerogative government and made certain that the law should be the King's will and not the King's will law. By denying the King direct control of the two most valuable possessions of his subjects, their liberty and their property, the Long Parliament had provided Englishmen with as much assurance as the law could give that the island kingdom would not become a despotism on a pattern then à la mode on the Continent.

The middle party had supported the great reform statutes of 1641 which set the limits on the Stuarts who returned in 1661. That alone gives its members a certain claim to distinction, but for that distinction they are not the sole claimants. The legislation of 1641 was not the private property of the middle-party men; in it they were but copartners. Men later of the peace party and moderate Royalists of the stamp of Hyde, Falkland, and Southampton had a full share in the early work of the Long Parliament. Of the groups responsible for placing insurmountable obstacles in the path of despotism, the moderate Royalists might with some show of reason boast that they had played the wisest part, since in the Restoration settlement they most nearly achieved their avowed ends. While the peace party and the middle party demanded a thorough remodeling of the Church of England in a Puritan sense, the

[21] For the legislation of the Long Parliament, see Gardiner, *Constitutional Documents*, pp. 144–155, 158–162, 179–197.

moderate Royalists were content with the Church as it stood after Parliament had taken away High Commission. It was not the austere church of the Puritans that the Restoration settlement established, but the church of the moderate Royalists, with all its endowments and all its Popish frippery. What the middle group got at last for all their insistence on root and branch reform was the Act of Uniformity, the Corporation, Conventicle and Five-Mile acts — the Clarendon Code.

Not only did the moderate Royalists come out better than the middle group in the Restoration settlement; they also out-theorized them at the beginning of the Civil War. Professor J. W. Allen has recently analyzed what he calls the "War of Manifestoes," the exchange of polemic that immediately preceded and accompanied the early stages of the real war between King and Parliament.[22] In the paper war, he points out as the Royalists did three hundred years ago, the Roundheads come off a poor second. On the King's side the declarations are clear, pointed, and consistent. Consistency seems to have meant nothing to the men who framed the apologia of Parliament. Not one of their declarations justifies the position of the Houses in the same terms as the preceding and succeeding declarations. Not only is the whole case of Parliament as presented in the sum of its manifestoes incoherent, but no single proclamation carries much conviction. Individually and as a whole the parliamentary declarations of 1642 and 1643 are ambiguous, obscure, and at times a little stupid. In one paper the Houses, disingenuously misinterpreting the law or citing a precedent that was no precedent at all, would claim something like full sovereignty for the two Houses without the King. In their next effusion they were likely to deny that they intended, made, or even suggested so radical a claim.

The theory has been advanced that the confusion of the parliamentary declarations stems from the reluctance of the men who wrote them to state their case clearly. The tendency of history in England, so the theory goes, was to exalt the

[22] Allen, *English Political Thought*, pp. 386–412.

representative body over the King. The middle-party men vaguely understood this but feared to say so; hence the confusion.[23] There is, however, a simpler explanation of the confusion of the parliamentary manifestoes. Those manifestoes show confusion on the surface because confusion is at the very core of them. They are the work of confused men, men in a predicament they did not envisage until it was upon them. The members of Parliament had to call soldiers to arms to fight against Charles I; they had called soldiers to arms to fight against Charles I; but, until shortly before they acted, they had never intended to do any such thing. The men who wrote the manifestoes were confused because they started to resist the King before they thought through the implications of resisting the King.

The declarations of the Houses indicate rather clearly that the Civil War was not the result of premeditation by the parliamentary leaders. They did not plan it; they did not foresee it. They were intelligent politicians. When intelligent politicians are at a loss to justify their deeds in a crisis, it is a fair guess that they did not expect the crisis. Had men of the caliber of Glynn, Hampden, and Pym thought in terms of armed resistance to the King before the Civil War, they would not have so ignobly muddled their attempt to justify armed resistance when the war broke out. They would have had a real answer to the Royalists, not a mere hodgepodge of fumbling non-sequiturs.[24]

The leaders of Parliament had never expected to take up arms against Charles I, and this in part explains their inability to justify their resistance to him. Still, once they found themselves in the middle of a Civil War, they might have picked any old justification of resistance that happened to be handy and used it for whatever it was worth in the way of propaganda. Unfortunately, no justification of resistance happened

[23] Allen, *op. cit.*, p. 397.

[24] It was by no means impossible to build a case for Parliament on a sound constitutional foundation. See Appendix B.

to be handy in the political tradition in which most of the Roundheads lived. They could not choose a story and stick to it, because the folklore of respectable squires and lawyers in the first half of the seventeenth century contained no stories in which decent men fought against their king. And almost everyone in the Civil War House of Commons was either a respectable squire or a respectable lawyer. In the political legends they had been raised on, kings were always reasonably virtuous and just, and the good subject was always obedient; and if an occasional king was not just, the good subject was obedient anyhow.

For a hundred years the obedience the subject owed the ruler had been the theme of orthodox English political theory. Men of many faiths and divers tempers had applied themselves to embroidering on the political doctrine of St. Paul:

Let every soul be subject unto the higher powers. For there is no power but of God; the powers that be are ordained of God.

Whosoever therefore resisteth the power, resisteth the ordinance of God; and they that resist shall receive unto themselves damnation.

Romans 13:1–2

In the sixteenth century the obedience of the subject to his lawful ruler was not merely desirable or useful; it was the very will of God. With equal fervor men on either side of the great religious controversy condemned resistance to the Lord's anointed. There were Catholic martyrs and Protestant martyrs — More and Fisher, Latimer and Ridley — who gave up their lives rather than stir active opposition to the ruler God set over them, though that ruler was a heretic. The Elizabethans were even more emphatic than their predecessors on the wickedness of disobedience. The anarchy of the War of the Roses was a living story to many of them; the anarchy of confessional strife in the Low Countries, France, and Scotland was a grim present reality just across the Channel or over the border. It is little wonder that in an age of faith men saw in the turmoil around them a sign of the hand of God punishing rebellion. The thin barrier that shielded England from anarchy was the unquestioning acceptance by Englishmen of the obligation to obey Elizabeth and protect her from all enemies. Under the circumstances *vox reginae* came very close to being deemed *vox Dei*. The feeling was natural enough. And Elizabeth was nothing loath. She encouraged the powerful public sentiment in favor of docility. The homily on "Disobedience and Wilful Rebellion," the work of an Elizabethan divine, must have been exactly to the Queen's taste.

> How horrible a sin against God and man rebellion is cannot possibly be expressed according unto the greatness thereof. For he that nameth rebellion nameth not a singular and one only sin, as is theft, robbery, murder, and such like; but he nameth the whole puddle and sink of all sins against God and man; against his Prince, his country, his countrymen, his parents, his children, his kinfolk, his friends and against all universally; all sins, I say, against God and all men heaped together nameth he that nameth rebellion.[25]

Such was the opinion of resistance to the ruler instilled into Englishmen by the most powerful organ of propaganda the time afforded, the pulpit of the Established Church.

Those very words about the cursedness of rebellion many Roundhead members of the Long Parliament had heard once a year since they had become of an age to go to church. What was worse, they could find no surcease from the demand for obedience even among their own spiritual ancestors, the Elizabethan Puritans. Those ancestors had grave fears of what God would do to England, if the realm were not shortly reformed unto righteousness; but they did not pretend for a moment to any right of rebellion in themselves or others in any circumstances whatever. "For procuring the reformation of anything we desire to be redressed in the state of our church, we judge it most unlawful and damnable by the word of God to rebel, and by force of arms to seek redress thereof." [26]

Only out of the dark and disreputable byways of Tudor

---

[25] *Certain Sermons or Homilies* (1864), pp. 609–610.
[26] John W. Allen, *A History of Political Thought in the Sixteenth Century* (1928), p. 223.

political thought came any defense of active disobedience to the ruler. One small group of men maintained that a prince who refused to rule religiously, lawfully, and justly not only might be disobeyed but should be disobeyed, overthrown, and deposed by the people.[27] This doctrine, considerably elaborated, might have quite well suited the book of the middle-party leaders, if it had emanated from just a reasonably presentable source. From the point of view of those leaders, however, the doctrine had the worst possible associations. It came from Catholics; more, it came from Catholics particularly fit to be blasted with the blighting epithets of Jesuitical and papistical. It was the work of émigré Englishmen who would have been quite willing to bring a Spanish army into England to force their mother land back into the Catholic fold.[28] Thus the one justification of rebellion that appeared in English political thought in one hundred and fifty years was doomed at its birth by a congenital taint. No one, not even the Jacobean Catholics, would have anything to do with it. For the Puritans of the early seventeenth century to adopt a theory so patently infected with Jesuitism was impossible.

While the justification of rebellion was neglected by the men who soon might need it, others developed, extended, and refined the doctrine of obedience. Boldly they came to grips with the crucial issue: What is the duty of the Christian subject of a heretical prince? With the splendid Christian fortitude of men who have no heretic prince in prospect the later Elizabethans accepted the doctrine of Latimer, who burned at the stake for his conviction, "When laws are made against God and His Word, then I ought more to obey God than man. Then I may refuse to obey with a good conscience; yet for all that, I may not rise up against the magistrate or make any uproar; for if I do so, I sin damnably. I must be content to suffer whatsoever God will lay upon me." [29] If the prince would lead you

[27] Allen, *History of Political Thought*, p. 261.
[28] Allen, *History of Political Thought*, pp. 199–209.
[29] Allen, *History of Political Thought*, p. 128.

to sin against God, follow God and suffer. Whatever else the prince commands, obey. Resistance to a ruler merely because he is a despot, because he takes your property and destroys your liberty, is not to be thought of. Though he make you a slave, yet he does not destroy your soul, which is, after all, what counts.

The doctrine of obedience was a theological theory of the state. It emphasized the divine origin of political authority, and surrounded that authority with a sacredness and an awfulness not of this world.

> Not all the water in the rough rude sea
> Can wash the balm off from an anointed king;
> The breath of worldly men cannot depose
> The deputy elected by the Lord.

This theological theory of political power had its most fervent exponents among the clergy of England and especially among the section of the clergy that found favor in the eyes of the earthly majesty it exalted. The more extreme Laudian churchmen were most vigorous in calling down divine judgment on subjects who presumed to question the duty of unfaltering obedience to the royal will in all matters secular.[30]

Nevertheless there were men in England in the seventeenth century who within limits disobeyed the King's will in secular affairs as a matter of course and right. They represented a tradition in English politics at least as old as the theological tradition the clergy upheld. The tradition was medieval and feudal in origin and respectable enough to have become imbedded in the ordinary procedure of the common law. For the sake of contrast we may call it the legal doctrine of the prerogative. Its chief proponents were the lawyers. Their basic conception was that the king's personal authority was not unlimited but defined by law. Any act of the King in Council affecting the lives, liberty, and property of the sub-

---

[30] For some extreme examples of the High Anglican position see *Select Statutes and Other Constitutional Documents Illustrative of the Reigns of Elizabeth and James I*, ed. G. W. Prothero (1913), pp. 357–359.

ject might be challenged in the courts of justice where the judges declared the law concerning the limits of the royal prerogative. In order to secure a test of the validity of the king's commands one had to make an issue of it in court by refusing obedience to the royal officer charged with enforcing the royal mandate. This limited kind of resistance forced a test of the king's prerogative in impositions and ship money and less directly in forced loans and imprisonment without cause shown. Far from holding that a subject must obey the personal mandate of the king, the legal doctrine of the prerogative imposed on the subject an obligation to disobey any mandate he deemed illegal until the voice of the law had spoken.

The legal doctrine went no further. It did not contemplate a situation where the king disregarded the declaration of his courts. Yet that is precisely what Charles I did in the matter of the forced loan. It did not provide any remedy against a king who, by dismissing independent judges and appointing subservient ones, procured a judiciary as amenable to his will as his own Privy Council. Yet the decision in the case of ship money showed that the King was on his way to securing just such a judiciary. The exponents of the legal doctrine of the prerogative refused to face the critical issue that Charles I's policy raised. Their impotence in the face of a policy that challenged every political tenet they held dear dramatizes the ascendancy the doctrine of obedience held in the minds of men who had every reason to shake themselves free of it. For a quarter of a century they had witnessed a trend of events the meaning of which they could not miss. Yet, while events moved, the legal doctrine of the prerogative stood still. It continued to stand still right through the eleven years of prerogative rule. In its old form it could not cope with the new condition of affairs. James Whitelock had as early as 1610 removed it from its old medieval framework of *dominium* and set it in the modern framework of sovereignty; [31] but nobody followed up Whitelock's work or developed the implication of it until 1643.

[31] For Whitelock's position see Appendix B.

Selden's dictum on the case of ship money is a sort of final petition in bankruptcy of the advocates of the old legal doctrine. If the King continued to collect ship money and avoided expensive follies (which he actually did not do) he could make himself as effective a despot as any in Europe. Yet after the decision in the Hampden case, Selden's counsel was the counsel of despair. "They that first would not pay ship money till it was decided did like brave men; . . . but they that stand out since and suffer themselves to be distrained . . . do pitifully, for so they only pay twice as much as they should." [32] Once a matter became *res judicata*, by whatever means the judgment of the court was secured, the adherents of the legal doctrine of the prerogative threw up their hands. After every defeat they threw them higher until by 1639 they had achieved a grotesque posture of political submission not unlike the one that preachers of obedience recommended to the subjects of a wicked prince.

With the summoning of the Short and then the Long Parliament the proponents of a legally limited prerogative saw a chance to vindicate themselves and their doctrine. Squires and lawyers poured into the House of Commons, resolved to tie the King to the law so tight that he could not shake himself loose. To that purpose they enacted the great legislation of 1641. At the end of a year of hard work they found themselves back where they started. The King had agreed to the restrictions the Houses set on him; but only the optimistic could believe that Charles had really seen the light. To believe that, a man had to blot out the memory of fifteen years of Charles's reign, pretend that Henrietta Maria had no influence over him, refuse to believe in the army plots, and pass off the King's attempt to seize by force five members of the House of Commons in the midst of a sitting of the House as a mere *faux pas*. At the end of all its work Parliament had to put a sword in the King's hand to quell the Irish Rebellion — or to quell Parliament, which was more annoying and nearer at hand. The only real alternative was for the Houses to take up the sword them-

[32] John Selden, *Table Talk*, under "Ship Money."

selves. If they did so, they must expect to use it not against the rebel Irish merely but against their own lawful king.

At this point the leaders of the middle party made a decision, perhaps the most important decision made in two decades of revolution. With little hesitation and no clear theory they decided that rather than leave themselves and their work at the King's mercy, they would resist him, if necessary actively and by force of arms. In so doing they turned aside the main current of English political tradition from the channel in which it had flowed for more than a century. By refusing to compromise the work of the Long Parliament — as they would if they submitted to the King — by their determination to sweep aside legal scruples once they had decided that they must fight for their cause, by placing considerations of justice above considerations of obedience, the men of the middle party vindicated through action the right of resistance not only against tyrants but even against a legitimate sovereign who broke the law that bound his people to him. The Houses did not pretend that the King's church policy was heretical or that it in any way tainted the legitimacy of his title to the crown. They only took up arms against their rightful lord because — so they asserted — the King misled by evil counsellors no longer would do justice according to law, but conspired to use force against the liberties of his subjects. They justified their disobedience on purely secular grounds.

Every measure proposed, every policy pursued by the middle party in its year of power, served only to implement the initial decision to fight Charles I. Misguided by ill-disposed men he had done wrongfully, and until he would do his people right he must be resisted. To resist meant to wage war, to raise armies and equip them, to levy taxes to support those armies, if necessary to seek allies. But to resist did not mean to forget that there was by right a king in England, and that his name was Charles Stuart. Under the guidance of John Pym the men of the middle party disregarded the clamor of the fiery spirits for a violent anti-royal policy and disregarded the clamor of the peace party for a ruinous submission to the King. They hewed consistently to their line of conservative but uncompromising resistance, and their consistency left a permanent mark on English political life.

No less important than the fact of resistance was the character of the men leading it. They were not wild-eyed fanatics rising in a moment of hysteria to frantic revolt. They were men of substance and wealth, men of broad acres with a stake in the country. To Royalist accusations that the war was the work of loose-tongued agitators, crypto-republicans, and sectarian wild men, the almost cloying respectability of Glynn and Clotworthy, Stapleton and Arthur Goodwyn, Gerard and Onslow and Hampden stood as an irrefutable answer. Although under the leadership of the middle party the Houses passed from one warlike act to the next as the occasion demanded, they never deviated in their assertions of loyalty to the principle of monarchy, of fidelity to the Stuart dynasty, and of allegiance to the person of the reigning king. In the light of what was actually happening in 1643 Parliament's professions of undying loyalty may have struck Charles I as somewhat inconsistent with its treasonous proceeding; yet it was in that first year of civil war that the middle party gave the English conception of the right of resistance its traditional form.

When the Cavaliers came back in 1660, they had a great hate in their hearts for the work of the middle party, work that for many of them had meant years of poverty in exile. Although they maintained those limits on the royal power that had passed into law in 1641, they reaffirmed and magnified the old theological doctrine of obedience. That doctrine called down divine wrath on any who would raise a hand against the King even in defense of the political principles the Cavaliers themselves adhered to. In so far as they could, the returned Royalists wrote the theological doctrine, refined of all ambiguity, into the law of the land. No doubt could now remain that the power, according to Paul ordained of God, was in England in the person and will of the reigning king. Any sub-

ject who refused to disavow unconditionally any right of resistance to the king was disqualified from holding municipal
or ecclesiastical office in the realm. The doctrine of nonresistance became "the distinguishing character of the English
Church." Clergymen denied hope of salvation to any man who
doubted the absolute unlawfulness of rebellion. The universities echoed the voice of the Church and burned all books that
maintained the right of the subject for whatever reason to disobey the king.[33] With press and pulpit thundering condemnation of the sin of disobedience and commination against all
resisters, one only listening to what men said, and not watching
what they did, might think that the work of the middle party
had been all in vain.

Yet even in listening one might detect a note of hysteria in
the Royalist denunciations of disobedience. The tone is not
that of men quiet and sure in the integrity of their convictions,
but that of men who carry a devil of doubt in their souls and
seek to exorcise it by denying its presence. The men of the
Restoration are a little like believers shaken in their faith,
who seek to reassure themselves by nervously reiterating its
formulae. Indeed they did protest too much. At the root of
their trouble lay an ineradicable inconsistency in their most
cherished political beliefs; along with the theological doctrine
of obedience they continued to cherish the legal doctrine of
the prerogative, and the middle party had shown unmistakably
that the latter doctrine might lead to rebellion. With the wisdom of the serpent or of his blessed maternal grandfather
Henry IV, Charles II perceived that the coat of loyalty his
Cavaliers wore was not so without seam as they proclaimed it
to be. He learned how much strain their loyalty would bear
by experimenting on it twice with declarations of indulgence to
Protestant and Popish dissenters. When the Cavalier Parliament after profuse expressions of eternal loyalty answered
the second Declaration of Indulgence with a Test Act, the one

[33] William E. H. Lecky, *History of England in the Eighteenth Century*, 8 vols.
(1878), I, 9–10.

Stuart who always learned and never forgot had his lesson. He doubtless would have gladly traded off a good deal of Royalist profession of unresisting compliance to the king's will for a little practical willingness on the part of the Royalists to give the king what he wanted. When he found no such willingness in that great prop of the monarchy, the Tory party, Charles II made it his business to ask for only such things as that party would be pleased to give him.

Charles II, epigrams to the contrary notwithstanding, was a wise man. He probably understood better than the Tories, who held it, whither the legal doctrine of the prerogative tends. He knew that the logic of that doctrine leads ultimately not to the obedience of the moderate Royalists of 1641 but to the armed resistance of the middle party. He may have realized, too, that, deeper than the logical incompatibility, a profound divergence in feeling and temper separates the theological from the legal doctrine. The inspiration of the former doctrine is essentially religious, that of the latter essentially secular and utilitarian. The one can only flourish in a mysterious atmosphere thick with pious awe and hushed reverence. The other thrives in the cold clear air of rational debate. Whatever their professions of faith may be, men cannot feel that the king is the very living image and deputy of God on earth and at the same time consider him, as Selden puts it, "a thing men have made for their own sakes, for quietness' sake; just as in a family one man is appointed to buy the meat." [34]

Selden's analogy has in it both the logic and the emotional level of the legal doctrine of the prerogative. He continues, "If every man should buy or if there were many buyers, they should never agree; one would buy what the other liked not, or what the other had bought before, so there would be confusion. But that charge being committed to one, he according to discretion pleases all; if they have not what they would have one day, they shall have it the next, or something as good." [35] One can conceive of the king as an earthly replica

---

[34] Selden, *Table Talk*, under "King."   [35] *Ibid.*

of Heavenly Majesty; one can think of him as a handy meat-buyer maintained for quietness' sake; but the combined conception of a divinely appointed meat-buyer is emotionally, if not logically, self-contradictory. Yet each aspect of this contradictory conception of royal power was formed in a matrix of ideals very dear to the Tory heart, and, as long as he could, the Tory clung to his composite picture of monarchy and disregarded the implication of the legal doctrine of the prerogative. The implication was obvious. If the man in charge persists in buying meat that no one in the family likes, it is time for members of the family to look to their rights and make him please them, or put in charge someone else who will. Stripped of all respectful verbiage, the legal theory of monarchy implies that the bonds of obligation binding the subject to his ruler are broken when the ruler destroys the very law by which he reigns. In such a political attitude there is no room for divine will, divine wrath, or divine right. Such was the lesson of the revolt of the Houses under the leadership of the middle party in 1642. The Tories tried hard to forget that lesson forever, but they did not succeed. They remembered it most effectively in 1688.

For a time, however, their rhapsodic descriptions of the beauties of nonresistance had the effect of shutting the eyes of the Tories to things they did not want to see and their minds to thoughts they did not want to think. They did not want to think that under any circumstances they would follow the example set by the middle party in 1642 and resist the King under the aegis of the legal doctrine of the prerogative. They did not want to see "that no logical process could reconcile the Tory political theory with their constitutional sense," and that the sterility of Katherine of Braganza and the conversion of James Stuart to Catholicism had prepared a set of circumstances fit "to strip off the intercepting veil of enthusiasm and to leave that inconsistency naked, repulsive and challenging." [36]

James II was a rare historical phenomenon, a man with a

[36] Keith Feiling, *History of the Tory Party, 1640–1714* (1924), p. 202.

truly unlimited capacity for making mistakes. Following the
history of his reign is a little like watching a tragic drama
played at such a breakneck pace that it becomes funny. In
three years James managed to do nearly all the wrong things
that his father, Charles I, had done in seventeen years. In
1685 he was crowned king of a people who yearned to respect,
obey, and love him. After a few months of harmony he began
to try the patience of his subjects to see how much they would
endure. Most of his subjects were Tories. He tried their
patience through the three years of his reign by a deliberate
campaign against the two English institutions closest to the
heart of the Tories — the Church and the law. As his father
had followed a policy ideally suited to combine Puritan squire
and common lawyer against him, so James did all he could to
join Anglican squire and common lawyer against him. He
cleared from the bench all judges who implied that the King
of England could not do exactly what he pleased. He dispensed
with penalties incurred for violating an act of Parliament,
the Test Act; and when his packed judiciary upheld him in this,
he proceeded to suspend the operation of the statute entirely.
He replaced loyal Anglicans in high office with Jesuits and
men who changed their religion to the shift of the political
wind. He turned colleges in England's two universities into
seminaries for Roman Catholic priests. Then he tried to force
the Anglican clergy to read the Declaration of Indulgence from
the pulpit. Years of careful calculation could not have produced a measure better suited mortally to offend the Tories.
The Anglican clergy had to read their congregations a document patently designed to destroy the Anglican establishment.
The Tories were invited to witness the wrecking of the Church,
a wrecking to be achieved through a flagrant violation of the
law of the land. James had not completely disregarded the
advice of his judges, as Charles I had done in the matter of
the forced loan; he had not levied taxes without the consent
of Parliament, as Charles had raised ship money; he had not
tried to coerce Parliament by armed force. But Englishmen

in 1688 might reasonably feel that not moderation but lack of the need or of the opportunity restrained James, that, given the chance or the necessity, the inclination would not be wanting. No more than their fathers and grandfathers in 1640 could the men of 1688 afford to blink at the fact that their king was governed by a fixed and rooted disinclination to submit his will to that legal definition of the royal prerogative which Englishmen deemed the main safeguard of their liberty and property.

The Tories could not deceive themselves forever. The king who ruled them was a king they could no longer trust, a king who was using his power to destroy much that they held dear, but also a king with a divinely sanctioned claim on their obedience. The Englishmen of 1688 were in a situation nearly analogous to that of the Long Parliament men in 1641. They had come to a parting of ways. Consciously and with premeditation the Tories had to make a choice between hard alternatives. They must follow the theological doctrine of obedience or the legal doctrine of the prerogative. Consciously and with premeditation, they chose. They engaged in a vast conspiracy to resist James II's will by force of arms; they planned to raise forces to achieve their purpose; they tried to disaffect the officers of the army to the King's service; they schemed to supply their own army of rebellion with the necessities of war; they invited foreign aid to carry their project to a successful conclusion. In a few months they did what it took the middle party a year and a half to induce Parliament to do during the Civil War. The prime movers in preparing the subjects of James II for rebellion were the seven men who invited William of Orange to invade England. It was they who "broke the ice and dared to pretend that reasons might be offered to justify disobedience." [37] Of the seven, three — Danby, Lumley, and Compton — were Tories. Of the three, one — Compton — was a bishop of the English Church. The seven who wrote to William were only the beginning of a plot that as it ripened

[37] Feiling, p. 224.

toward execution involved literally thousands of men, including the most eminent Tories in the realm — bishops, dukes, earls, generals, and admirals.[38] Like the members of the middle party in 1642, these men had decided to resist their lawful king and to take all the steps necessary to make that resistance effective. It may be said that while the middle party had scarcely half the nation behind it, the men of '88 acted as the channel of a well-nigh unanimous public opinion. This is true. Yet it is not irrelevant to reflect that the unanimity of England in the Glorious Revolution may owe more than a little to the pioneer work of resistance to an untrustworthy prince that the middle party undertook in the Civil War. Men find a thing less difficult to do if someone has done it before; and once the cords of the doctrine of obedience had been snapped, it did not need much initiative or courage to snap them again.

From the moment the Anglican clergy refused *en masse* to read the Declaration of Indulgence that James commanded them to read, the Tories had embarked on a course of action leading straight to revolt. They had taken the political line not of the moderate Royalists but of the middle party. In 1688, with anguish and foreboding, no doubt, but none the less thoroughly, the Tories shook loose from the doctrine of non-resistance and followed the legal doctrine of the prerogative along the path the middle group had opened in 1642. The Tories said that King James had broken the law and in so doing had forfeited his claim on the obedience of his subjects.[39] They were saying what Pym and his friends had said almost half a century before. Having said what Pym and his friends had said, they proceeded to do what Pym and his friends had done. What the Anglican clergy offered as an excuse for disobedience, the Tory laity used as an excuse for rebellion. In the critical hour of the history of the party the Tories acted as heirs not to the moderate Royalists, who trusted and obeyed, but to the middle group, that doubted and rebelled.

[38] Feiling, p. 226.
[39] *Cobbett's Parliamentary History of England*, 36 vols. (1806–20), v, 32–108.

CHAPTER X

PYM

WE HAVE now surveyed the history of the middle group and dealt with what we may call its indestructible essence. If instead of trying to see the middle group as a whole over the whole period of its active existence, and even beyond, we examine it minutely at any single moment in its career, we lose the sense of its fundamental unity. We hear a Babel of voices and see a muddle of men — Puritans of various hue and intensity, the officers of the Lord General's army, the great Hampden-Barrington connection, a not altogether reliable set of City fathers, an equally unreliable set of London ministers, and a scattering of independent members of Parliament. And, seeing and hearing, we do not wonder that an alliance constructed of such miscellaneous materials, drawing its strength from the bonds of interest in one case, family ties in another, religious sympathy in a third, political agreement in a fourth, and common fears in a fifth, one day collapsed. It was full of inner tensions and vulnerable points, and that it fell apart at the death of John Pym, who had held it together, is nothing remarkable. The really remarkable thing is that in the midst of defeat, disappointment, and panic it did for a time actually work as an effective political entity, and that by means of it Pym built a war machine that would occasionally fight without completely destroying a debating society much more anxious to talk.

Such was the dual aspect, the essential nature and the ephemeral structure, of the group Pym led in 1643. What of the leader himself? What was the basic policy behind his fascinating display of tactics? What was the motive and the profit and the goal of all his labor? We will try to answer these questions; but let us first point out a simple assumption we intend to make about Pym.

After living a while on terms of intimacy (historically speaking) with a great man out of the past, the historian is bound to become curious about the springs of action which moved that man, in modern terms is bound to ask sooner or later what made him "tick." In working out an answer to that question the author usually wrestles with an old, old dilemma: Was this man conscientiously seeking the public weal or was he trying to win power for himself? In our search for the springs of action that moved Pym, we will simply disregard the dilemma. It seems reasonable to assume that a man without ambition rarely lands on top of the political heap. To get there a man must want to get there; to stay there a man must want to stay there, must fight to stay there. Pym landed on top of the political heap, and he stayed there for three years in the midst of a revolution. He fought to stay there. So Pym was ambitious; that is, he wanted power. So did Edward Hyde, and Oliver Cromwell, and William Laud, and Henry Vane. Yet none of these men wanted power merely for its own sake. In a quarter of a century the uses they made of the might they fought for led two of them to the block, one to death in exile, and one to undisputed rule of England, Ireland, and Scotland; the uses they made of their power, the ends they aimed at, were worlds apart.

So we shall assume that Pym was ambitious and wanted power, and shall ask why he wanted it and what he did with it when he had it. Even with this limitation our problem is anything but simple. History rarely grants her devotees a "natural" like Pepys, who for years pours out his whole mind and what he has of a soul on paper, so that he who runs may read the man in his writings. Yet anything less than Pepys is something less than satisfactory. The latest monumental study of Cromwell reveals to us how unsure we must always be even of those who have left big tracks for us to examine in the record of the past.[1] Cromwell scattered his soul abroad in writing, sporadically but frequently, for a quarter of a century; yet when we

[1] W. C. Abbott, *Writings and Speeches of Oliver Cromwell*, vols. I–II.

read the record of everything he is known to have said and done we still wonder whether he was the Archangel Michael or Old Nick. Very likely we join the greatest authority on the subject in concluding that Oliver Cromwell was not altogether the one or the other, but at least a little of both.[2] If this is the closest we can come to a judgment on Cromwell, who so freely opened his heart to so many friends, how can we hope to understand Pym, who, as far as any evidence we have goes, opened his heart to no one at all? Actually the only intimate glimpse of Pym we get, the only sign we have of what once was a strong surge of feeling, is a letter of stern parental warning he wrote his erring son Alexander. Even this is well-nigh useless. Since we have no notion of the scope or nature of Alexander Pym's fall from grace, we cannot guess whether John was an outraged righteous father or a nasty ill-tempered martinet.[3]

Yet this lack of any data on the personal life of Pym is only the beginning of our difficulties. Far more embarrassing is the lack of the faintest trace of Pym's political opinions in the years when his opinions would have given a master clue to the inner man — that is, in the two decades that followed his death. The times that would have really tried his soul came only after he had been safely tucked underground in Westminster Abbey. Instead of decently conforming to the Aristotelian canon and beginning *in medias res*, the tale of John Pym ends *in medias res*. It breaks off, as it were, in the middle of a chapter and leaves us wondering how the story was supposed to come out. When there is merely the ordinary dearth of evidence to go on, the historian, in a sense, plots his subject's actions as a series of points on the events he lived through and then, considering all the points, tries to get a picture of the general curve and direction of his subject's life. Thus with young Henry Vane we can follow his career through a sufficiently varied set of happenings to feel in the end that we have some understanding of his own peculiar curve, of the man's

[2] Abbott, I, esp. pp. 401–759.
[3] For Pym's letter, see C. E. Wade, *John Pym*, p. 339.

place among other men of his time. Vane lived until his actions made a fairly complete, consistent, and intelligible pattern on the background of events; Vane lived until it was logical for him to die, and then Charles II in a moment of happy inspiration took his head off. So it was with Vane.

So it was not with Pym, who inconsiderately died just a few months before things began happening that would have forced him to reveal himself to us. Up to 1643 Pym's political curve was almost perfectly congruent with the curves of a dozen other men who followed strangely divers courses in the decades that come after 1643, but what course Pym would have taken we can never know and can hardly guess. Yet for one little clue as to how he would have reacted to the Committee of Both Kingdoms, the new modeling of the army, the Parliamentary church settlement, and Pride's Purge we could afford to give away half of Pym's politician speech-spinning and still be richer in our understanding of him.

As a politician Pym did and said whatever seemed best suited to his general purpose in a particular set of circumstances. If circumstances once in a while required that he say one thing and do another, who but his enemies and a handful of purists would presume to criticize? And he was too old a hand in Parliament to let carping from such sources bother him. We must be careful, however, in evaluating even his most eloquent enunciation of noblest principles. Perhaps we must be most careful when Pym's principles seem most noble. His speech on the majesty of the common law, the law which alone keeps the bounds between good and evil, is brilliant, powerful, fine, a truly moving thing. He may have believed every word he said on that occasion at the time he said it, and, if he did not, at least a lot of other people did. It is not beside the point, however, to notice that the object of this fine oration was to secure the judicial murder of the Earl of Strafford by a piece of dubious special pleading which the impeached lord at once tore to bits.[4] Pym's love of the law had about it a certain quality of inter-

[4] John Rushworth, *The Tryal of Thomas Earl of Strafford* (1680), pp. 661 ff.

mittency. He turned it off when he praised the London mob
for rioting on the right side, and when he argued as few of his
associates dared or desired to argue, that while the common law
was a fine thing in fine times, necessity imposed another sort
of law in civil war, and that for the nonce legal arguments were
a waste of energy.[5] In his religion, too, he combined a judicious
amount of Puritan zeal with a judicious vagueness as to particulars, so that he always left himself enough room for a
graceful about-face. In 1641 Pym wanted to reform episcopacy and the Prayer Book, not to abolish them; [6] but in 1643
he did not scruple to advocate the uprooting of the former and
the outlawing of the latter as a *quid pro quo* to the Scots for
marching an army into England.

His attitude on this matter of church reform in relation to
the Solemn League and Covenant was refreshingly frank and
simple. It contrasted favorably with the line taken by a number of his "unco guid" fellow members. Some of the godly
commoners raised loud paeans to the Scots and indulged in
an orgy of frantic adulation of the Covenant, which their later
treatment of both Covenant and Scots proved to be either
hypocrisy or self-deception. Other members had a hard tussle
with their consciences before they could agree to the utter
extirpation of episcopacy. Pym took the very forthright position that if you really wanted a commodity in a seller's market, you had to pay the seller's price for it, and that in the
particular case in point Parliament would be justified in turning
over to the Scots anything short of their own souls in return
for the Covenanting army.[7]

In one of the debates on the Covenant, Pym laid bare the
workings of his mind as he had rarely, if ever, done before.
John Glynn had proposed that the oath for the extirpation of
prelacy be struck from the body of the Covenant or modified
because bishops might in part be lawful and consistent with

[5] *Y.*, 18777, fol. 92.
[6] *Clar. H. R.*, bk. vii, par. 410.
[7] *Y.*, 18778, fol. 30.

the Gospel. He had qualms about taking an oath to uproot them when they might be reformed to righteousness.[8] Pym by leave of the House answered Mr. Recorder. "Suppose," he said,

that a law is in some points deficient. Can we not lawfully make a new law so long as the former law may be reformed? Though bishops may be reformed in time, yet we are in a present necessity. We must take care to remedy our present necessity, and not stay for a convenient time to reform the bishops; for in the meantime we may be destroyed. If a man have a disease in his body and a medicine in his hand to cure it, but before he can take it one comes to him sword in hand to kill him, shall he not cast away his medicine and betake himself to his sword; or shall he take the medicine and suffer himself to be killed? [9]

Pym's analogy was not rhetorically neat, but it made the main point clear and made it quickly. Pym took little delight in the flowers of rhetoric for their own sake but only in so far as he could use them in wooing the House of Commons.

What was the main point as Pym saw it? Simply that in politics men must ask not what is ideally best but what is the best possible under existing conditions; and that when those conditions include civil war the distance between the ideally best and the really best may be painfully great. The stateman who always does what he ought to do, forsaking all worldly considerations, may store up a treasury of grace for himself in Heaven, but he will achieve precious little here below; and Pym was not made for the blessed role of martyr-statesman. To him half a good cause still alive was infinitely more valuable than the best dead cause in the world. Given perfect freedom to choose, he, as well as Glynn, might have preferred a purged episcopacy to any other form of church government;

[8] *Y.*, 18778, fol. 30: "It may be there is something of Episcopacy lawful and may consist with the Gospel. How then can I swear to extirpate that which I am persuaded being purged may consist with the propagation of the gospel. Therefore he would have us add one word to the explanation of the assembly — *present government*, for the present government is abominable."

[9] *Y.*, 18778, fol. 30.

but that freedom did not exist. If one could only get the Scottish assistance necessary to save the remainder of a good cause by throwing over the bishops, why, then one had to throw them over, and one did it, and there was an end to all argument.

Pym's analogy of the intruder with a sword in his hand gives us a vivid insight into his conception of the events for the three years preceding his death. In 1641 Parliament had set about ministering to the ills of the body politic, a very sick body indeed. Yet those were happy days when for a time it seemed that what could be done for England and what was best for England were one. Before the cure was finished, while the nation was yet but half healed of its sickness, the enemy, the man with the sword, came against it. So the cure must be suspended to save the life; for a partly cured England was better than an England with the spirit and the cause and the life killed within it. Since the day when the enemy, the man with the sword, had broken in, there had been little time for the curative work of reform. And that work must be postponed yet a while, and some part of it perhaps even sacrificed, if the patient was to be saved alive from the assault of the enemy. Pym knew that Parliament had to have the help of the Scottish army to stave off the onslaught, and since Parliament had to have it, Pym was ready to take the quickest and the surest way to get it, leaving no lingering doubt as to his motives. The Solemn League and Covenant which to militant Puritans was a thunderbolt of God wherewith to smite the Romish harlot was to Pym just another, but a very necessary, weapon of defense against the enemy, against the man with the sword in his hand, against Charles I of England.[10]

Perhaps in that last phrase "against Charles I of England" we have the most consistent note in Pym's career. Others in Parliament may have had as good or better reason to dislike

[10] In reading over what I have thus far written I note that I have instinctively taken Pym's point of view and described even his most aggressive ordinances as part of his "program of Parliamentary defense." However those ordinances may appear under the aspect of eternity, I am quite certain that Pym thought of them as defense measures.

Charles — holders of royal forest lands whom he dispossessed, unruly northern men whom he had reduced to order, common lawyers whose courts he tried to undermine. Some members certainly had better reason than he to hate Charles — Rouse and Tate, who had seen the austere religion they loved trampled on at the King's behest, and a decorated idol set up in its place; [11] Strode and Valentine, who had suffered at his hands eleven years of imprisonment without trial. But none of these knew so immediately the things Pym knew about King Charles, none had so carefully traced the tortuous line of his trickery, none had been so early informed of each new instance of his deceit.[12] Of all the members of the Long Parliament Pym had the most cogent reasons for distrusting Charles I. Strafford's supposed intention of landing an Irish force in England,[13] the army plot,[14] and the elaborate and unremitting intrigues of the Queen — Pym knew about all of them before they became common property. What royal plottings, how many subtle devices and underhand schemes, he heard of from that industrious busybody and cunning intriguer, Lady Carlisle, we cannot with certainty say; [15] but we know that for each step Parliament took toward reform the King planned a secret counter move showing his hostility to the change, and we also know that Pym learned of many of those contemplated counter moves only a little after the royal mind conceived them. So Pym's distrust of the King grew and grew, and he communicated that distrust to Parliament, both to the members who eventually followed him, and even to those who at last followed the King. Then Charles made his catastrophic mistake; he broke into the House of Commons with soldiers behind him

[11] Rous and Tate were probably the deepest-dyed Presbyterians in the House (Baillie, *Letters and Journals*, II, 120, 157, 198, 237, 333).

[12] It may be argued that each of Charles's ventures into deception was justifiable. The point is, however, that they were deceptions, and one cannot expect the men on whom they were practiced to justify, sanctify, and beatify them.

[13] Gardiner, *History of England*, IX, 229.

[14] Gardiner, IX, 317.

[15] Sir Philip Warwick, *Memoires of the Reign of Charles I*, p. 204; *Clar. H. R.*, bk. IV, par. 14, 78n, 149n; Gardiner, *History of England*, IX, 376.

and tried to arrest Pym and four other members. Pym escaped arrest; but from that day, says Clarendon, he was inveterate against the King.[16] By his violent breach of the privilege of the House, Charles I hardened against himself many hearts besides Pym's. Now others fully understood what Pym may have known all along, that the only way to keep Charles from cutting under their work of reform was to tie his hands. Since Charles naturally refused to be tied, his opponents could only choose between civil war and surrender. Pym realized that in a civil war between two parties, each distrustful of the other, the only outcome can be the submission of one or the other party. So he made it his business to see that the King submitted to Parliament, not Parliament to the King. It was, it seems, as simple as that.

If we seek further than this for the basis of Pym's policy, we are likely to reverse the customary procedure and miss the one real tree in a futile quest for an imaginary forest. We follow Pym's painstaking labors, his deft craftsmanship in making Parliament a relatively mobile and efficient instrument capable of waging war; and naturally we look for some grandiose ideal as the purpose of all his work. It is hard to avoid the conclusion that having forged and beaten Parliament into a well-tempered weapon he sought to conquer some new height with it, to cut through the enemy to some new goal of achievement. Vane and Cromwell, the great successors of Pym, considered and used Parliament as a means to an end; and when it would no longer serve, they cast it aside. The analogical argument from Vane and Cromwell to Pym is very simple and very tempting — and it will not work at all. Every effort to define the new goal that Pym was working toward fails. He was not a dogmatic republican like Martin [17] nor a staunch Presbyterian like Harley.[18] He never showed any sympathy for Independency, and his previous parliamentary career does not incline

[16] *Clar. H. R.*, bk. VII, par. 413.
[17] See, above, p. 60.
[18] *Correspondence of the Scottish Commissioners*, ed. H. W. Meikle (1917), p. 102.

one to believe that he yearned for a policy of religious toleration.[19] The attempt to ascribe any clear new ideal to Pym involves a fundamental misunderstanding of the man. Not a political theorist like Ireton,[20] and not a religious theorist like Vane,[21] he had nothing in him of the architect of brave new worlds. He was a political tactician, a political engineer.

One of the reasons for Pym's effectiveness as a political engineer was that he did not have to waste his time and energy fitting his actions to a new and unfamiliar plan or trying to fit the new plan to recalcitrant circumstances and situations. In straining our eyes to see Pym's great ideal beyond the horizon we overlook the commonplace little scheme right under our nose. Pym was a middle-party man, and such aspirations as he had were the aspirations of that group. For what it is worth we can bring the evidence of an *ipse dixit* to prove this statement. A few months before he died Pym wrote his political apologia. He called it a *Declaration and Vindication of John Pym, Esquire*. In it he roundly disavows "anabaptism, Brownism and the like." Of his "detestation of those gross errors . . . every man that hath any acquaintance with my conversation can bear me righteous witness." [22] Equally he detests the bishops; yet he detests them not for what they are but for what they have done. They have "punished men's bodies instead of serving their souls," and have introduced Arminian or Popish practices and ceremonies into the Church.[23] No private grudge against the bishops made Pym "adverse to their function, but merely my zeal to God's cause." He does not wage war against the bishops as individuals or even against prelacy as an institution. He fights lordly prelacy, the "too extended authority" of those "who according to the purity of their institution should have been men of upright hearts and humble

[19] Gardiner, *History of England*, IV, 242–243; VII, 36.
[20] For Ireton's political thought see *Clarke Papers*, I, 194–199, 294–303; Gooch, *English Democratic Ideas*, pp. 126–140.
[21] Sir Henry Vane, *Retired Man's Meditation* (1655).
[22] *Declaration and Vindication of John Pym, Esquire* (1643), p. 4.
[23] *Declaration*, p. 5.

minds." [24] In a word, Pym was not a fanatic and not a sectarian. Probably he was not even a Presbyterian. He was a militant Puritan. So was almost every associate of his in the middle party. So, for that matter, were a goodly number of his opponents in the peace party. The differential, if there was one, lay in the militancy, not in the Puritanism.

Pym's vindication of his politics is of a piece with his vindication of his religion. He does not deal with the accusations of republicanism leveled at him by the Royalists. Very likely he could not imagine that anyone would believe such palpable nonsense. He is more concerned to announce his unfaltering loyalty "to his Majesty," whom he acknowledges to be "my lawful King and sovereign, and would spend my blood as soon in his service, as any subject he hath." [25] Since he had for the better part of the year devoted his energy to devising methods for exterminating those subjects whose services the King accepted, Pym's declared zeal to spend his blood for Charles I looks like an act of supererogation by one already irretrievably damned. Yet there is a good chance that Pym meant what he wrote, that he believed, or very much wanted to believe, that no act of his went beyond what was "warranted by the known law of the land and authorized by the indisputable power of Parliament." [26] If Pym's actions and even his words in the House of Commons were not always completely consonant with his profession of faith, we do well to remember that perfect consistency is a virtue rarely vouchsafed to any but saints and philosophers. Pym was neither of these; he was a party leader, and in a party leader we have a right to expect only a rough general coincidence between profession and practice.

John Pym's *Vindication* is a dull piece of pamphleteering. The repudiation of sectarianism on one extreme and lordly prelacy on the other, the avowal of perfect fidelity to the King coupled with the determination to fight on until His Majesty returns to his duty as a lawful sovereign, the exaltation of

[24] *Declaration*, p. 6.
[25] *Declaration*, p. 6.
[26] *Declaration*, p. 7.

laws of the land and the indisputable powers of Parliament —
all these things had been done before and done much better
than Pym could do them. The *Vindication* is merely a belated
statement of middle-party policy, inadequate and uninspired.
But it is a statement of middle-party policy and nothing else.
It does not vary a fraction from the ideas common to the
whole group. It is in no sense an original piece of work; but
by the end of 1643 there was little room for originality in
expounding middle-party ideas, and such room as there was
we should not expect John Pym to occupy. After all he was
not a publicist.

Of course the argument *ipse dixit* demands confirmatory
evidence. In Pym's case his career as leader of Parliament in
1643 furnishes that evidence. If all the foregoing pages mean
anything they mean that Pym was leader of the middle party
in 1643, and that it was through the middle party that he ruled
the House. As long as the middle group held together, the men
in it remained under Pym's leadership, apparently confident
that his general aspirations were one with theirs. In evil times,
when some of his followers deserted to the right and some to
the left, he stuck immovably to his line until the deserters came
back to him. In doing so he was exercising a free choice. His
influence and prestige in Parliament were such that he could
have commanded any group he associated with and through
that group dominated the Commons. It would have been easy
for him in the summer of 1643 to desert the unpopular Essex
and take over the leadership of the then prevailing war party;
but he did not do so. Instead, endangering his control of the
House, he remained faithful to Essex and stood by him and
the policies they had maintained together. When a politician
risks a position of great power to uphold a particular policy,
we may be sure that whatever principles he has are somewhere
embodied in that policy. Pym stood by the middle-group policy
because he believed in it.

The historian is usually tempted to ascribe to the great men
he deals with some clairvoyance, some talent for anticipating

specific future developments. Thus in the late nineteenth century it was the custom to distribute halos liberally to all precursors of democracy. But whether we consider the anticipation of the future by three hundred years or one hundred years a sign of divine inspiration or a species of insanity, we must, if what we have just said about Pym is correct, eschew all such ambitions for him. In the main stream of moderate political thinking in the seventeenth century we find no distinct ideas of the shape of things to come. Isolated instances of what appear to be anticipations of the future can always be explained by reference to the past. The right to veto the King's appointments to the Council, demanded by the Houses in the Nineteen Propositions of June, 1642, seems to look forward to the whole development of responsible parliamentary government.[27] The privilege of reading history forward, however, is vouchsafed only to historians. For the men the historian seeks to understand, history unfolds itself not forward into the future but backward into the past. Where we look beyond the veto proposal in the Nineteen Propositions and see the great series of ministers responsible to Parliament — Walpole, and the Pitts, and Peel and Disraeli and Gladstone — Pym could only look back and see Strafford and Laud and Cottington, Weston and Buckingham, and more dimly, at the beginning of his political memory, Carr, Earl of Somerset, and the ravenous Howards. We must remember that to Pym and his like Burghley and Walsingham were only memories of a tale their fathers told them, while the almost living past was Black Tom Tyrant and the Archbishop of Canterbury, and the very living present was the mercurial Digby and the slippery Jermyn. Though some

[27] In connection with the Nineteen Propositions it is well to remember that the attempts of the politically active subjects of the realm to control the advisors of a King they had reason to distrust were as old as the days of Henry III and the Provisions of Oxford. From 1258 to the coming of the Tudors such attempts form a recurrent pattern in English politics. Among a people as conscious of their past history as the English were in the seventeenth century and under kings so incapable of understanding the conditions of their tenure of power as the Stuarts, a revival of the ancient tradition with regard to the King's councillors was almost inevitable.

dreamers may have had an inkling of what the future held for England, still busy men like Pym find a more powerful incentive to action in a sense of past grievances than in vague visions of things that are not yet. A future of responsible ministers had less to do with the demand for a veto power over royal appointments than a past of irresponsible ones.

So every other apparent anticipation of the future can be explained more plausibly as a reaction from the past or as a hasty remedy for a present difficulty. The claim Parliament put in for the right to ratify the future marital arrangements for the King's children was based less on a subtle plot to get an indirect control of foreign policy than on the simple and perfectly sound conviction that two or three more rounds of Spanish and French marriages would permanently wreck England. And what may appear to us as Parliament's outrageous attempts to seize sovereign power by controlling the militia probably represented to Pym only the age-old solution to an age-old dilemma: "If either thou or I must suffer, better it should be thou than I."

What distinguished Pym from his collaborators in the middle group was not any schism between them in theory; it was the intensity with which Pym realized this matter-of-fact dilemma. He was perhaps the first in England after Strafford clearly to grasp the fundamental truth, which Hyde only understood in later years, that in the pass affairs had come to between King and Parliament one could not grow greater without the other growing less. Pym might have preferred a reversal of Hyde's statement of the case: "The highest terms of honor and security for the Parliament could be neither secure nor honorable for the King."

The situation that made this true had developed rapidly during more than a decade. As Charles I cut through, one after another, the barriers that separated him from arbitrary power, the residual responsibility for restraining him fell upon Parliament. By collecting ship money he had wrenched himself free of the embarrassing alternative of living off his own or getting supply in a constitutional way. By the successive dismissals of

Crew and Heath, by appointing the judges *durante bene placito*, he had destroyed all hope that the ordinary courts of justice might keep him within the limits of the law. There remained only Parliament. Only to it could men look for redress of their grievances; so that by his very success in setting aside all other institutional restraints on his will the King had himself unwittingly magnified the importance of the Houses. And if the King was to become less, then Parliament must become greater still, because on account of the King's own acts and by his own showing Parliament was the only safe depository of powers he could no longer be trusted to exercise within the law. The Civil War only intensified the need for a weapon of defense against a king who when his hands were free had a dangerous itch to lay about him on all sides.

The forger of that weapon was John Pym, and the weapon he forged was the Civil War House of Commons. Looking back at it with a knowledge of what it became, we tend to see it as a sword. That is because we see the thing that Vane and Shaftesbury made of the House. If, however, we carefully focus our vision, if we try to see the House as it appeared at Pym's death, as it probably appeared to Pym himself, it has more likeness to a shield than to a sword. And yet it is neither. It is one in the process of becoming the other. It may well be that Pym had no clear idea what the instrument he was making would look like when he finished it. There have been other men like that in history. Gregory VII never seemed quite sure how great he wanted the Church to be; he was only sure that it could not stay as it was, and that if the Church was to become greater the Empire must become less. Luther, too, cried out for the liberty of the Christian man without precisely defining the extent of that liberty; but he knew that it must be greater than it had been, and that it could grow only at the expense of the Church of Rome. It was for the Urbans and the Calvins and the Shaftesburys to put the finishing touches on the structures of other men and to clarify the meaning of work that had been by no means clear to the worker. It was for Luther and Gregory and, on a smaller scale, Pym to build without knowing how well or how largely they built.

To men like Pym the blueprint, the design, means little; the functioning of the machine means much. If through some lack of foresight or of practical knowledge on the part of the designers, or through unforeseeable circumstances, the machine breaks down, the man of many expedients adds a gadget to make it work again. And to improve it yet further and to meet new emergencies he adds another gadget and yet another. And then he cuts out parts that were in the original design but that have since lost their function; and in the end he has a machine only vaguely corresponding to the plan he started from. Yet so engrossed has he become in his work that he is quite unconscious of the difference between the finished machine and the machine he began to build. So Pym no doubt would have in all sincerity maintained that the juggernaut he had constructed was that modest House of Commons called for by the scheme for a moderate legal monarchy. Wherein he illustrates the profundity of his greatest contemporary, who said that no man goes so far as he who knows not whither he is going.[28] Surely Pym did not know whither he was going; probably he did not even know how far he had already gone.

And so we search Pym's mind in vain for a consistent theory of state with even a touch of novelty in it. For him reality was not a theory of state; it was this day's battle and that day's treaty, a bill on the way to becoming an ordinance, this measure accepted and that measure dashed; it was the Grand Remonstrance with its hundred odd grievances, its dozen adopted remedies and its dozen more proposed reforms. The reality was not a theory of limited monarchy but Charles I, King of England, a man with a sword in his hand who could not be trusted. And when Pym fought, it was not against monarchy but against an untrustworthy man with a sword. The Nineteen Propositions and the articles of the Oxford treaty are not tentative constitutions of a new political order; they are the verbal

[28] Abbott, *op. cit.*, I, 472.

expression of the resolution of Pym and his friends to chain
up Charles of England on both sides.[29]

Parliament had to grow so that the Stuart could be tied.
Whether it ever occurred to Pym that it was unreasonable to
expect the King to accept impotency with good grace, we do
not know. Perhaps it did. His answer we may guess; good
grace or ill grace, surrender or fight, the King must be bound.
And Parliament must grow greater. Not to this or that or the
other importance in the constitution, but somehow and vaguely
greater. All who occasionally grasped that fundamental fact
were his allies. All rules and law must bow down before it;
an army must be kept in the field; an ally must be sought in
the north; and, above and before all, the men at Westminster
must present at least the semblance of a united front against
the King. To preserve the unity of Parliament and keep fighting
until Charles accepted his fate, that was the policy of Pym,
and it was a policy that as a dominant force in the history of
the Long Parliament died with him.

[29] The phrase is a modification of the slogan of John Selden, who wanted to
bind the clergy precisely as Pym wanted to bind the King (Selden, *Table Talk*,
under "Clergy").

APPENDICES

APPENDIX A

NEWSBOOK WRITERS AND OXFORD REPORTERS

IN dealing with political developments on the Parliamentary side the historian is frequently handicapped by lack of specific and discriminating information. There is a particular dearth of information on events outside Parliament that affected the action of the Houses. Dewes and Yonge usually give adequate reports of proceedings in the House of Commons, and Dewes occasionally indulges in a parenthetical observation on behind-the-scenes politics. Those observations are unfortunately infrequent. The Venetians occasionally report rumors of the schemes and devices of various groups in London; but both Giustinian and Agostini had insatiable appetites for anti-parliamentary rumors, and such precise news of secret doings as they got probably came from the Earl of Holland, with whom they had commercial dealings (*C. S. P. Venetian* XXVI, 199, 200, 212). Holland was not likely to be very reliable on matters he did not know about directly.

Since detailed news is so scarce, we must take it where we find it. We have two sources of spot news — London and Oxford. Our London news comes from the newsbooks that mushroomed into being mainly during 1643. Before we venture to use them, however, we must evaluate them and arrive at some conception of their accuracy. The intimate history of the London journals is an unexplored field. The only study of the "new journalism" is by J. B. Williams [Muddiman], *A History of English Journalism to the Foundation of the Gazette* (1908). The work is comprehensive, but the author's interest in the shades of parliamentary politics is too slight to make the book useful in determining fluctuation of opinion among the newswriters, or to enable us to judge the exact political connection of a particular newswriter. Godfrey Davies in his *Bibliography of British History* (1928) attempts to classify the various news-books, probably basing his surmises on Williams' work. The very first item Davies lists illustrates the futility of simple classification. It is *"The Kingdomes Weekly Intelligencer . . . Presbyterian"* (p. 244). Yet it is certain that, in the first two and a half years of the Civil War, there was no live sectarian issue among the factions in Parliament. It is also certain that the *Kingdomes Weekly Intelligencer*, a

"Presbyterian" paper, was in 1643 hostile to Essex, the future chief of the "Presbyterian" party. It is doubtful if the single word "Presbyterian" meant a great deal at any time during the Interregnum. Most assuredly in the first years of the war it meant nothing whatever.

The most accurate of the London journals, *The Perfect Diurnall* is not very useful, because, save for war news, it prints little beyond what can be found in the *Journals* of the House of Commons and the House of Lords. For new data one must turn to less reputable sheets: *Mercurius Civicus, The Parliament Scout, Certaine Informations, The Kingdomes Weekly Intelligencer.* Needham, who wrote *Mercurius Brittanicus,* is a hopeless liar. What one can find in the London newsbooks is a reflection of temper in London and the attitude of the more belligerent Londoners on parliamentary activity, both military and legislative. Scattered in with the more purely hortatory sections of the newsbook are occasional bits of news about affairs in the City. These reports and rumors in so far as they stick to London usually are verified by later events reported in more reliable sources. Thus, besides indicating the rising distrust of Essex in the summer of 1643, the newsbooks give us our first inkling of the plans and plots to get rid of him. This news, borne out by the later petitions of the City and a group of citizens, comes to us at a time when Yonge is silent altogether and Dewes has little to say.

Out of Oxford come occasional reports of London matters from Hyde in his *History of the Rebellion* and from *Mercurius Aulicus.* The question of Hyde's reliability has long been a moot point. C. H. Firth has analyzed in several articles the structure and date of composition of the great *History* ("Clarendon's 'History of the Rebellion,' " *English Historical Review* [1904], v, 26–54, 246–262, 464–483). He has shown to what a great extent Clarendon must have relied on a not too strong memory and a powerful imagination for his statements on parliamentary affairs after the middle of 1642. Most of Hyde's information came through rumor from London to Oxford, and Oxford was a poor place for even a rumor long to hold its own original shape. Moreover, Hyde wrote years after the events he describes. Most of what he says, then, is little better than the faded memory of dubious gossip. Yet there are occasions when the circumstantial character of Hyde's tales must give us pause. Both the abundance of detail and the rarity with which such full reports appear lead us to look further. There are two points at which we are treated to exceptionally lavish reports of parliamentary episodes. We get a particularized tale of Holland's attempt to seduce Essex into treason to Parliament in August 1643 (see p. 146, above) and another of the politics of the Self-Denying Ordinance in December 1644. In the latter case we know that royal emissaries were in London at the time, and that they were visited by members of the Houses. Probably their visitors were friends of the Earl of Essex, and from those friends they heard complaints about the queer dealings of the faction out to ruin the Lord General (*Clar. H. R.*, bk. VIII, par. 181–204). They carried the stories, already somewhat garbled, back to Oxford, where Hyde heard them. He carried them around in his head for a number of years and then wrote them into the *History*. So the details of the affair are confused, and yet the general account on basis of more direct evidence seems to be sound. Again, in the Holland-Essex affair, Hyde had an extraordinary source to draw on. When Holland fled from London to Oxford, he was coldly received. Only Hyde befriended him (*Clar. H. R.*, bk. VII, par. 189), and one may well imagine that Holland poured out his tale to Hyde at a time when it was fresh in his memory. In several details of the affair Clarendon receives independent corroboration from Dewes (*D.*, 165, fol. 150). So here again Hyde's narrative is probably the best we have. In general we may say that, when there is good evidence that Hyde could tap a special source of news, his story, despite inaccuracy of detail, is likely to contain a kernel of substantial truth.

Mercurius Aulicus is doubly damned. He is an Oxford reporter and therefore removed from his source of information on parliamentary affairs. He is a pamphleteer rather than a news retailer, and in the capacity of Royalist pamphleteer is a conscienceless liar of the same magnitude as Marchmont Needham on the parliamentary side. Yet we cannot dismiss *Aulicus'* rumor-mongering as altogether worthless. When he reports violent language used about the King in 1643, and a few years later we find just such language reported in unimpeachable sources, we must admit a certain plausibility in *Aulicus'* story. Moreover, even in giving details of transactions in the House of Commons *Aulicus* sometimes gets support from good authority. His tale of the expulsion of Martin and of Pym's part in and reason for securing it coincides exactly with the narrative of Dewes and Whitelock (see pp. 148–149, above). Provisionally we may conclude that, although we must use both newsbook and Clarendon with great caution, we may through such cautious use obtain details on parliamentary affairs otherwise not available.

APPENDIX B

A CONSTITUTIONAL BASIS FOR THE MIDDLE-GROUP POLICY

THE task of answering the Royalists was not impossible, and one Roundhead pamphleteer did, in fact, produce a justification of the parliamentary call to arms that, had it been available to them, would have met the need of Pym and his friends. Unfortunately, Philip Hunton's *Treatise of Monarchie* did not appear in print until May 1643,[1] several months after the conflict between the King and the Houses had passed from the forum of debate to the field of battle. Because lines of war were already too sharply drawn for persuasion to matter much one way or the other, men of action paid little attention to Hunton's work. His thesis evolved out of a theory of the nature of the English constitution. The theory was not fantastic, and it was not new. It was in the direct line of parliamentary tradition, as that tradition had developed under the Stuarts. In 1610 James Whitelock in the debate on impositions gave the classical exposition of the conceptions Hunton used.

"In every commonwealth and government there be some rights of sovereignty . . . which regularly and of common right do belong to the sovereign power of that state . . . which sovereign power is *potestas suprema*, a power that can control all other powers, and cannot be controlled but by itself. . . . Then is there no further question to be made but to examine where the sovereign power is on this kingdom. . . . The sovereign power is agreed to be in the King; but in the King is a two-fold power; the one in Parliament as he is assisted with the consent of the whole state; the other out of Parliament, as he is sole and singular, guided merely by his own will. And if of these two powers of the King one is greater than the other, and can direct and control the other, that is *suprema potestas*, the sovereign power, and the other is *subordinata*. . . . The power

---

[1] Gooch (*op. cit.*, 95–96) treats Hunton's work with an entirely undeserved contempt. Allen (*op. cit.*, 449–456) gives it a more ample discussion. For an adequate appreciation of the fundamental theoretical soundness of Hunton's thesis, however, one must turn to the scholarly essay of Professor C. H. McIlwain, "A Forgotten Worthy, Philip Hunton, and the Sovereignty of King in Parliament," *Politica* (1934), I, 243–274. In the following discussion of the validity of Hunton's argument as a justification for the policy of the middle group I have relied extensively on Professor McIlwain's work.

of the King in Parliament is greater than his power out of Parliament and doth rule and control it. . . . Appeal is from the King out of Parliament to the King in Parliament . . . for in acts of Parliament . . . the act and power is the King's, but with the assent of the Lord and Commons, which maketh it the most sovereign and supreme power above all and controllable by none."

All Hunton did was draw out the implications of Whitelock's conception of the fundamental law of English monarchy, a conception that almost every man at Westminster and a good many with the King at Oxford would have subscribed to. Sovereignty lies with the King in Parliament, for in the King, Lords, and Commons is the power to make law; not in any one or two of them, but in the three together. Parliament then is, to use a modern term, the corporate sovereign of England; there is no power above it, no power equal to it. Here Hunton asks the fatal question: What happens if the members of this corporate sovereign fall out, if the King and the Houses find themselves irreconcilably at odds? Who is to arbitrate between them? The answer epitomizes the tragedy of civil war: there is no judge. Only a power superior to the King and the Houses could judge between them. And above the highest earthly power there can be no higher power on earth. When King and Parliament fall out, the bonds of allegiance are dissolved, because there is no longer any single supreme authority to claim allegiance. The State itself has ceased to be. If that happens, each man must examine for himself the causes of the strife between the King and the Houses and look into his own conscience. Then he must do what his conscience dictates. Philip Hunton's conscience told him to side with the Houses.

Such is the essence of Hunton's theory. It is not brilliant, and certainly it is not radical. It conforms to an analysis of the fundamental law of England altogether tenable in the seventeenth century. Taken with the bill of particulars in the Grand Remonstrance, it offers a sound theoretical basis for the action of the Houses in raising arms against the King. The Houses might have said, "Together with Charles I we have been the supreme power, the legislative sovereign of England. Now it is no longer possible for us to act with him. You, people of England, must choose between us. On one side you have the author of the forced loan and ship money, the jailer of the innocent, the enemy of an independent judiciary and the opponent of Parliaments, the friend of Papists and persecutor of sincere Protestants. On the other hand you have an assembly of laborious men who, whatever their mistakes, have struggled mightily to undo the damage one man has done. That man now says he has seen the light and seeks only to rule according to law. By the scheming of the Papists around him, by two army plots against Parliament, by his coming with an armed force into Parliament lawlessly to seize six members of the Houses you may judge the real worth of his professed reformation. Now, you people of England, choose." Such a defense of their position the Parliamentarians might have made. The Royalists would not have found an attack on it easy. It was based on a theory of the English constitution at least as tenable as their own.

BIBLIOGRAPHY

ABBREVIATIONS

A.O.I.	*Acts and Ordinances of the Interregnum, 1642–1660*
B.	Correspondence and Papers of the Family of Barrington, British Museum, Egerton MSS, 2646–2647
C.J.	*Journal of the House of Commons*
C.S.P.	*Calendar of State Papers*
C.W.	Samuel Rawson Gardiner, *History of the Great Civil War, 1642–1649*
Clar. H.R.	Edward Hyde, Earl of Clarendon, *History of the Rebellion and the Civil Wars in England*
D.	Sir Simond Dewes, Journal of the Parliament begun November 3, Tuesday, A.D. 1640, British Museum Harleian MSS, 164–165
D.N.B.	*Dictionary of National Biography*
H.M.C. Report	*Reports of the Historical Manuscripts Commission*
L.J.	*Journal of the House of Lords*
M.H.S. Collections	*Collections of the Massachusetts Historical Society*
M.H.S. Winthrop	Winthrop Papers, Massachusetts Historical Society
Rushworth	John Rushworth, *Historical Collections*
W.	Laurence Whitaker, Diary of Proceedings in the House of Commons, British Museum, Additional MSS, 31116
Whitelock	Bulstrode Whitelock, *Memorials of the English Affairs*
Y.	Walter Yonge, Journal of Proceedings in the House of Commons, British Museum, Additional MSS, 18777–18778

BIBLIOGRAPHY

I. PRIMARY SOURCES

MANUSCRIPTS

Correspondence and Papers of the Family of Barrington. British Museum, Egerton MSS, 2646–2647

Dewes, Sir Simond: Journal of the Parliament begun November 3, Tuesday, A.D. 1640. British Museum, Harleian MSS, 164–165

Manuscript Collections Relating to Norwich. British Museum, Additional MSS, 22619

Rossetti Correspondence. Public Record Office Transcripts, 9:23

Salvetti Correspondence. British Museum, Additional MSS, 27962

Verney MSS, at Claydon, Bucks.

Whitaker, Laurence: Diary of Proceedings in the House of Commons. British Museum, Additional MSS, 31116

Whitelock, Bulstrode: Memorials. British Museum, Additional MSS, 37343

Yonge, Walter: Journal of Proceedings in the House of Commons. British Museum, Additional MSS, 18777–18778

PRINTED MATERIAL

Contemporary Pamphlets and Sermons

Bowles, Edward, *Plaine Englishe*, London, 1643

Certain Sermons or Homilies, London, 1864

Cotton, John, *The Way of the Churches of Christ in New England*, London, 1645

A Declaration of the Proceedings . . . at Merchant Taylors Hall, London, 1643

The Earle of Essex His Letters to Mister Speaker, London, 1643

Goodwyn, Thomas, and others, *An Apologeticall Narration*, London, 1644

Hill, Thomas, *The Militant Church Triumphant over the Dragon*, London, 1643

Hunton, Philip, *A Treatise of Monarchie*, London, 1643

Instructions and Propositions Drawn and Agreed on by Divers Well-Affected Persons, London, 1643

"Letters from Mercurius Civicus to Mercurius Rusticus," *Somers Tracts*, ed. Sir Walter Scott, 13 vols., London, 1809–15, IV, 580–597

Marshall, Stephen, *Threnodia*, London, 1644

"Monarchy Asserted to be the Best, Most Ancient, and Legal Form of Government," *Somers Tracts*, v, 346–401

Pym, John, *A Declaration and Vindication of John Pym, Esquire*, London, 1643

Rudyerd, Sir Benjamin, *Sir Benjamin Rudyerd His Speech for Propositions of Peace*, London, 1642

Three Speeches Delivered at a Common Hall, London, 1643

Vane, Sir Henry, Jr., *The Retired Man's Meditation*, London, 1655

Newsbooks

Certaine Informations

Kingdomes Weekly Intelligencer

Mercurius Aulicus

Mercurius Civicus

Parliament Scout

Perfect Diurnall

State Papers and Documents

Acts and Ordinances of the Interregnum, 1642–1660, ed. C. H. Firth and R. S. Rait, 3 vols., London, 1911

Acts of the Privy Council of England, London, n.s., 1921–

Calendar of State Papers, Domestic Series, The Reign of Charles I

——, *Commonwealth and Protectorate*

——, *Reign of Charles II*

Calendar of State Papers, Colonial Series

Calendar of State Papers relating to Ireland, Adventures for Land

Calendar of State Papers relating to Ireland in the Reign of Charles II

Calendar of State Papers and Manuscripts relating to English Affairs . . . in the Archives . . . of Venice

Calendar of the Proceeding of the Committee for Compounding

Calendar of the Proceeding of the Committee for the Advance of Moneys

Constitutional Documents of the Puritan Revolution, 1625–1660, ed. S. R. Gardiner, Oxford, 1888

Journal of the House of Commons

Journal of the House of Lords

Minutes of the Sessions of the Westminster Assembly of Divines, ed. A. F. Mitchell and J. Struthers, Edinburgh, 1874

"Records of the Company of Massachusetts Bay," ed. S. F. Haven, *Archaeologia Americana* (1857), vol. III

Reports of the Historical Manuscripts Commission, MSS of the House of Lords, Report v, appendix i, pp. 1–134

Rushworth, John, *Historical Collections*, 7 vols., London, 1659–1701

——, *The Tryal of Thomas Earl of Strafford*, London, 1680

Select Statutes and Other Constitutional Documents Illustrative of the Reigns of Elizabeth and James I, ed. G. W. Prothero, Oxford, 1913

Private Correspondence, Diaries, Memoirs

Baillie, Robert, *The Letters and Journals of Robert Baillie*, ed. D. Laing, 3 vols., Bannatyne Club, 1841–42

Burton, Thomas, *Diary of Thomas Burton, Esq.*, ed. J. T. Rutt, 4 vols., London, 1828

Clarke Papers, Selections from the Papers of William Clarke, ed. C. H. Firth, 4 vols., Camden Society, 1891–1901

Collections of the Massachusetts Historical Society, ser. 4, VI, VII; ser. 5, I

Commons Debates, 1621, ed. W. Notestein, F. H. Relf, and H. Simpson, 6 vols., New Haven, 1935

Correspondence of the Scottish Commissioners, ed. H. W. Meikle, London, 1917

Cromwell, Oliver, *Letters and Speeches of Oliver Cromwell, with Elucidations by Thomas Carlyle*, ed. S. C. Lomas, 3 vols., London, 1904

Debates in the House of Commons in 1625, ed. S. R. Gardiner, Camden Society, 1873

Henrietta Maria, *Letters of Queen Henrietta Maria*, ed. M. A. E. Green, London, 1857

Hyde, Edward, Earl of Clarendon, *The History of the Rebellion and the Civil Wars in England*, ed. W. D. Macray, 6 vols., Oxford, 1888

Lightfoot, John, "The Journal of the Assembly of Divines," *The Whole Works of the Rev. John Lightfoot*, ed. Rev. J. R. Pitman, 13 vols., London, 1825–42

Original Letters and Papers Addressed to Oliver Cromwell, ed. J. Nickolls, London, 1743

Pythouse Papers, ed. W. A. Day, London, 1879

Reports of the Historical Manuscripts Commission
    MSS of the Duke of Sutherland, Report V, app. i, pp. 135–214
    MSS of Sir Harry Verney, bart., Report VII, app. i, pp. 433–509
    MSS of Mr. G. A. Lowndes, Report VII, app. i, pp. 537–589
    MSS of Lord Braye, Report X, app. vi, pp. 104–252
    MSS of the Earl Cowper, II, Report XII, app. ii
    MSS of the Duke of Portland, I, Report XIII, app. i
    MSS of the Duke of Portland, III, Report XIV, app. ii
    MSS of the Duke of Hamilton, Supp. Report
    MSS of Reginald Hastings, II
    MSS of Lord Montague of Beaulieu

Selden, John, *Table Talk*, London, 1906

Verney, Sir Ralph, *Verney Papers*, ed. J. Bruce, Camden Society, 1845

Waller, William, "Recollections," *The Poetry of Anna Matilda*, London, 1788, pp. 103–139

Warwick, Philip, *Memoirs of the Reign of King Charles I*, London, 1702

Whitelock, Bulstrode, *Memorials of the English Affairs*, London, 1682

Winthrop Papers, Massachusetts Historical Society, vol. 1, 1929

II. SECONDARY WORKS

Abbott, Wilbur C., *The Writings and Speeches of Oliver Cromwell*, 2 vols., Cambridge, Mass., 1937–39

Allen, John W., *English Political Thought, 1603–1660*, London, vol. 1, 1938

——, *A History of Political Thought in the Sixteenth Century*, London, 1928

Berens, Lewis H., *The Digger Movement in the Days of the Commonwealth*, London, 1906

Brown, Louise F., *Political Activities of the Baptists and Fifth Monarchy Men*, Washington, 1912

C(okayne), G. E., *Complete Peerage*, 8 vols., Exeter, 1887–98

Craven, Wesley Frank, "The Earl of Warwick, a Speculator in Piracy," *Hispanic-American Historical Review* (1930), X, 457–479

Davies, Godfrey, "The Parliamentary Army under the Earl of Essex, 1642–1645," *English Historical Review* (1934), XLIX, 32–54

Dictionary of National Biography, ed. Leslie Stephen and Sir Sidney Lee

Feiling, Keith, *A History of the Tory Party, 1640–1714*, Oxford, 1924

Firth, C. H., "London during the Civil War," *History* (1926), XI, 25–36

Forster, John, *The Debates on the Grand Remonstrance*, London, 1860

Foss, Edward, *The Judges of England*, 9 vols., London, 1848–64

Gardiner, Samuel Rawson, *History of England from the Accession of James I to the Outbreak of the Civil War, 1603–42*, 10 vols., 1883–84

——, *History of the Great Civil War, 1642–1649*, 4 vols., London, 1893

Gooch, George P., *English Democratic Ideas in the Seventeenth Century*, Cambridge, 1898

Haller, William, *The Rise of Puritanism*, New York, 1938

Hexter, J. H., "The Problem of the Presbyterian Independents," *American Historical Review* (1938), XLIV, 29–49

Lecky, William E. H., *A History of England in the Eighteenth Century*, 8 vols., New York, 1878

McIlwain, C. H., "A Forgotten Worthy, Philip Hunton, and the Sovereignty of King in Parliament," *Politica* (1934), I, 243–274

May, Thomas E., *A Treatise on the Law of Parliament*, 12th ed., London, 1917

Newton, Arthur P., *The Colonizing Activity of the English Puritans*, New Haven, 1914

Notestein, Wallace, "The Establishment of the Committee of Both Kingdoms," *American Historical Review* (1912), XVII, 477–495

Parker, Henry A., "The Feoffees of Impropriations," *Publications of the Colonial Society of Massachusetts; Transactions* (1906–1907), XI, 263–277

Pease, Theodore C., *The Leveller Movement*, Washington, 1916

Redlich, Josef, *The Procedure of House of Commons*, 3 vols., London, 1908

Relf, Frances H., "The Petition of Right," *University of Minnesota Studies in the Social Sciences* (1917), VIII

Rose-Troup, Frances, *John White, the Patriarch of Dorchester*, New York, 1930

——, *The Massachusetts Bay Company and Its Predecessors*, New York, 1930

Sharpe, Reginald R., *London and the Kingdom*, 3 vols., London, 1894–95

Shaw, William A., *A History of the English Church during the Civil War and Under the Commonwealth*, 2 vols., London, 1900

Verney, Frances P., and Margeret M., *Memoirs of the Verney Family during the Civil War*, 2 vols., London, 1892–94

Victoria History of the County of Essex, Westminster, 1903–

Wade, C. E., *John Pym*, London, 1912

Williamson, H. R., *John Hampden, a Life*, London, 1933

INDEX

INDEX

Any special utility this index may have will depend on the guidance it offers to the activities of the members of the Civil War Parliament and to the work and structure of the Parliament itself as they are related in the text. It therefore contains full entries on these matters. The names of members of the Civil War House of Commons before the recruiting of Parliament in 1645 are followed by the designation "M.P." In the case of members of the House of Lords, subheadings are used only for those peers who took part in the deliberations after the outbreak of the Civil War.*

A

Abbott, George, Archbishop of Canterbury, 76

Administration, lack of in Civil War Parliament, 15

Adwalton Moor, 129, 149

Agostini, Geronimo, Venetian secretary, 37, 52 and *n*, 119, 141, 211

Allen, Professor J. W., quoted, 175

Anderson, William, 88

Army of Earl of Essex, voluntary principle in, 15; condition of, 21, 109, 112, 117, 138–140; endangered by peace negotiations, 71; size exaggerated by press, 108; London petition for reform of, 110; loyalty to Essex, 121; officers align with peace party, 134; officers thwart scheme against Essex, 138; Commons resolves to recruit and pay, 140–141

Army, New Model, 5, 27, 92, 136, 146*n*, 169, 194

Army, Parliamentary, 34, 128–130, 132, 135–137. *See also* Devereux, Robert, Earl of Essex; General rising; Impressment; London, militia of

Army of the Protectorate, 171

Army, Royalist, 20, 29, 109, 117, 120, 121, 127, 128, 129

Army, Scottish, of the Covenant, 132

Armyne, Sir William, M.P., resists forced loan, 83*n*, 87; Lincolnshire knight in Rich Eastern Gentry connection, 87

Ash, John, M.P., political theory of, 165; offers crown to Cromwell, 165

Ashurst, William, M.P., member of committee on general rising, 132*n*

Assessment, of London, 17–18, 48; general, 18; monthly, 18, 27; of non-contributors, 18, 19, 24, 26, 31, 38; weekly, 18, 19, 22, 26, 31, 134; favored by Common Hall, 20. *See also* Taxation

Association, principle of, accepted by Civil War Parliament, 28; Pym's attitude on, 28–30; favored by London clergy, 29; favored by London, 29; Commons indifferent to, 29; oath of, 31, 32, 113. *See also* Solemn League and Covenant; Vow and Covenant

Ayscough, Sir Edward, M.P., resists forced loan, 83*n*, 88; Lincolnshire knight, 88; feuds with fellow officers, 129

B

Bancroft, Richard, Archbishop of Canterbury, 76

Barebones' Parliament, 172

* The author takes this occasion to express his thanks to Mrs. Emily Adler for her assistance in compiling this index.

Barnardiston, Sir Nathaniel, M.P., Presbyterian elder, 83; Winthrop's friend, 83; resists forced loan, 83n, 87; in Rich Eastern Gentry connection, 87

Barrington, Sir Francis, 83, 86, 87

Barrington, Sir Thomas, M.P., connection with Earl of Warwick, 44–45, 86; friendship with Clotworthy, 44; connection with Pym, 45–46, 89–90; connection with Providence Island Company, 78; position among Puritans, 78; resists forced loan, 83n, 87; in Rich Eastern Gentry connection, 87; leader of middle group, 88n; proponent of Grand Remonstrance, 161

Barrington family, *see* Hampden-Barrington connection, Rich Eastern Gentry connection

Baxter, Richard, 82

Baynton, Edward, M.P., attacks Pym, 60; member of committee on general rising, 123n

Bedford, Earl of, *see* Russell, Francis, 3rd Earl; Russell, William, 4th Earl

Bedford Western Gentry connection, 88; colonial entrepreneurs in, 84; structure of, 84–85. *See also* Connection; Kinship groups

Bellingham, Richard, 87

Bendish, Sir Thomas, M.P., attacked by war party, 104n

Berkshire, 128

Blakistone, John, M.P., member of war party, 20n; defends Essex, 110–111; member of committee on general rising, 123n

Bolingbroke, Earl of, *see* St. John, Oliver

Bond, Denis, M.P., raids chapel of Queen's Capuchins, 38; attacks member of peace party, 105n; member of committee on general rising, 123n

Bowles, Edward, 105, 106, 112–113

Boynton, Colonel Matthew, 129

Bradstreet, Simon, 87

Brereton, Sir William, M.P., subscriber to Massachusetts Bay Company, 79n

Bristol, 128, 141, 149

Brook, Baron, *see* Greville, Robert

Brown, Samuel, M.P., Erastianism of, 98

Bruce, Thomas, Baron, opponent of Pym, 58n

Buckingham, Duke of, *see* Villiers, George

C

Calvin, John, 205

Carlisle, Countess of, *see* Hay, Lucy

Carr, Robert, Earl of Somerset, 203

Cary, Lucius, Viscount Falkland, 174

Case, Thomas, 105, 118

Catholics and Catholicism, 20–21, 29, 76n, 106, 126n, 161–162, 179, 188

Cavalier Parliament, 184–187

Cavendish, William, Earl of Newcastle, 20, 29, 128, 129

Cecil, David, Earl of Exeter, opponent of Pym, 58n

Cecil, William, Earl of Salisbury, opponent of Pym, 58n

Certaine Informations, 212

Charles I, relations with Parliament (to 1642), 4, 5, 182; calls a Parliament (1640), 5; attacks Brentford, 17; rejects peace proposals, 17; refuses safe conduct to commissioners, 17, 50; declares Parliamentary customs and taxes illegal, 19; rejects truce overtures, 20; letters to Duke of Newcastle, 20, 29; relations with Catholics, 20, 23; answers peace proposals, 21; ensures passage of money measures, 21; proclaims county associations traitorous, 23; rejects armistice, 23; attitude of parties in Parliament on, 36; attacked by all parties, 50; duplicity of, 55; attacked by war party, 57, 59, 60; sends counter proposals in Oxford Treaty, 67; avoids calling Parliament, 77; Puritan opposition to Church policy, 81–82; Puritans resist forced loan, 82–84; power of taxation in ship-money case, 82; animosity to Hampden, 93; attitude weakens peace party, 104; attacked by City and clergy of London, 105; attacked by Bowles, Case, and Peters,

Hampden-Barrington connection, 74*n*, 98, 191. *See also* Rich Eastern Gentry connection; Connection; Kinship groups

Hampshire, 128

Harley, Robert, M.P., Presbyterian, 199

Harman, Richard, M.P., despairs of Parliamentary cause, 130*n*; on prospects of Western Campaign, 143

Harvey, Colonel Edmund, 144*n*

Harwood, George, 82*n*

Haselrig, Sir Arthur, M.P., pallbearer of Pym, 5*n*; engages with Army, 5*n*; takes engagement to Commonwealth, 6*n*; executed at Restoration, 6*n*; opposes peace negotiations, 51; contempt for King, 57*n*; attacks House of Lords, 58*n*; career of, 78; Saybrook patentee, 78; relations with Winthrop, 80; in Bedford Western Gentry connection, 85

Hay, Lucy, Countess of Carlisle, 198

Heath, Sir Robert, 205

Henrietta Maria, Queen of England, 40, 71, 106, 182, 198

Herbert, Philip, Earl of Pembroke, opponent of Pym, 58*n*

Hertford, Marquis of, *see* Seymour, William

Heyman, Sir Henry, M.P., member of committee on general rising, 123*n*

High Commission, 162, 174, 175

Hill, Thomas, 118

History of the Rebellion, see Hyde, Edward

Holcroft, Sir Henry, 144*n*

Holland, Cornelius, M.P., attacks Committee of Safety, 59*n*

Holland, Earl of, *see* Rich, Henry

Holles, Denzil, M.P., pallbearer of Pym, 5*n*; one of the eleven members, 5*n*; arrested in Pride's Purge, 6*n*; receives peerage at Restoration, 6*n*; activity before November *1642*, 9; leader of peace party, 9, 70, 140*n*; role in preparing peace proposals, 14; denounces Popery, 20*n*; opposes sequestration ordinance, 39; attacks King's refusal of safe conduct, 50; wants to abolish episcopacy, 97; opposed by Presbyterians, 103*n*; favors inquiry on loss of West, 140*n*

Holles, John, Earl of Clare, opponent of Pym, 58*n*

Homily on Disobedience and Wilfull Rebellion, 178

Hopton, Sir Ralph, 120, 121, 129

Hotham, Sir John, sr., M.P., deserts Parliament, 8*n*, 129; feud with fellow officers, 129

Hotham, Sir John, jr., M.P., deserts Parliament, 8*n*, 129; feud with fellow officers, 129

House of Commons, leadership in, 3; desertion of members to Royalists, 8; passes and extends London assessment, 18; recommits money bills, 19; passes assessment of non-contributors, 21; receives answer to peace proposals, 21; relations with House of Lords, 22, 23; attitude on taxation, 22; passes weekly assessment, 22; passes sequestration ordinance, 23–24; passes excise, 25; antipathy to Catholicism, 29; hostile to measures proposed by Pym, 32; conflict over sequestration, 32; procedure in divisions, 33–34; supports Pym's legislation, 34; division on Army reforms and Committee of Both Kingdoms, 34; controlled by St. John and Vane, 34; sources on, 35; *Journal* as source, 35, 52, 63–64; recommends Glynn as recorder, 42; position of middle group in, 47; dominated by peace party during Oxford Treaty, 49; Pym real leader in, 49; character of division in, 64; maximum attendance, 67; effect of kinship in, 74–75; low opinion of Essex, 90; religious issue in, 97; submits to petition for general rising, 123; humiliates Essex, 124; ratifies appointment of Waller, 125; receives Martin's report on general rising, 126; refuses coercive powers to committee on general rising, 127; Pym loses control of, 133–134; controlled by war party, 133–134; renews weekly assessment, 134; attitude on common law, 134; passes impressment ordinance, 135; in rapprochement with Essex, 138–143; resolves to recruit and pay army of Essex, 140–141; establishes Council

Long Parliament, division lists lacking in, 35; Clotworthy elected to, 44; split between Royalist and Parliamentarian in, 74; connection in, 75; religion in, 96; work maintained at Restoration, 173–174; legislation, 162–163, 173; peace party and middle group in, 174; political theory of, 182; relations with Charles I, 182. *See also* Civil War Parliament; House of Commons; House of Lords

Lovelace, John, Baron, opponent of Pym in House of Lords, 58n

Luke, Sir Oliver, M.P., resists forced loan, 83, 87; in Rich Eastern Gentry connection, 87

Lumley, Richard, Viscount, 189

Luther, Martin, 205

Lyttleton, Sir Edward, Lord Keeper of Great Seal, 37

M

Mainwaring, Colonel Randall, 144n

Manchester, Earl of, *see* Montague, Edward

Mandeville, Lord, *see* Montague, Edward

Manifestoes of Parliament, 175

Manners, Henry, 7n

Marshall, Stephen, 3

Marston Moor, 136

Martial law, 162

Martin, Henry, M.P., republicanism of, 9, 199; hostility to King, 28n; leader of war party, 49, 70; on King's refusal of safe conduct, 50; opposes peace negotiations, 51, 57n, 60n; collaborates with Pym, 56n; seeks to break off peace negotiations, 57n; expresses contempt for King, 57n; attacks principle of monarchy, 58n; attacks Committee of Safety, 59n; attacks Pym, 60; expelled from House of Commons through Pym's influence, 60, 148; attacks royal family, 60; typical member of war party, 67; attacks Essex, 110; member of committee on general rising, 123n, 127; speech at celebration for Waller, 125; character and career, 125;

Cromwell's judgment on, 125; opinions on religion, 125–126; reports to House of Commons on general rising, 125, 138n; favors toleration for Catholics, 126n; military plans for Waller, 127–128; refuses to go to Lord General's army, 130; opposes apology to Essex, 133; Pym's enemy, 137; deserted by middle-group associates of Hampden, 138; fails as leader of Commons, 142

Masham, Sir William, M.P., elder of Presbyterian Church, 83; in Rich Eastern Gentry connection, 87; resists forced loan, 87; an Independent, 98; member of middle group associated with presbyteries, 98n; member of committee on general rising, 123; despairs of Parliamentary cause, 130–131

Massachusetts Bay Colony, 44, 105, 158

Massachusetts Bay Company, 79, 83, 86

Maurice, Prince, 121, 128

Maynard, John, M.P., peace-party member on the Great Seal, 37; against sequestration ordinance, 39; leader of peace party, 49; typical member of peace party, 67; opposes abolition of episcopacy, 97

Mazeres, Colonel de, 144n

Merchant Taylors' Hall, 125, 127

Mercurius Aulicus, 212–213

Mercurius Brittanicus, 212

Mercurius Civicus, 212

Michell, John, 85

Middle group, 52; difficulty of controlling Commons through, 10; position in Commons, 47; as trimmers, 63; divisions indicate split in, 64; Clotworthy as typical member, 67; number indicated in division on peace negotiations, 70; splits on peace negotiations, 70–72; kinship in, 73–75; connection in, 75; transient nature of, 75, 160; Puritanism of, 76, 96, 165; prewar Puritan leaders of, 88; political operation of, 89; led by Pym, Hampden, and Essex, 91; importance of Essex to,

Rich, Robert, 2nd Earl of Warwick, 44; Lord Lieutenant of Essex, 44; influences elections, 44; political alliance with Sir Thomas Barrington, 44, 86; signs petition of twelve peers, 45; connection with Pym, 45–46, 58n, 89; Puritanism of, 77; connection with Providence Island Company, 77, 85; Saybrook patentees, 78; in Rich Eastern Gentry connection, 85; career of, 85; leader of middle group, 88

Rich, Robert, Baron, 85

Rich Eastern Gentry connection, 84–88. *See also* Connection; Kinship groups

Ridley, Nicholas, 177

Rigby, Alexander, M.P., proclaims right of Houses to levy taxes, 9; on the menace of Popery, 20n; favors association against Catholics, 29n; leader of war party, 49; attacks Committee of Safety, 59n, 60; connection with Winthrop, 80; associated with presbyteries, 98n; member of committee on general rising, 123n

Rivers, Countess of, *see* Savage, Elizabeth

Robartes, John, Baron, Providence Island Company adventurer, 78n; in Rich Eastern Gentry connection, 86

Rolle, Robert, 41

Roosevelt, F. D., 53

Roundway Down, 121, 129, 137, 149

Rous, Sir Anthony, 85

Rous, Francis, M.P., suffers at hands of Charles I, 198

Royalists, 3, 8, 74, 128–129, 161, 165. *See also* Army, Royalist

Royalists, moderate, role in legislation of Long Parliament, 174; attitude on Church, 174–175; political theory of, 175–176

Rudyerd, Sir Benjamin, M.P., on the dangers of war, 8; on the menace of Popery, 20n; Providence Island Company adventurer, 78n

Rump Parliament, 166, 170

Rupert, Prince, 109, 128

Russell, Francis, 3rd Earl of Bedford, 84–85

Russell, William, 4th Earl of Bedford, opponent of Pym, 58n

S

St. John, Sir Beauchamp, M.P., resists forced loan, 83n, 87; in Rich Eastern Gentry connection, 87

St. John, Oliver, Earl of Bolingbroke, ally of Pym, 58n

St. John, Oliver, M.P., pallbearer of Pym, 5n; engages with Army in 1647, 5n; Lord Chief Justice of Commonwealth, 6n; exiled at Restoration, 6n; method of controlling Commons, 34; as Independent, 74n, 98; connected with Providence Island Company, 78; career before Long Parliament, 78; lawyer to Earl of Bedford, 85; in Bedford Western Gentry connection, 85; in Rich Eastern Gentry connection, 86; leads Presbyterians and Scots in opposition to Essex, 103n; political theory of, 166–170; career and character, 168

Salisbury, Earl of, *see* Cecil, William

Saltonstall, Sir Richard, 79n, 85–86

Salvetti, Amerigo, Florentine resident, 52n, 126

Savage, Elizabeth, Countess of Rivers, 113–114

Say and Sele, Viscount of, *see* Fiennes, William

Saybrook patentees, 78–80, 83–86

Scarborough, 129

Scotland, alliance with, 28, 30, 46, 132, 134–135; Pickering sent to, 30; relation with Civil War Parliament, 46; relations with England, 46. *See also* Pym, John, and the alliance with Scotland; Solemn League and Covenant

Scots, rebel against innovation of Laud, 5; support Vane and St. John, 103n, 168; send army of the Covenant to England, 132

Selden, John, M.P., favors toleration for Catholics, 126n; peace-party member opposing inquiry in loss